12/2014

W9-BXG-232

THE LOST BOOK OF MORMON

ALSO BY AVI STEINBERG

Running the Books:
The Adventures of an Accidental Prison Librarian

THE LOST BOOK
OF MORMON

A Journey Through the
Mythic Lands of Nephi, Zarahemla,
and Kansas City, Missouri

AVI STEINBERG

NAN A. TALESE | DOUBLEDAY
NEW YORK LONDON TORONTO
SYDNEY AUCKLAND

This is a work of nonfiction. Nonetheless, some of the names of the individuals involved have been changed in order to disguise their identities. Any resulting resemblance to persons living or dead is entirely coincidental and unintentional.

Copyright © 2014 by Avi Steinberg

All rights reserved. Published in the United States by Nan A. Talese/ Doubleday, a division of Random House LLC, New York, and in Canada by Random House of Canada Limited, Toronto, Penguin Random House companies.

www.nanatalese.com

DOUBLEDAY is a registered trademark of Random House LLC. Nan A. Talese and the colophon are trademarks of Random House LLC.

Grateful acknowledgment is made to Oxford University Press for permission to reprint the bar graph from "Reassessing authorship of the *Book of Mormon* using delta and nearest shrunken centroid classification" by Matthew L. Jockers, Daniela M. Witten, and Craig S. Criddle (*Literary and Linguistic Computing*, December 2008, Vol. 23:4, page 478). Reprinted by permission of Oxford University Press, administered by Copyright Clearance Center.

Map illustration by Emily Wong
Jacket design by Emily Mahon
Jacket illustration by Jason Ford/Heart Agency

LIBRARY OF CONGRESS CATALOGING-IN-PUBLICATION DATA
Steinberg, Avi, author.
The lost Book of Mormon : a journey through the mythic lands of Nephi, Zarahemla, and Kansas City, Missouri / Avi Steinberg.
pages cm
ISBN 978-0-385-53569-4 (hardcover)
ISBN 978-0-385-53570-0 (eBook)
1. Book of Mormon—Geography. 2. Church of Jesus Christ of Latter-day Saints—History. 3. Mormon Church—History.
4. Travelers' writings, American. I. Title.
BX8627.S779 2014
289.3'22—dc23
2014009464

MANUFACTURED IN THE UNITED STATES OF AMERICA

1 3 5 7 9 10 8 6 4 2

First Edition

To my father, for teaching me *maddah*

To my mother, for teaching me *midrash*

*Literature was born not the day a boy crying "wolf, wolf"
came running out of the Neanderthal valley with a big
gray wolf at his heels; literature was born on the day
when a boy came crying "wolf, wolf" and there was no
wolf behind him. That the poor little fellow because he
lied too often was finally eaten up by a real beast is quite
incidental. But here is what is important. Between the
wolf in the tall grass and the wolf in the tall story there is
a shimmering go-between. That go-between, that prism, is
the art of literature.*

—VLADIMIR NABOKOV

*There can be no doubt that such a creature exists, for in
our museum we have its tail and bones.*

—FATHER ATHANASIUS KIRCHER

CONTENTS

LOOMINGS

Happy people don't think about angels. And they certainly don't see them. As for holding extended conversations with angels, that's only for the truly, irretrievably miserable. Despite our best painters' best efforts to ennoble this kind of behavior, we are, in the presence of our angels, just like that depressed donkey in the Bible who sees the heavenly messenger standing on the highway, where others see nothing. What choice did he have but to give up and crouch down in the middle of the road? What good is being a prophet when you're a donkey?

That the vast majority of Americans believe in the existence of angels—80 percent, according to most counts—is usually cited as proof of our foolishness or our piety. But that's all beside the point. What it really says, simply put, is that we are one of the unhappiest peoples ever to walk the face of the earth.

And they're everywhere, these angels. There are, to paraphrase an old mystical tradition, as many angels as human worries. Which means the number is staggeringly large and ever multiplying. It has been calculated, for starters, that 133,306,668 angels were cast out of heaven. That's about the size of the population of Germany, Spain, and Portugal. It should be noted that this number was but a fraction of the original quantity of angels, and that when you factor for population growth—and the precipitous rise of human worries—since the Great War in Heaven, the sum total jumps a few orders of magnitude, each angel representing a discrete unit of discontent, and each tailor-made to fit the unique dimensions of that discontent. One angel, known as Sandalphon, stands five hundred *years* tall. Sometimes unhappiness is exactly like that.

Young Joseph Smith swore that late one night in the fall of 1823, a spirit, barefoot and luminous, visited the cramped bedroom he shared with his brothers and told him the hidden history of America, a history that was engraved on gold plates—that is, gold pages, bound by three large rings—buried in a hill down the road from the family farm. When Joseph dug up the gold book, which he did only with great difficulty, he translated it from its ancient language, also with great difficulty, and published it in 1830 under the title *The Book of Mormon.*

It tells the saga of the descendants of Nephi, a sixth-century BCE Israelite man, from the beginning, when Nephi and his extended family take a boat from the Middle East to the New World, to the end, in the fourth century CE, when the Nephite people are destroyed in a giant apocalyptic battle. The stories told in the Bible and in *The Book of Mormon* basically roll along simultaneously for about a thousand years along two parallel tracks, one in the Middle East and the other in America. Like the Bible, *The Book of Mormon* is organized as a collection of books, each named for its first-person narrator, starting with Nephi himself, who was born in Jerusalem, and concluding with Moroni, who was born somewhere in the Americas. The complete book is named for Moroni's father, Mormon, the scribe who edited and engraved the final version of the gold plates.

Two years before *The Book of Mormon* was published, author Israel Worsley wrote a book in which he documented the popular belief that American Indians were among the Bible's ten lost tribes. The Indians, he wrote, "once had a holy book . . . [but] they lost it and in consequence of the loss fell under the displeasure of the Great Spirit; but they believe they shall one day regain it—they are looking for and expecting someone to come." As Joseph walked along the glacial hills of northern New York, he came to believe that he was that man, that he would deliver the lost book.

Joseph, like many on the American frontier, had long been impressed by the mysterious Indian burial mounds that dotted the terrain. The angel who'd visited him had explained that the mounds were in fact ruins from the time of the Nephites, that the big hill near his house held the Nephites' great literary treasure. The first run of *The Book of Mormon* was sold to the public as an account of ancient Indians, a prehistory of settlement in the New World.

Joseph said that the angel who visited him was the spirit of the long-dead Moroni, the last Nephite. The angel had spoken about a world he had personally known and lost. It was he, when he'd lived as a mortal, who had buried the book all those years earlier. To Joseph, the angel Moroni (rhymes with *snow glow guy*) wasn't a metaphor for something, a literary convention, or a figure in a dream. He was a handsome Maya, fluent in Hebrew, who lived 1,400 years earlier and came back looking better than ever and with a lot to say about everything.

I wanted to hear it all. As a youngish, still struggling writer, I was enthralled by Joseph's stories, and particularly by his impressive run as an underdog, an underground American writer—a cult author, you might say. A few years ago, as I nervously worked on the manuscript for my first book, I developed a particular interest in his experience as a literary rookie, a "debut author," as we like to say. I was touched and amused by the writerly moments of his life, such as running into one of his collaborators shortly after the publication of *The Book of Mormon* and pumping him for sales information, only to be bummed out to learn that it wasn't selling at all. I felt only affection for him when I discovered that he'd received a prophecy telling him it was time to seek a Canadian copyright for his book—and, when that fell through, received another prophecy chastising him for being too hasty about copyrights.

The Book of Mormon is about writing books. Every few pages, the story's various narrators describe to us how the writing of this book is going. Every narrator in *The Book of Mormon* describes how he wrote, why he wrote, where he wrote. Moroni tells us that he was tired of writing but wrote anyway. Jacob frets neurotically about his talent. It can feel like a freshman writer's workshop with these guys. They work hard and complain a lot. They seem to be fishing for compliments.

In a narrative with scores of characters and plots and subplots, the one constant is the story of how this book became a book. Its narrative arc follows the real-world physical process of creating manuscripts, of how the book was written, preserved, edited, and archived and passed along through history, usually under the worst of conditions. A thousand years and thousands of miles separate Nephi on the first page from Moroni on page 584, and another thousand years and thousands of miles separate those ancient guys from Joseph, the book's translator. But the one steady character throughout the story is the record itself, the book, the various manuscripts that Mormon edited down into the gold plates, which Joseph eventually excavated and translated.

Joseph's ambition to publish his bible struck me as a refreshingly honest acknowledgment of what it means to be a writer, a regular Joe with an unreasonable faith in oneself and in literature. I felt that there must be something in his story that would be of value to an American writer today trying to stay afloat in the stormy world of letters. He had taken on the problem of life and writing—that dangerous question of where one ends and the other begins—by going at it like the best American picaresque heroes, like Saul Bellow's Augie March: "head on, as he taught himself, free-style, making the record in his own way, first to knock, first admitted, sometimes an innocent knock, sometimes a not so innocent." The difference, of course, was that Joseph was a real person. Madly he turned his whole life, every aspect of it, into high literature and literature into life, casting himself as the hero of a recklessly improvised live-action epic.

And what about that recklessness? Was that what happens when a literary project becomes too ambitious? What kind of person dares write a sequel to the Bible? Was Joseph's compulsion for sequels the kind of promiscuous creativity that might lead a man to marry dozens of women? He was run out of Kirtland, Ohio, in 1837 by an angry mob in the middle of the night after the bank he'd founded went belly-up (turned out that it didn't have any money). In what should have been a clear warning to his clients, the bills he'd been issuing pictured not great leaders but rather bucolic images of shepherd boys. Is the kind of daring required for his literary projects necessarily anarchic, even criminal? Joseph was always right on the edge. These seem like good things to think about if you're throwing in your lot as a writer.

Joseph's failures were as stirring to me as they were inevitable. But it was his success at publishing his book *as a bible*, conceived in Jerusalem and born in American soil, that truly amazed me. Even after all my travels through the lands of his book, it still amazes me.

———

For a period of a year and a half, or more—it's hard to say how long—I entered into the mysteries of *The Book of Mormon* by way of quest, by traveling along the path set out by the characters in the book: from Jerusalem to America. My travels took me from the Middle East to the ruined Maya cities of southern Mexico and Guatemala—known in *The Book of Mormon* as the Lands of Nephi and Zarahemla, among others—to upstate New York, where Joseph Smith unearthed, translated, and published his bible.

I vowed that if I survived that journey in good health, I would make a visit to the spot in the Old West where a band of vigilantes found the prophet in prison—a smuggled revolver, a bottle of cheap wine, and *The Book of Mormon* at his side—and lynched him.

Every journey is propelled by a series of motivations, large and small, known and unknown, but it always boils down to what Melville's Ishmael said when examining his own motives for adventure: the allure of the open sea, the air, deep optimism, deep depression, restlessness, vengeance, art, money. But "chief among these motives," said Ishmael, is "the overwhelming idea of the great whale himself."

I wanted to see the thing itself, in its own habitat, to experience the overwhelming *idea* of it, the kind that compels a person to drop everything, cross continents and oceans, and become someone new.

But it wasn't just about me. As far as I was concerned, American literature got serious at Hill Cumorah. The discovery of the gold plates at the hill in 1823 can be seen as a founding myth for American letters: Joseph, a frontier peasant boy—a restless Puritan—unearths a book from deep in the soil of the country, the promised land, and discovers a story written in the language of the Old World but shaped by the landscape of the New, an American epic about Indians who came from Jerusalem. If Joseph, or his protagonist,

Nephi, was a picaresque hero, an American Don Quixote, he was one of the earliest—a generation or two before Melville's Ishmael or Twain's Huckleberry Finn. Joseph was one of the first, and arguably the most successful American, to take up Emerson's challenge to renew the ancient literary tradition in the New World: "I look for the hour when that supreme Beauty which ravished the souls of those Eastern men, and chiefly those of the Hebrews, and through their lips spoke oracles to all time, shall speak in the West also."

Just months before Emerson made those comments, in 1838, Joseph was riding through Missouri, unearthing the remains of ancient Hebrew warriors and their altars, remnants of the story told in his great, recently excavated book. Joseph spent his life digging into the soil and finding artifacts, footnotes to his *Book of Mormon.* He was one of the first ravished souls to take on the big American literary project, the call to writers of the New World to venture deep into the interior, to blaze a trail, to describe the land, its rivers, its political and natural histories and myths, its tribes and wars and tragedies, and to collect all of it, the whole of this giant continent, and synthesize it into a single, bulging narrative filtered through the energetically deluded first person, to create America in words and deliver it to the people in a book as big and shameless and unruly and haunted and deeply problematic as the country itself.

Still, most of us frankly don't know what to make of *The Book of Mormon.* We feel the need to distance ourselves from it. It is spoken of amid nervous laughter. Consider the punch line of a recent chat on NPR between the writer Tom Bissell and host Brooke Gladstone about the fate of the world's great books:

> TOM BISSELL: And it's just sheer chance that any of Aristophanes' plays survived. I mean, most of them didn't. The ones we have, we have no idea if they're his stinkers.

BROOKE GLADSTONE: The good stuff doesn't always rise to
the top.

TOM BISSELL: No. And I'd like to imagine an alien civilization who has only, say, *The Firm*, Sidney Sheldon's
collected works [BROOKE LAUGHS], and *The Book of
Mormon* to determine what we were like today.
[LAUGHTER]

Tom Bissell may be more prescient than he cares to be. In a couple thousand years *The Book of Mormon* may well be on the short
shelf of American books. At 150 million copies and counting, in 83
languages, it's in for the long run. We Americans are unreformed
angel-seekers, and for this reason alone *The Book of Mormon* may
be one of our most representative stories. It may well be one of the
stories future people, or aliens, or algae-fueled cyborgs will use to
determine what we were like today. Maybe it's time we got used to
it. Maybe it would be better if we owned it.

To be a fan of *The Book of Mormon* is to walk a lonesome road. You
have almost no one to talk to. None of your friends have read the
book. None have had it assigned in school. There are many people
who don't realize, or have forgotten, that it is in fact a book, not
just a hit musical. It isn't merely socially acceptable to mock and
dismiss it, it's a prerequisite for being taken seriously. When the
mood to talk about the book strikes you, you end up chatting with
missionaries, which is satisfying for a while, until it becomes panic-
inducing. Out of necessity, then, you end up describing the book
to people who haven't read it.

At an early point on my quest I found myself in New York City,
having a lunch meeting with James Frey, the man best known as the

author of the notorious, partly fabricated memoir *A Million Little Pieces*. Frey was supposed to write a script for the pilot episode of a TV series based on my first book. The production company had brought him into the project on the strength of his screenplay for a 1998 romantic comedy starring David Schwimmer, a movie whose title the producers could not name and, from what I could tell, did not show the slightest interest in looking up.

The producers had told me that they and everyone in the biz were "hungry for original content." With a faltering national economy, the industry was in a conservative mood and wasn't taking many creative risks. Everywhere you turned, people were doing either remakes of old material or lame sequels. But *our* collaboration, they said, would be bold and original. This was clearly intended to flatter my ego, but as a writer of prose, my ego dwelled elsewhere. As far as I was concerned, their adaptation of the story would in fact be exactly that: a remake, a spin-off, or a sequel, depending on how they did it. For better or worse, the book had been the "original content."

But there was no need to get academic about it. So it would be a secondary version of the thing—so what? People have been apologizing for sequels for as long as the concept has existed. After the smashing success of *Robinson Crusoe*, Defoe published the much less adventurous *Farther Adventures of Robinson Crusoe*, in 1719, and included a highly defensive preface in which he vowed that this new installment was "every Way as entertaining" as the original, even though he confessed that "Second Parts" were generally crap. But for some reason, probably owing to my affection for ambitious failures, I happen to like sequels, and was excited to see an uncanny facsimile of my book. Even a bad one would be fun.

On my way downtown to meet Frey, I found myself on a subway car plastered with ads for the *Book of Mormon* musical, a sequel to

Joseph Smith's original *Book of Mormon*, which itself was a sequel to the New Testament, which was a sequel to the Old Testament. Earlier that day I had seen a gigantic billboard for the musical on the side of a passing bus, one on top of a taxi, another grinning down at me with shimmering menace from the top of Times Square.

When I met Frey, he was a busy man. He was running a start-up—described ungenerously by *New York* magazine as a literary sweatshop—in which he'd hired grad students to cook up books about belligerent aliens. He also had a new novel of his own coming out. On top of that, he was working on a series pilot for an HBO show about porn starlets, if I remember correctly. And some other project, vaguely alluded to, involved his sitting on a porch in the desert, on what could only have been a creaky rocking chair, musing on life and love with retired Hells Angels.

Frey looked roughly the way I imagined him. A worn navy blue polo shirt—collar curling in at the edges—over a pink T-shirt, a trim beard, designer glasses, exhausted eyes, thinning curls. The air of a charming depressive who conserved his charisma for his many projects. He told me that Sonny Barger, the notorious former leader of the Hells Angels, had told him that Hunter Thompson was a chickenshit. "I believe that," I heard myself say in response.

He'd brought us to his usual spot, a fancy farm-to-plate bistro near his SoHo office. As we waited for our server, Frey offered me a piece of Nicorette gum ("fuckin' love this shit"). For a moment we sat there, chewing contemplatively, absorbing the mild nico-buzz and gauging the restaurant's carefully cultivated look of rustic simplicity, suggestive of a swanky lounge designed by the Amish. On the wall was a giant glossy photo of a studious farmer, a man of plain looks, of deep, scowling moral seriousness and vaguely affronted Protestant rationality, a man possibly of Dutch extraction, standing atop a bale of hay. His pursed lips communicated a message of unimpeachable authenticity. Frey briefly glanced up from his menu and said, "Yeah, I don't know what that guy's deal is."

At a table across the restaurant an old man wearing a peasant blouse sat alone, slowly polishing off a pile of hard-boiled eggs, one egg after another. If you pay attention, you'll see such lonesome egg-eaters anywhere. I mention this instance only because hard-boiled eggs weren't on the menu.

Frey and I chatted about the difference between writing books and writing scripts for the screen. He told me that his heart was in books. I considered asking him about the Schwimmer picture, which I'd looked up. Titled *Kissing a Fool* and directed by Doug Ellin (previous film: *Phat Beach*), it had been characterized by the *Kalamazoo Gazette* as a "pleasant surprise hiding inside an unpromising package" and featured Schwimmer as a womanizing TV sportscaster who gives up his hedonistic ways when he falls in love with a bespectacled book editor. I wondered whether this scenario had been a dramatization of Frey's own personal conflict between TV and books. Instead, I glanced down at the menu and asked him how he imagined the opening scene of our sitcom. He replied without hesitation.

"I love that scene in your book when the rabbi punches you in the face."

"Uh-huh, yeah."

"That's definitely how I'd open. The wedding, the bad interaction with the rabbi. Cut to later in the wedding, the dancing, and *wham.*" Frey smacked his fist into his palm, raising eyebrows among our fellow lunch patrons. "We see the rabbi again, he's throwing the punch to the face—your face, obviously—then cut to opening credits."

"Okay, yeah, I can see that," I said.

I took a drink of water. In an attempt to keep the conversation going, I added, "That's an interesting departure from the book, which is totally fine, of course . . ."

"What do you mean?" said Frey. "That was right out of your book."

"Not really. But that's fine, it doesn't matter. It doesn't have to be the same. The book was the book and this . . ."

"Yeah, I know. But seriously, that was right there in the book," said Frey.

"Well, okay, the rabbi didn't *actually* punch me in that scene in the book. During the wild dancing, someone *accidentally* smacked me, then I saw the rabbi standing there and speculated crazily that it was him. It was like a projection of my anxiety about him."

"Nah," said Frey, shaking his head.

"You . . . disagree?"

"He definitely punched you."

"No, I'm pretty sure . . ."

"I'm telling you," said Frey, "he definitely punched you. I know these guys. They're tough mothers."

I noticed that I'd stopped chewing my Nicorette. I was genuinely confused. Why was James Frey insisting that this former rabbi of mine, this frail man who could barely keep order in my high school Bible class, had thrown a punch, even though he most certainly did not throw that punch, or any punch, ever, in his entire life?

Was I getting a taste of Frey's talent for mythmaking? Like so many other people, I'd watched the Frey scandal and not quite known what to make of it. But whenever I think back on his memoir, I'm amazed by what little difference the commotion made. Perhaps that was his plan all along: to tell a story so good that the fabrications didn't matter. And that was more or less what happened. After it was revealed that a man whose face is bleeding profusely, whose teeth have been knocked out, and who's pissed his pants would never be allowed to board a plane in the real world—as he claimed he had in the opening to *A Million Little Pieces*—people grew angry over the fictionalization and over the subsequent revelations about others. But even after Frey was pilloried in the media and beaten down by Oprah for the pleasure of a live studio audience, the majority of his readers quickly forgave him. All they cared about, it turned out, was what happened next to the bloody guy on the plane. Even Oprah, following some particularly cleansing yoga session, called Frey and made peace with him. Frey received a nice contract for his next book. His readers didn't care about the genre, they cared only about the story.

At the heart of my *Book of Mormon* quest was an effort to understand the difference between prophecy and fabrication, angels and inspiration, delusion and fact. I'd already learned a lot about Joseph Smith, but the more I read, the more facts I accumulated, the less I understood him. I couldn't pin him down. To be honest, I could barely keep up with him. What was remarkable about Joseph's talent for self-creation wasn't simply that he remade himself so many times over, but that he never discarded the old selves along the way. As he pushed west—after the book's publication—getting run out of towns from Ohio to Missouri to Illinois, the fictional selves just kept accumulating. He became the protagonist-author of dozens of different American stories. By the time he was murdered, in 1844, he had been the mayor of a rapidly growing city—a rival to Chicago—the head of a bank, a city planner, editor in chief, ditch digger, respected amateur wrestler, museum curator, church president, author, translator, seer, general of a large militia, chief of police, chief of secret police, renowned practitioner of white magic, proprietor of a general store, collector of ancient Egyptian mummies and papyri, land surveyor, fugitive in two states, farmhand, landlord, would-be arsonist, hotel manager, and Planet Earth's one and only prophet of the living God. His bid to unseat James K. Polk for the office of president of the United States ended abruptly when he became a martyr. He died at age thirty-eight, survived by at least forty-eight grieving widows. After his death, he was sighted as an angel. And even then the beat went on. Records show that still more women, including medieval Catholic saints, were wed to him posthumously. Joseph didn't just have plural wives, he had plural lives to match, as if he, a literalist to his core, had married each of his personas to a different woman.

The more I learned about the man, the less I could imagine having a conversation with him. The facts were so odd and sensational that the mystery of the person only deepened. Did he believe his own story? Or was he so deeply invested in it that he no longer knew what was story and what was fact? How did he keep it all straight? It occurred to me that Frey, because of his experience, could shed some light on these questions. And since he, like almost everyone else I knew, hadn't read the book, I described it to him.

The first story, I told him, was narrated by a guy named Nephi (rhymes with *cream pie*). Nephi's father, Lehi (which also rhymes with *cream pie*), was a Jerusalem prophet 580 years before the birth of Jesus, a contemporary of the biblical prophet Jeremiah. Because Lehi proved to be a constant nuisance to the city's corrupt elites, his life was threatened. He was forced to collect his family and flee Jerusalem at once.

The premise follows a now-familiar formula for a sequel: the retrospective discovery of a hidden storyline belonging to heretofore unknown relatives of the original story's characters, a scenario in some ways like that of *City Slickers II: The Legend of Curly's Gold*, in which Jack Palance reprises his hard-boiled cowboy character, Curly—who died at the end of the first movie—by returning, unexpectedly, as Curly's uncannily hard-boiled twin, Duke Washburn. Like *City Slickers II, The Book of Mormon* begins in the original work's setting, in this case biblical Jerusalem, and stars newly introduced blood relatives of the original heroes. And like *City Slickers II*, the story involves a wild treasure plot, as evidenced in the tale's first action sequence (translation mine):

1 Nephi tells us that his family—father, mother, and brothers—Laman, Lemuel, and little Sam—have escaped Jerusalem abruptly, leaving behind all of their possessions. **2** After some time in the wilderness, it becomes clear that they cannot ever return home; their flight into the desert will be the start of a long adventure. **3** But before they can set out on their journey, they must recover one critical possession: a book. **4** The book, which Lehi describes to Nephi as "the record of the Jews and also a genealogy of my forefathers," is written on "plates" of brass. **5** Lehi orders his sons to return to Jerusalem and recover this metal book, which was in the hands of a relative, Laban. **6** It is very important that they succeed in this mission, says Lehi, because this book will be the means by which they "preserve the language of our fathers." **7** Nephi's brothers Laman and Lemuel are far from pleased about this task. **8** Still, they depart. **9** Sitting outside Jerusalem's walls, Nephi and his brothers draw lots to decide who will risk his life to reenter the city. **10** Laman draws the short stick. **11** He approaches the house of his kinsman Laban, a member of the corrupt Jerusalem nobility. **12** After some time, Laman returns to his brothers, empty-handed and feeling "exceedingly sorrowful." **13** He tells them that Laban furiously expelled him and vowed to kill him if he returned. **14** Laman and Lemuel, who hadn't wanted to make this trip to begin with, are ready to quit. **15** Nephi hatches a new plan: return to their family's Jerusalem residence, gather up the gold and silver that they'd left behind in their haste, and offer it to Laban in exchange for the desired book. **16** At Laban's residence the brothers make their offer, and Laban accepts. **17** But just as the exchange is under way, Laban grabs the treasure—without relinquishing the book—and violently expels the brothers. **18** Laban's servants chase the brothers out of the city. **19** In a cave outside Jerusalem, Laman and Lemuel become furious with Nephi for failing the mission, for losing the family's fortune, and for almost getting them killed. **20** They viciously beat Nephi. **21** An angel arrives and saves Nephi.

1 Nephi decides to make a third effort to obtain the book. **2** He enters the city, alone this time, in the dead of night, "not knowing beforehand the things which I should do." **3** As he approaches Laban's house, he notices a man lying on the ground, passed out drunk. **4** The drunk man is none other than Laban himself. **5** Nephi draws Laban's sword from its sheath and admires it: "The hilt thereof was pure gold, and the workmanship thereof was exceedingly fine, and I saw that the blade thereof was of the most precious steel." **6** A voice tells him to kill Laban. **7** (This voice is identified not as a god or an angel but as *the spirit.*) **8** Just then, a second voice, in his heart, tells Nephi not to kill Laban. **9** His heart tells him that he isn't a murderer and that he shouldn't do it. **10** But then the spirit speaks and makes a series of arguments for killing Laban: **11** Laban stole his family's property. **12** Laban was a bad person. **13** And, the main argument: Laban held a book that his family absolutely needed for the sake of their future descendants. "Better that one man should perish," says the voice, "than that a nation should dwindle and perish." **14** The voice suddenly drops its reasoned arguments and becomes demanding: *Slay him*, it says.

1 Disregarding the voice in his heart, Nephi raises the sword and beheads the sleeping man. **2** He dresses himself in Laban's clothes. **3** At Laban's treasury, the guards take the disguised Nephi for their master and give him the coveted brass book. **4** After a dramatic chase sequence, Nephi escapes the city walls. **5** Once outside, Nephi connects with his brothers. **6** They run back to their father's desert hideout. **7** Nephi arrives, bruised, sweaty, and breathless. **8** He drops the precious book into his father's hands.

(In the action-movie version, the screen would go to black and, in a crescendo of percussive theme music, the titles BOOK. OF. MORMON would pound the screen.)

I asked Frey what he thought about this opening. Why does the story begin like this? The Hebrew Bible begins with the creation of heaven and earth; the New Testament begins with the mysterious birth of a boy god. What kind of bible starts off in a dark creepy alley, with a sleazy drunk guy and a gruesome murder/robbery? This sounded more like Dostoyevsky than Genesis.

To Frey, that was precisely the intended effect. "You've got to do something different in this version," he said. "You have to remind readers why the story is still hot. You have to let them know that actually the plot is just starting to thicken, that we're just arriving at a crossroads. You have to be clear about what the stakes are—and that they're serious. You want to remind the reader that this story is about life and death."

Frey thought for a moment.

"You know what?" he continued. "I think it's like this. There's a question at the beginning of this story: what kind of book is so important, what kind of story is so important, that you would kill for it—literally *kill*? Well, this is that kind of book."

"And," I replied, "that's why Nephi opens the story with his shocking confession: he knows all about this because *he* has already killed for it."

"*Exactly*," said Frey. "Hacked the motherfucker's head right off."

After lunch, I walked Frey a few blocks up Sixth Avenue back to his office. He'd named his start-up Full Fathom Five, after the song of Ariel, the captive spirit from *The Tempest*: "Full fathom five thy father lies; / Of his bones are coral made; / Those are pearls that were his eyes."

"You know," Frey said as we waited for the light to change, "you're talking to the right guy about all of this. I just wrote a kind of bible myself."

It was, I now gathered, during his research for this book that he had determined that rabbis are "tough mothers." It was called *The Final Testament of the Holy Bible* and, I soon discovered, it came with this note:

James Frey isn't like other writers. He's been called a liar. A cheat. A con man. He's been called a savior. A revolutionary. A genius. He's been sued by readers. Dropped by publishers because of his controversies. Berated by TV talk-show hosts and condemned by the media. He's been exiled from America, and driven into hiding. He's also a bestselling phenomenon. Published in 38 languages, and beloved by readers around the world. What scares people about Frey is that he plays with truth; that fine line between fact and fiction. Now he has written his greatest work, his most revolutionary, his most controversial. *The Final Testament of the Holy Bible* . . . We've waited 2,000 years for the Messiah to arrive. We've waited 2,000 years for this book to be written.

Frey was right: I was talking to the right guy. It's easy to forget, and not entirely easy to grasp, that scripture is in fact a subgenre of *nonfiction*. The audacity of scripture, the way in which it far outfictions fiction, is in its claim, its absolute insistence, that it is thoroughly factual. It made perfect sense that someone like Frey—or Joseph Smith—would be attracted to writing a bible. If you substituted "Joseph Smith" for "James Frey," the description on Frey's book could appear on the back of *The Book of Mormon*.

Perhaps if James Frey had grown up on the frontier in the 1820s he would have *been* Joseph Smith. Or maybe if Joseph was alive today he'd have a fancy agent and a successful alien-lit start-up. I'd been having a difficult time imagining what it would be like to hang out with Joseph, but it turned out I'd just had lunch with him at an overpriced place in SoHo.

But meeting Frey, who, after all, was probably not an actual karmic incarnation of Joseph Smith, only highlighted how difficult it was to encounter Joseph in the flesh—a particularly frustrating problem as so many details of Joseph's story are so tantalizingly fleshy. The popular version of how Joseph obtained the gold plates—that the angel delivered the book to him—understates the bodily struggle of the operation. It was far from an effortless, elegant process. In every version of the story, in the many conflicting accounts recorded by Joseph, his friends, family, enemies, and deputies, the common theme is the worldly nature of the action. The story of the gold plates unfolds as a series of intensely physical experiences.

It took years for Joseph to excavate the book out of the hill—much more time, in fact, to extract the book from the ground than to translate it. From September 22, 1823, when the angel Moroni first revealed the burial spot, four years would pass until Joseph would hold the gold book in his hands, and three additional years until it was published as *The Book of Mormon*. Joseph spent about a third of his adult life just trying to dig up the book and prepare it for publication.

On his first attempt to unearth the book, in 1823, Joseph was roused in the middle of the night by the angel, who showed him a vision of the hill where it was buried—and then more or less talked his ear off all night. Working in the field the next day, reaping wheat, Joseph fainted from exhaustion. Later, when he finally made his way to the hill three miles down the road, he dug a ditch, then used a lever to roll away the stone slab that covered the box in which the plates were stored. When Joseph put his hands on the gold plates for the first time, he was sent reeling from a terrific jolt, like an electric shock. Three times he tried to touch the plates; three times he was violently repelled, causing him to scream out in agony. Apparently he wasn't ready to receive them. When Joe, the impoverished farm boy, first saw the gold plates, all he could see was gold.

Moroni reappeared. Having spent the entire previous night

warning Joseph not to turn a profit from the gold, the angel was furious.

Given Joseph's employment at that time, it was a reasonable concern. He was working with a team of men who were digging up a hill in Pennsylvania, the supposed site of an old Spanish silver mine. Mining for precious metals was in those days a collective mania among westward-moving settlers. Joseph's neighbors eagerly searched their new lands for gold. In a couple decades' time some of these same ex–New Englanders, including followers of Joseph, would take part in the California gold rush. Joseph joined a number of "money-digging" expeditions, groups of men who banded together to mine precious metals, promising each other to share the spoils.

It was during this period, when Joseph was about twenty years old, that his older brother Alvin, the family's main breadwinner, died suddenly (his last words to Joseph were "obtain the Record"— the excavation of the gold plates had become a family obsession at that point). Shortly thereafter, the family, sinking in debt, lost their farm. Hard up for cash, Joseph redoubled his desperate effort to dig for the solution to his problems. It was on these expeditions that he sharpened his skills with various occult practices. With the help of divining rods and seer stones, he earned a reputation as a seer who specialized in identifying dig spots. He became well enough known that in 1826 he was brought up on charges of being a "disorderly person and imposter" for using occult methods to find lost objects. He confessed and was found guilty.

Even after burrowing into hills all over the region, Joseph believed that the gold plates, buried three miles down the road, were still his family's best prospect. But the more he worked at treasure digs in the hills of New York and Pennsylvania, the more his angel criticized him and warned him that he would never obtain the gold plates.

At the command of the angel, Joseph made an annual pilgrimage up the hill, each year on the Autumnal Equinox, September 22, to attempt once again to dig up the book. Four times in five years Joseph tried and failed to obtain the book (he skipped a year because he was working a job out of state). Over the years people in the region had learned about this young seer and his buried "gold bible." Even before he had anything to show for himself, Joseph managed to create an aura of anticipation, jealousy, admiration, and rage. His annual September 22 pilgrimage became known to some in the area. In preparation for his final journey up the hill, he had his father spy on the neighbors to make sure they weren't spying on him. When he arrived at the hill that night, on September 22, 1827—actually just after midnight of September 21, to throw off his foes—he finally succeeded. Joseph could now feel the weight of the gold plates in his hands, estimated between 40 and 60 pounds.

But this process was only the beginning of the arduous effort to protect the gold plates, then translate and publish them. The first task: to find a secure location. He hollowed out a log somewhere in the woods and stored them there until he could afford to have a chest made. In order to raise the necessary funds, he departed to a nearby town, Macedon, for a well-digging gig. The next day, a notorious soothsayer, who Brigham Young would later say "possessed as much talent as any man that walked on the American soil, and was one of the wickedest men I ever saw," led a gang of men to find and steal the much-discussed gold plates—but the plan was detected by Joseph Senior. Young Joseph urgently rode to the site where he'd buried the plates and, for the second time that week, he unearthed the book.

The new plan involved storing the gold book at the Smith home, where it might be safer. But the trip between the hiding spot and the family home was treacherous. According to his own account, Joseph was brutally assaulted by anonymous men three times during the trek through the woods back to his family farm. In the first of these attacks he was ambushed and struck by an assailant with a blunt object, forcing him to wrestle the man down. After that, Joseph ran the remainder of the way through the forest, clutching the heavy book like a running back dashing up a football field. He arrived home with a dislocated thumb and one side of his chest heavily bruised.

These events only deepened the intrigue of the treasure, eliciting the curiosity and occasionally the burning greed of the Smiths' neighbors. Joseph had made enemies of his former team of money diggers, who argued that, pursuant to their agreement, all found treasure must be shared equally among the men. Joseph wasn't showing, much less sharing, this major find. But these men weren't the only ones eager to get their hands on the treasure, or at least see it. The secrecy surrounding the find, the buildup of years, was driving people wild.

Reading the accounts of what happened to the plates once they were in Joseph's hands, you will inevitably lose track of their whereabouts, of how many times and in how many places Joseph buried and reburied the book. First he hid it under the heavy hearthstone in the house. After a gang of armed men raided the home in search of the treasure—and were repelled—Joseph reburied the plates in the farm's cooperage shop. Shortly thereafter, another gang entered and ransacked the shop but somehow missed the plates. You can visit these sites today at the fully restored Smith farm.

Joseph leveraged the treasure-mania of his neighbors for alliances and some financial support. A wealthy farmer named Martin Harris agreed to bankroll him, to pay off his debts and support him while he worked at translating the book's ancient text. Harris eventually mortgaged his farm to pay for the book's publication.

As the months went by, more mobs of local people, villagers and farmers, gathered and demanded to see the reputed treasure. People threatened to tar and feather Joseph if he didn't exhibit his find. He armed himself and his wife with clubs, packed up his wagon—hiding the gold plates in a barrel of beans—and relocated to his in-laws' farm in Harmony, Pennsylvania, where he would begin the translation. In Harmony, it all happened again: he hid the plates in the woods; local people became curious; some became aggressive. This cycle would continue throughout the process of the book's publication.

All of which is to say, the process was physically taxing and quite real. Whatever the gold plates were or weren't, nobody disputes that rumors of their existence caused many bodily and emotional hardships. It is a documented fact that Joseph Smith was armed and on the run *on account of the gold plates*.

A similar mix of mystery and fact surrounds the "translation" of the gold book. Since Joseph didn't know how to read the hieroglyphs on the plates, he employed his seer stone, the same device he'd used to locate treasure. He would put it into his hat, and then, in the darkness of the hat, gaze deep into the stone, where the text would appear as though on the glowing screen of an iPhone. At other times he used the ancient Israelite seer stones known as Urim and Thummim, which Moroni had buried along with the gold plates. Joseph would recite the revealed text to a scribe, usually Oliver Cowdery but also other friends or his wife, Emma. Since only Joseph was permitted to see the plates, he often strung up a veil between himself and his scribe, an image frequently reproduced in *Book of Mormon* art.

The translation process took over a year and was beset by logistical challenges, lost pages, money problems, conflicts between prophet and scribe, typos, interruptions, fatigue. If you visit the print shop where the book was first published—today a museum—you can see selections from Joseph's original manuscript, 75 percent of which is lost, and you'll see scribbles and notes all over the bible in progress. On one line you'll see a word crossed out and the word *angel* scrawled in above it.

As with the excavation of the gold plates, the hazy, magical images of the translation process ultimately resolved into the sharp focus of real-world facts. Joseph obtained a copyright in June 1829 from the clerk of the U.S. district court for the Northern District of New York. Nobody disputes that there were two original manuscripts, one that Joseph kept and one that was given to the printer, and that Joseph had Oliver Cowdery deliver the latter, unpunctuated, written by hand on foolscap paper, to the Grandin Print Shop in Palmyra, New York, in August of 1829. The book was set in type there and published in March of 1830 in a first run of five thousand leather-bound books. Nor does anyone question that a local newspaper somehow filched the first pages of the book and printed them early, and desisted only when Joseph threatened legal action.

Though later editions would be divided into numbered verses, like a bible, the first edition was laid out in paragraphs, like a novel. On the title page, Joseph Smith, Jr., was listed as "Author & Proprietor." As an introduction to the book, Joseph explained that the plates were discovered in Manchester County, New York, and he gave an account of translating them into *The Book of Mormon*. He thus entered the story as its protagonist.

The Book of Mormon, in other words, can be read as a story within a story: the ancient saga of the Nephite people framed by the modern drama of Joseph becoming that saga's author and proprietor. I read those two narratives—Joseph's and the Nephites'—as one interlinked story, which together form a modern American novel. That novel is what I talk about when I talk about *The Book of Mormon*.

The frame story of the book, the story of Joseph and the gold plates, is still a work in progress. We still haven't sorted through all the stories connected to the discovery of the gold plates. One of the Smiths' acquaintances insisted that he'd heard young Joseph describe "something down near the box that looked something like a toad that rose up into a man which forbid him to take the plates." Fifty years after Joseph's death, the *New York Herald* reported that Joseph once said that the entire hill seemed to be on fire, that he saw an "enormous toad" morph into a "flaming monster with glittering eyes," the image of a ferocious treasure guardian, typical of local treasure-hunting lore.

In the 1980s a controversy arose over whether the treasure guardian Joseph saw wasn't a toad but rather a salamander. Someone tracked down a book in Joseph's local library that included an entry in which the name Moroni was said to derive from the name of a type of salamander.

Devout scholars will rightly point out that the salamander-man theory was exposed as a fraud based on forged documents. But there's something particularly odd in debunking the salamander theory while holding true to the equally weird theory that the plates were revealed by the spirit of a dead guy. To any outside observer, both explanations—that Moroni was a magical salamander/treasure guardian and that he was the ghost of a Semitic Maya—are equally bizarre and clearly the result of forged evidence.

To me, they are renditions of a myth, each possessing its own literary worth, each offering its own insight. Isn't it beside the point to argue whether the forbidden fruit in the Garden of Eden was actually an apple or, as others have variously contended, a fig, grapes, wheat, or a psychoactive mushroom? Isn't the fact of multiple versions a sign that a story is interesting enough to provoke many readings and subtle enough to support all of them?

Nobody, starting with Joseph himself, told the stories the same way twice. Every retelling introduced new elements, glaring omissions, and substitutions. In later published versions of the story, Joseph omitted key elements that he had mentioned previously. In early versions of the story, the angel was named Nephi, not Moroni; in later versions he was unnamed; and in the final, official versions, he was called the "the angel Moroni." The word *angel* is itself a late addition. Earlier versions of the story didn't identify his species. This ambiguity leaves open the possibility that Joseph himself wasn't certain at first of the spirit's origin. Accounts of a toad-man or salamander-man support the theory that Joseph didn't know whether he'd met an angel or a figure from magic or the demon world. In later versions, Joseph also glossed over his original motive of seeking profit, and thus also omitted both the moment when the angel chastised him and the three shocks he received.

But that redacted treasure plot might hold important clues about the story's origin. For Joseph's fellow money-diggers and occultists, the biggest prize was a giant hoard of gold and gems that the British pirate William Kidd supposedly buried somewhere on American soil. Expeditions regularly explored rumored spots from Nova Scotia down the eastern seaboard. A cottage industry of seers and sorcerers cropped up to help find the lost treasure.

Over the years, the legend grew in folk songs and popular retellings. Almost every nineteenth-century American author, from pulp writers to Emily Dickinson, spun some version of doomed Captain Kidd.

As it turned out, the best way to acquire riches from the Kidd treasure was to retail it as a published story. Edgar Allan Poe's most financially successful short story during his lifetime, "The Gold-Bug"—an inspiration for Stevenson's *Treasure Island*—centered on the discovery of Kidd's loot in South Carolina by the ingenious application of cryptography, a more scientific version of the discovery and translation of the gold plates.

One standard legend maintains that Captain Kidd ordered one of his men to bury the treasure, then immediately turned and killed him—and it was the vindictive spirit of that murdered man who guarded the loot for all time. Most versions include similar elements: the discovery of the treasure in a night vision or through the use of divining rods, the sudden vanishing of the treasure if the would-be digger hadn't proceeded according to the guardian's directions, the burial of the treasure in a large stone box whose top had to be rolled off. Was Joseph influenced by the circulating Kidd legends of buried gold and fierce treasure guardians? Did he, like Poe, find his treasure in the publication of a Kidd-inspired story?

There might be a clue in the Comoro Islands, an archipelago in the Indian Ocean, off the east coast of Africa. The Comoro Islands and Madagascar were Kidd hot spots, and it just so happens that the name for the islands on old maps was the Arabic *Camora*, which just so happens to match Joseph's early spellings of *Hill Cumorah*. And the capital city of Grand Comoro, the archipelago's largest island: Moroni.

The myth of the gold plates, like all stories, was born of other stories. What makes it different from most is that it continued to grow and evolve, and only got bigger, more layered, and unique as the years went by.

Decades after the publication of *The Book of Mormon*, in the State of Deseret—aka the Utah Territory—the prophet Brigham Young, Joseph's disciple and successor, told yet another version of the story, which he claimed to have heard from Joseph himself. He said that the angel had told Joseph and his scribe Oliver Cowdery to return to the hill with the plates and deposit the book back where Joseph had found it. When they arrived there, said Brigham, the hill opened up to reveal a giant hidden cavern. In this cave Joseph and his scribe discovered "more plates than many wagon loads . . . piled up in the corners and along the walls."

More books! Countless volumes of books! One book alone stood two feet tall. The book that Joseph and his scribe had just labored to translate was but a tiny part of a much larger untold story that was—and is—still buried and that continues to emerge slowly, piecemeal, in unexpected places. Brigham's tale isn't just a tale but an invitation to seek. It *exists*, says Brigham, and can be found if you look for it.

Even before *The Book of Mormon* was published, a living mythology sprouted up alongside Joseph's early revelations. It started with many people, from Joseph's mother to his scribes and confidants, his neighbors, both friendly and not, who gave their first-draft versions of what happened on the hill. And it continued to develop after they were gone. And it continues today. We aren't that far from the event, after all. The biblical Book of John was likely written over a hundred years after the crucifixion of Jesus. The big stories take shape slowly and collaboratively. And they grow because people continue to believe in them.

To insist that a story is literally true is to raise the stakes for the characters in that story. If, for example, the gold plates were a real object that took up real space in Joseph's home, what, then, were the consequences? Fawn Brodie, one of the earliest serious biographers of Joseph Smith, slyly conjectured that the physical presence of the gold plates in the Smith home created a wedge between Joseph and Emma, that the imposition of this object was in fact the beginning of the end of the happy Smith marriage, the original sin of their union. By refusing to allow Emma to see the treasured book, Joseph damaged her trust and raised suspicions about their marital alliance. This distrust only deepened with the ensuing years, the rising ambitions, and the accumulating wives. A direct line can be drawn, as well, between the gold plates and Joseph's eventual bloody demise. The gold plates weren't merely real, nor merely consequential to Joseph's life, they were the most consequential thing in his life. That is what made the book a bible.

Hundreds of years later, the allure of *The Book of Mormon* is still in its insistence on being a completely true story that describes real places and real people, a true history of this continent translated from an actual gold book buried in our backyard. For some reason, I have come to feel the need to submit to its charms, to take it at its word, to *believe* the story—not necessarily because I do believe in the story, but because belief in the story may be the closest thing to reading it in its original language. Does believing in the story make one a believer? No more than learning Russian makes one a Russian—and isn't that the best way to read Gogol?

If Joseph was able to translate his gold book even though he couldn't read its language, maybe I too could find a way to translate it. I could return to a source even more primary than the plates themselves: the settings described in the plates, the material stuff of the story. If the events that happened in these places really did happen, there would be physical evidence left to explore. And so I set out on a journey through the exotic locales of this lost Great American Novel. I would rewrite *The Book of Mormon* by rereading it, and reread it by retracing its physical trail, following the book where it would lead me.

LEAVING JERUSALEM

In Jerusalem, the city where *The Book of Mormon* opens, it is nearly impossible to find a copy of *The Book of Mormon*. An official Hebrew translation was abruptly halted, and even that half-completed version is out of print for the foreseeable future—which in Jerusalem-time means at least a few centuries. You certainly won't find it in the city's bookstores and public libraries. Your best bet is to look for an English-language edition in one of the over-stuffed expat bookstores—not that any of them had a copy when I visited. In the very city where Nephi was born and raised, his book is absent.

Perhaps it just isn't in the stars. Even within *The Book of Mormon*, the prospect of a Hebrew edition is beset with problems. Moroni tells us that Mormon had planned to engrave the gold plates with Hebrew letters but didn't have space enough on the pages. He needed a more economical language and thus the short-hand version of Egyptian hieroglyphs.

But the modern Hebrew edition was thwarted by more than mere typographical logistics. Like everything in Jerusalem, the problem can be traced back to a fishy real estate deal. When construction plans for a Jerusalem center of Brigham Young University were revealed in the mid-1980s, some religious Israelis threw a fit.

This is a city where the equilibrium is so delicate that rival Christian sects must entrust the key to the holiest shrine in Christianity, the Holy Sepulchre, to a Muslim custodian; they simply cannot find a way to work together. Any new variable thrown into the mix threatens to plunge the city into crisis. In this instance, some religious Jews in Jerusalem promised that an official presence of Mormons, known for their aggressive—and successful—missionary work, would not be tolerated.

Mostly this was about hazing. The local thinking goes something like this: Since every other sect had to carve out its little space in the city by force at least ten centuries ago, what makes these Mormons, the new kids on the theological block, think they can just roll into the Holy City in an air-conditioned car service and establish permanent residence on one of the most sought-after plots of land on earth with nothing but a friendly American smile and a handshake? No. To gain a foothold in Jerusalem, you must take the deal at a painful loss. Even God had to sacrifice his only begotten son just to get himself a musty little sepulchre in which to stretch his legs out. And so the Mormons were offered a deal: cease missionary operations in Israel and to Israelis abroad and indefinitely halt publication of a Hebrew edition of *The Book of Mormon* in exchange for permission to build a center on the sacred Mount of Olives.

During my search for *The Book of Mormon* in Jerusalem, I was living in Nah'laot, the old Iraqi-Kurdish section of town, where I was supposedly hard at work revising the manuscript of my first book. The book had nothing to do with Jerusalem, at least not directly. After a monthlong sublet in a tin-roofed shanty that belonged to two traveling circus clowns, Shiri and Dondush, my girlfriend and I settled into a first-floor apartment hidden at the end of a passionflower-lined path on Euphrates River Street. Nobody outside the neighborhood knew it was called Euphrates River Street because it was unmarked, save for one ancient, virtually invisible sign that read EUPHRATES CREEK STREET. This little street emptied into the Valley of the Cross, a forested park and popular barbecue spot where roughly 1,977 years earlier a tree had been cut down and fashioned into the cross upon which Jesus would spend his agonizing final hours. It seemed like just the place to finish up a book.

Except that I wasn't trying to finish the book. Or rather, I was actively trying to *not* finish it. This wasn't hard to do. I even found ways to make progress on the manuscript that somehow still wouldn't put me in any danger of finishing it, like a literary version of Zeno's paradox, the old thought experiment that imagines a guy who runs toward the finish line of a race but will never reach it because he must first arrive at the halfway point, then at the quarter point, then at the eighth, and continues to arrive at these half-milestones infinitely—and if he's truly splitting the difference infinitely, he can't ever be said to have arrived at the end point. Spending an afternoon reading about Zeno as "book research," for example, brought me another half-measure not closer to finishing my book. So did taking off entire afternoons to search for *The Book of Mormon* in a city where there was no *Book of Mormon*.

I'd also come up with other time-killing activities. I was doing some professional networking for my circus clown subletters, booking gigs for them in the English-speaking expat community. (I found myself on the phone saying things like "These guys can *really* juggle.") I'd also begun attending hearings at Tel Aviv Municipal Court, where the National Library of Israel was sparring with a German literary archive and a few other interested parties over ownership rights to a large cache of unseen papers that contained handwritten material by Franz Kafka—notes, manuscripts, letters, and drawings—that was ostensibly being held at the Spinoza Street apartment of a notorious cat lady. (I visited the apartment but was repelled by a spectacular force field of dander.) The Kafka trial had been dragging on for months, with no sign of letup, and proved to be a wonderfully productive misuse of my time. The search for missing books, Kafka's and Joseph Smith's, was a reliable, ostensibly respectable way to avoid finishing my own book, and so I kept at it, expanding my search to the city's extensive network of junk shops.

The first shop I visited was the one in which I worked. I didn't quite realize that I was working there until one rainy winter morning when the junk shop's proprietor, a sleepy-eyed Georgian named Shabtai, asked me how much I wanted to be paid. I laughed. But Shabtai, it turned out, wasn't in his usual joking mood that morning. "How much?" he asked again. "Don't be a shy one"—and then he proceeded to give me a lowball offer.

His shop was located around the corner from my place, deep within the big outdoor market, Mahane Yehuda, a galaxy of hyperactive commerce, the kind of place that smelled powerfully of whatever was in season. Most stalls specialized in something: produce, kugel, challah, meats, fishes, halvah, spices, cheese, juices, schmattas, olives. And then there were a few places, like Shabtai's, that sold everything but nothing in particular. Rusty harmonicas. Old photos of Turkish soldiers with magnificent mustaches. Binoculars. Creepy candelabra shaped into the visage of a well-known local miracle-maker.

For customers he liked, Shabtai would make a clay figurine on the spot; for those he really liked, he'd make an erotic figurine, usually a donkey with a giant schmuck. The women on the receiving end of his idolatrous come-ons typically forgave him on account of his soulful eyes and the earnest way in which he spoke of his forlorn merchandise. He could flirt in six languages. Somehow, whenever

I saw Shabtai I heard sad, wistful accordion music playing in my head. He was that kind of guy.

When I'd become a regular at the shop, he invited me to sit with him and have horrible coffee and stale cookies; this was a major step forward in our relationship. From there, he started to ask me to watch the shop while he . . . it wasn't clear exactly what he was doing. It seemed he had other business in the market, possibly involving certain female acquaintances. He had a serious flirtation going with the chain-smoking woman who sold dishrags and mops.

During my time as deputy junk man, I got to know the shop regulars. There was the cabbie who would come in after his shift in search of radios and call me "sweetie"—which in Hebrew is considered a macho thing for men to call each other—and who would inevitably begin speechifying and tell me that when I returned to the United States, I should "tell the Americans" whatever slightly frightening political opinion he happened to hold that day. There was a very old, very pious woman who inspected every item with Orthodox exactitude and usually ended up buying her grandson a coin from a distant, long-obsolete country. Sometimes I would end up watching the shop for a few hours, but I didn't care. For better or, more likely, for worse, minding a junk emporium in the Jerusalem outdoor market was kind of a dream job for me.

But most of the time Shabtai hung around his shop. We would sit on mismatched chairs that were probably 50 percent duct tape and we'd chat. He told me the story of how he got his name: he was born at the very moment that the Sabbath started. Unsatisfied by my degree of enthusiasm at this disclosure, he grabbed my shoulders, looked me deep in the eyes, and said, "Do you hear what I am telling you? The *exact* second!"

He told me that he was a writer, and if I didn't believe him, I was invited to check out the article that he'd framed and mounted on the wall of his shop. After a few minutes sifting through clanking piles of junk, he located this wall and, shortly thereafter, the framed newspaper clip. The article indeed reported that my very own Shabtai had in fact won a writing contest by adapting stories his grandmother had told him back in a village south of Tbilisi. A younger Shabtai was pictured posing with a family-friendly version of one of his little homemade clay idols.

At some point I asked him to keep an eye out for *The Book of Mormon*. For days he rummaged around his back room looking for a copy. Shabtai hated not being able to track something down. When people came around to sell him junk, he'd ask if they had a *Book of Mormon*. No one did; few had any clue what it was. Shabtai himself didn't know what it was. One day, shortly after one of his errand boys showed up with a plate piled high with broken sesame cookies—courtesy of the biscuit guy a few stalls away—Shabtai asked me about the book.

As I told him the story of Nephi and his boat journey to America, he closed his eyes and got very quiet and contemplative. If he hadn't been nibbling on a cookie, I might have thought he'd fallen asleep. At every turn in the Nephite saga, he would shake his head and softly intone *Wow*, which in Hebrew sounds like the English word *why* and always makes me feel like I'm talking to an inquisitive child.

When I wrapped up my tale, after giving him a summary of the life of the prophet "Yosef Shmeet," Shabtai opened up his eyes and decisively brushed the cookie crumbs from his sweater vest.

"We must find you this book," he said.

And so onward we searched, for a book that didn't exist—thus ensuring that the book I was supposed to be bringing into existence would also never exist.

In retrospect it's pretty clear that I was afraid of finishing my book. I feared what was to come: the certain public shaming, the critical floggings, the editorial recriminations, the horror that would surely attend the publication of my book. Since I couldn't admit to fear, I spun a slightly different version of it, which went like this: I had grown to love the sprawling physical mass of manuscript, the towers of paper that colonized my kitchen table like a small, proud boom town, forever growing, forever rising, forever new. What could be more hopeful than that? Were I to gather these pages, box them up, and send the bundle to my publisher, that optimistic feeling, the openness of the manuscript, the limitless possibility for revision, for perfectibility, would disappear forever. This was my first effort as an author, the one with all the promise, before everything came crashing down. At night I would have lame, painfully literal nightmares in which a childhood friend's father clobbered me over the head with the rigid spine of a book. I also had pleasant book-related dreams, but those were always about the unbound manuscript.

The writers who used to live in my neighborhood, those ancient scribes, also dreamed about books. In the Bible, Ezekiel dreams of eating a book, which he claims is delicious. Isaiah imagines taking a giant scroll and, for no obvious reason, writing "quick to the plunder, swift to the spoils" across it. Zachariah dreams of a scroll opening in the sky. That was how I felt about my manuscript: a wide-open scroll endlessly unfurling as though of its own creaturely will, rolling elegantly toward an infinite Zeno's paradox of a horizon. These kinds of things used to happen in the Jerusalem sky.

Today, however, the heavens above the Holy City are rarely disturbed. After so many centuries of celestial activity, it seems the sky over Jerusalem is finally tapped out, retired. You can sit all day on a bench overlooking the walls of the Old City without seeing a single airplane pass by. At best you might see a few lost and dehydrated birds. Meanwhile, forty-five minutes down the road, on the coast, cosmopolitan, tech-booming Tel Aviv roars with airplane engines, streaking high in the sky, landing low over the Mediterranean. People come from all over the world to watch spectacular bird migrations between Africa and Europe over the Tel Aviv beachfront. But inland, in Jerusalem, up in the Judean Hills, the skies are as silent as a crypt.

Being disconnected from the world, isolated, would perhaps feel lonely if that weren't the whole point. The city desires to be singular, set apart as the dwelling of the One True, the creator of all, that violently monogamous god of gods. *You shall have no other gods but me.* That is the first commandment. His city, like him, is an end unto itself. According to his prophets, it is indeed the place where the world will end, the destination point of history. As a matter of convention, old maps placed Jerusalem at the center of the world. To fly a plane past Mount Zion, out of Jerusalem, isn't just a sacrilege but a grave navigational error.

Which, in a way, explains why *The Book of Mormon* is banned in Jerusalem: the story told in the book puts Jerusalem not as the destination but, sacrilegiously, as its point of departure. It's a story about *leaving* Jerusalem—and not returning.

And yet Jerusalem is what binds *The Book of Mormon* with the Bible. Before the story dares to depart from the city, it must pass through. The city of Jerusalem is the only point on the map at which the Bible and *The Book of Mormon* converge. *The Book of Mormon* cycles through its own characters and conflicts and, significantly, its own geographical settings; but for one brief moment, at its beginning, the two sagas cross paths in Jerusalem.

The Jerusalem opener of the book is action-packed—but brief. This is the result of a horrible accident. The first draft of Joseph's translation of the gold plates included much more Jerusalem back-story. But a novella-sized chunk of text, the first 116 handwritten pages of the original *Book of Mormon* manuscript, are lost to us.

Joseph and his then scribe, Martin Harris, had labored for months on these opening chapters set in Jerusalem. Meanwhile, Harris's wife had been growing increasingly furious. Not only was her husband sitting around indoors, scribbling, instead of tending the family farm, he was also dropping significant sums of cash to finance the Smith boy, a notorious money-digger and small-time neighborhood sorcerer who passed his days with his face planted in a stovepipe hat, where the words of a new bible were supposedly appearing on a magical stone and being dictated to her gullible Martin.

Lucy Harris was convinced that her husband was being taken in by a con man. She demanded to see the manuscript and, when rebuffed, demanded some more. After Harris hassled Joseph, the young prophet finally consented to let her see their work in prog-ress. Harris took the manuscript home to Lucy. It was never seen again.

Some people believe that Lucy, and/or some other, nameless party, destroyed the only existing copy of *The Book of Mormon*'s original opening, most of the Jerusalem saga. (Later, when Martin Harris mortgaged his farm to pay for the publication of the book, Lucy left him.) To Joseph, the incident of the lost 116 pages was a major crisis. For days he raged around his parents' home, crying and begging for his angel's mercy. He'd spent four years trying to convince Moroni that he was worthy of the gold plates. But maybe the angel had been right the first time: maybe he wasn't worthy. Joseph was upset in that way you might imagine being upset after carelessly throwing away the only extant copy of the first revealed divine oracle to come into the world in almost two thousand years.

I've always found that part of the story particularly compelling. Even with the direct intervention of heaven-sent angels, with the aid of powerful magic and clairvoyance, producing a book turns out to be an unbelievable pain in the ass. This seems very true to life.

After almost a year of soul-searching and grieving, Joseph finally regained the angel Moroni's trust and was able to get back to work. Even though he could have used his seer stone to produce a perfect replica of the lost 116 pages, he feared that his first draft, if it still existed, may have landed in the hands of a foe who would alter the text and use the discrepancies to discredit him. Joseph decided to cut his losses and, with the help of his scribes, begin translating the story again from a new starting point. This second draft wouldn't open with the now-lost Book of Lehi but instead with the Book of Nephi.

Perhaps the story of Nephi killing Laban and stealing his book was Joseph's defiant message to Lucy Harris and to all his enemies. With Nephi, Joseph reverses the roles: instead of the bad guys stealing a book, the hero gets to steal it—and also gets to lop off the head of the person who tries to deprive him of his rightful ownership of it. Maybe what Joseph dreamed of doing to Lucy, Nephi in fact does to Laban.

But whatever personal meaning lay behind the account of Laban's murder, that story became the centerpiece of the book's new opening. We don't have any more background story for Nephi and his family's life in Jerusalem. The original is lost and gone forever.

Now that I'd outsourced to Shabtai the impossible search for a copy of *The Book of Mormon* in Jerusalem, I decided to seek out the story in a more direct way. I set out for a walk through the Old City to examine *Book of Mormon*–related ruins, if such sites existed.

Because so little of *The Book of Mormon* happens in Jerusalem, not many ruins in the city are directly connected to the story—but there is one. Right in the middle of the Old City is a modest, rumpled city wall that has been unearthed from under 2,500 years' worth of construction projects and rubbish that have accumulated over it.

In preparation for my visit, I reviewed a program by a young *Book of Mormon* adventurer-geek who identified himself as an "investigative journalist and explorer." The introduction to the show indeed featured a montage of him both investigating and exploring. We find him sprinting through a forest, dodging low-hanging branches; then wearing fatigues and taking off in a helicopter, issuing critical orders to the pilot; and finally in a desert, taking a giant running start before awkwardly leaping onto an enormous boulder. The host explains that he's "launching an investigation into Nephite archaeology" in Jerusalem.

But of course he mostly just hangs out with that wall. The wall, he says, helps us visualize Nephi's murder of Laban. Although we can't be certain, it is distinctly possible that the killing happened *right on this spot*, beside the small area of wall visible today. He points to a wider part of the ruin and identifies it as a gatehouse. He asks us to recall that Laban, a member of the nobility, was a guardian of the gate, which means that the events of that night might have happened right there. Nephi's brothers would have been on the other side of the wall, waiting for him. Once he'd gotten his hands on the book, Nephi may well have exited the city through that very gate.

When I myself reached the Old City and stood at the very spot where Nephi once struggled with his conscience before decapitating Laban, I couldn't help but think about Mark Twain's skeptical takes on Jerusalem's sites during his famous pilgrimage in 1867.

His experiences in the Holy Land were fodder for his travelogue *The Innocents Abroad*, his biggest bestseller during his lifetime. The specious claims of biblical tourism had given him ample material to lampoon; during more fatigued moments, his humor became a grievance.

"I must begin a system of reduction," he wrote. "I have got everything in Palestine on too large a scale."

He lamented that the biblical Land of Israel was not as big as a continent, as he'd been raised to believe. The great kings of the Bible were in fact small-time clan leaders; the grand battles more closely resembled shepherds' squabbles. The hollow grandiosity of biblical tourism offended his practical-minded American sensibilities. Mark Twain was from a country that was in fact growing as large as a continent and whose conflicts and leaders were truly grand. America's Abrahams and Ulysseses were real-life heroes, not mere legends.

He was certainly right about the physical scale. The Israelites were far from great builders. Their structures were never impressive. Their landlocked territory lacked natural resources. Their militias were never any match for their neighbors. They were basically hillbillies, new to urban life. The monomaniacal hatred they harbored for their neighbors to the south, in Egypt, was probably just a case of raging civilization envy. Their claim to having dealt the mighty Egyptians a humiliating defeat remains one of history's most extravagant and widely propagated wish-fulfillment fantasies. The first mention of Israel in the archaeological record comes not from the early Israelites—who, as pastoralists tend to do, left almost no trace—but from their enemies, in an engraving in which a pharaoh brags that "Israel is laid waste." The moment they arrived in history, they were already gone. It's as though the

Israelites appeared on the record solely for the purpose of confirming the fleetingness of their existence. Nothing about the physical remnants of the Hebrew Bible era would suggest that these people were particularly favored by an all-powerful god.

Literary critic Edmund Wilson made similar observations during his visit to Hill Cumorah in 1968. Standing at the top of the hill and taken by the prettiness of the New York countryside, Wilson allowed himself, for a moment, to imagine the view through the eyes of Joseph Smith. Like Mark Twain, Wilson adopted a "system of reduction." What Joseph's vision amounted to, for Wilson, was garden-variety megalomania. Sure, he concluded, some semiliterate farm boy looking down on his small, picturesque world from atop his hill might imagine greatness in himself, but what does that really amount to? The view from on top of the hill only confirmed his suspicion that Joseph Smith was small-fry.

But Wilson did manage to see in rural New York what Mark Twain could not in Jerusalem: that the lavishness of a biblical imagination is sometimes born out of the poverty of space and resources, from a poor person's urgent need to amplify. The dullness of the Bible's physical remains is precisely what is impressive about them. To the people who built them, imagination mattered because imagination was the best they had. In the end they staked their entire identity on their stories—instead of architecture, a kingdom of words. So it was with Joseph, landless and broke, standing on a small hill imagining Nephi escaping from ancient Jerusalem late one night through the city wall, book in hand. Nephi's story is about a dispossessed person who reclaims his rightful literary inheritance by forcibly removing it from the grip of the upper classes.

According to the prophets, it is the place where the world will end.

After I left Nephi's wall in Jerusalem, I made my way southwest through the Old City, downhill, through the Arab market. As I descended, the nearby Dome of the Rock seemed to set over the city's jumbled buildings like a startlingly proximate gold planet. I bought some sumac and a pack of gum and walked through a few Stations of the Cross—in reverse order, which seemed like a pleasanter way to tell that story—until I reached the gate to the Haram ash-Sharif, a monumental wooden door like the hull of an old ship. There, at Islam's third holiest shrine, I hung a right and immediately got swept into Hasidic foot traffic en route to afternoon prayers at the Western Wall. I rode this sweaty express train all the way to the southern exit, the unfortunately named Dung Gate, and walked out of the city walls.

I was headed toward the center of Hebrew Bible–era Jerusalem, which can be found in the modern neighborhood immediately outside the city's southern wall. This older Old City is no longer a city but an archaeological site known as the City of David, after one of the early biblical names for Jerusalem. Today it is located in the middle of the Arab neighborhood of Silwan. Signs on the other side of town, in Jewish West Jerusalem, advertise this tourist site with goofy cartoon characters and the ominous slogan SEE WHERE IT ALL STARTED.

Book of Mormon–wise, I had just walked from the old outer wall, near where Nephi had killed Laban, to the center of that same ancient city. This site, Where It All Started, was where young Nephi used to hang out—probably. We can only assume, for the story of Nephi's time in Jerusalem has been lost, thanks to the wrath of Lucy Harris.

Visiting this part of Nephi's hometown is always a thrilling and disconcerting sort of literary tourism. Walking through the ancient structures, today mostly the knobby suggestion of rooms, the bases of doorways, a toilet, an odd bath or two, you come into direct contact with all that is seductive and unfulfilling and deeply depressing about revering a literary text.

That afternoon I found myself standing on a shiny new stone porch built with the gift of prosperous right-wing American land developers who were taking their earnings from building suburban malls in Ohio and pouring them into the construction of Jewish settlements on the West Bank and in Arab East Jerusalem. These days the oldest part of Jerusalem is a violently divisive, heavily fortified, but completely family-friendly archaeological park. In an unprecedented and surely dodgy move, Israel's Antiquities Authority turned over management of the City of David archaeological site to a West Bank Jewish settlement NGO, which runs everything from security to the actual dig. It also offers Segway guided tours, great for bar mitzvah groups.

From the heights of the new porch, I was trying to assimilate the views of old Jerusalem, Nephi's Jerusalem: a steep mountain spur dipping down into a thin strip of dry gulley, known as the Kidron Valley, site of the future Judgment Day, according to the prophets of old. Facing me from the other side of the valley was the Mount of Olives, home to the BYU center and the spot where the Messiah will one day appear, or reappear, or definitely not ever appear, according to one's taste. In the meantime, the view was dominated by a densely populated Arab town, in which old Toyota flatbed trucks dodged children playing soccer and mules carrying nuts and dates and China-made toys to market. In the odd ventriloquial acoustics of desert hills and valleys, isolated sounds from this village—a mother shouting to her son, an engine struggling to climb the hill, a jackhammer—carried with astonishing clarity and reached my ear in rapid, clipped breezes which just as quickly cut out, like a soap bubble bursting. It's easy to imagine how these

distant whisperings of unknown provenance might seem to someone with prophetic and/or schizophrenic sensitivities. But of course
there's no need to imagine: some of them took the time to tell us all
about it, often eloquently and always at great length, filling entire
books with these murmuring revelations.

I was suddenly surrounded by two dozen newly minted Israeli
paratroopers, boys eighteen years old or so, bearing their heavy
weapons. Their uniforms and their faces were brand-new, but their
rifles were well worn. Like me, they were on a field trip. Their unit
was led by two tour guides, a short guy with a pithy mustache who
spoke continuously, and a tall one with a long bushy beard, who
said not a word.

"Look over the valley, fellas," said the mustachioed guide. "This
is the view that King David had from his royal palace. This. Is. It.
The very land King David—may the memory of the righteous be a
blessing—conquered through courage and shrewdness. And three
thousand years later, this is the very same land that your battalion
liberated in his name."

I saw one of the soldiers, a bookish sort, sling his rifle over his
shoulder so that his hands were free to take a photo of a shepherd
boy who was crouching on a boulder down in the valley and flicking pebbles into the air absentmindedly as his flock grazed around
him. Behind me, on a bench, two of the teenaged soldiers leaned
against each other in a deep nap.

The guide's spiel eventually, and inevitably, turned to Bathsheba. At the City of David archaeology park, there was a lot of
excited talk about her. The story of Bathsheba bathing on her roof
is of course an old favorite, made legend in centuries of art and
literature and Leonard Cohen covers. Who can resist the particular
thrill of talking about naked ladies during a Bible tour? The City
of David guides certainly couldn't. They took evident pleasure in

asking tourists to look down from atop the palace ruins to "see what David saw."

For someone like me, who's read the story on a continuous loop starting in childhood, there is indeed some kind of visceral feeling, an immediate physical reaction to standing at the peak of the oldest part of Jerusalem. It's not a positive feeling, exactly. You sense a tug of vertigo in your knees, the pull of gravity. In that small impulse, you feel the charged moment when David, restless with success, stands at the top of his world, at the literal height of prestige, gazes down into his royal capital, and sees Bathsheba. That moment, which happens at both the apex of the story and the apex of the city, is the moment when noble David takes a terrible turn for the worse. In a manner that can barely be described as consensual, he sleeps with Bathsheba, impregnates her, and, in an increasingly desperate effort to cover his tracks, murders her husband, who happens to be away fighting in one of David's wars.

Gravitational pull is heavily implied in the scene of David standing on his roof. The repeating word *descend*, which the site's literal-minded lead archaeologist had taken as a topographical clue, was in fact a poetic refrain: the man was teetering on a precipice. David, the beautiful shepherd boy, the sweet singer, the soldier and beloved working-class hero, could go no higher in the world. And so he fell. This is one of the rare ancient ruins where a visitor who is attuned to the narrative might actually *feel* the narrative by standing there.

But this gut feeling has nothing to do with David. In the ruins of his city, it isn't David who has been unearthed but the *authors* of David. You don't see what David saw, you see what the author who created David saw. Perhaps in the vertigo that touched the body of that anonymous scribe, he came to understand his fictional version of David and the gravity-heavy story of how It All Started. What the biblical text matched with the biblical site "proves" isn't so much the existence of the historical characters or events described in the story but rather the tangible, if elusive, presence of the people who once came here and drew a story out of the shapes of the land and the buildings, and out of the visceral experience of standing at that particular height.

Edmund Wilson felt it when he stood atop Hill Cumorah. He interpreted the signal he received up there as counterevidence. And yet he felt something. Though unmoved by the religious sectarian façade, Wilson nonetheless sensed the very human striving of an author, the struggle between his dreams and delusions.

The professional tour guides at the City of David, dressed like car rental clerks in their congenial polo shirts and nameplates, omit the awkward details of the story—namely, that the tale of Bathsheba is about the spiraling nature of corruption and overreach. Why demoralize visitors by mentioning that the story of David's downfall is high tragedy, the kind that is supposed to elicit disgust and pity? Who wants to hear that the "Palace of David," a structure hastily excavated in 2005, is, according to many scholars, very dubiously linked to any historical person named David? What tourist wants to hear that this structure, if it was in fact the royal abode of the biblical David, would carry the heavy curse placed on it by the prophet Nathan as a chastisement to David's heirs and to any arrogant power-grabber throughout history? In the City of David, the powerful have always seen whatever they wanted to see, whatever was most pleasing to the eye. That blindness was the cause of the curse and is itself the curse.

At the City of David gift shop, newly refurbished, you will find a full array of T-shirts, books, jewelry, and ice cream. Inside, a novice tour guide, licking a blue Popsicle, will excitedly tell you all about the archaeological park's plan to expand farther down into the valley, inaugurating a section that will be called the Garden of the King, and, with the help of God, create an adjoining Jewish residential area, all of which, it's true, will necessitate the demolition of a few pesky Palestinian homes in the area. "Which, by the way, don't have proper papers anyway," he explains.

To Mark Twain, ancient Jerusalem's ruins were a big zero, proving once and for all that the whole thing was a farce and a humbug. To another kind of traveler, the modest surroundings quietly attest to the triumph of the literary imagination. As I encountered at the City of David, that is also its curse. In the end, it's all of these things: at once ridiculous, inspiring, and dangerous.

Not long after my day trip among *Book of Mormon* ruins in Jerusalem, I found myself back at Shabtai's junk shop, where I was supposedly employed. Something happens at the marketplace every day at around 3:35 p.m., some collective draining of oxygen and hope. It becomes nearly impossible to stay awake. My friend and semiboss Shabtai never put up much of a fight. Neither did his neighbor to the right, the produce guy who specialized in Persian cucumbers. When I arrived, at roughly 3:35, both men were slumped unconscious in their chairs, Shabtai leaning back with his arms crossed over his chest, the produce guy leaning precipitously forward, threatening at any moment to somersault face-first into a giant pile of fennel bulbs.

When conscious, these men didn't care much for each other. The cucumber man scorned Shabtai's junk as mere junk and disparaged his enterprise as bad for *real* business; meanwhile, Shabtai snobbishly dismissed the cucumber man as a mere cucumber-monger whose customers were boorish, disreputable cheapskates. Often they argued over petty things, like who really owned the totally revolting fold-up table that separated their stalls, even though neither man had the slightest intention of touching that table himself. And now, joined in slumber, they still didn't quite get along, but their quarrel took on a more dignified air, with both men snoring mightily, animatedly, and in succession, like two grizzly bears engaging in a spirited but respectful debate.

The moment I walked into the shop and began to quietly organize a recently arrived hoard of exotic egg cups, Shabtai sprang to life.

"Good, good," he said, slapping me on the back. "You'll watch the shop."

Before I could respond and tell him that I shouldn't stay long, that I had to get back to my manuscript, Shabtai was tossing his scarf around his neck, tipping his cap to me, and pointing to his mournful little coffeemaker, as though offering me an irresistible incentive, or at least perfectly fair compensation. Before I knew it, he was shuffling down the fish-gut-and-lettuce-covered market to wherever it was he went.

That day he stayed away longer than usual. I began to grow antsy. The moment another of Shabtai's flunkies showed up, a tiny elderly Russian man with a trimmed beard and much-too-large leather jacket, I immediately said to him, "Good, good, you'll watch the shop," patted him on the back, and hit the road.

I walked through the mostly empty market until I hit a major traffic jam, and wiggled my way to the front of the crowd just in time to see the cause of the commotion. A burly youth threw open the grimy tin shutters of a shop to reveal a large, shimmering holy ark within; at just that moment, a pomegranate juice–stained hand poked out of the crowd and grabbed the cord to the ark, pulling open its felt curtains to reveal a large Torah scroll, which was also clothed in felt and embroidered with pomegranate prints. At the sight of the scroll, the gathered masses began singing and chanting and jumping and clapping and beating hand drums. The scroll was heaved out of its perch in the holy ark and hoisted high in the air. A bar mitzvah boy was catapulted onto the burly youth's shoulders, and high above the cheering crowd, the scroll and the boy danced a wobbly jitterbug. A whoop went up and a man shrouded in a tallit was catapulted onto someone's shoulders; he too got a spin with the scroll. In the midst of whirling around, the tallit came loose. I was shocked to discover that this veiled man, wildly waving his arms and singing, was none other than sleepy old Shabtai. After a few minutes he saw me and excitedly motioned for me to come over.

"Mazel tov," I said to him, but he didn't hear me over the din.

Sitting on the sweaty shoulders of an overweight army reservist, Shabtai leaned down and shouted in my ear, "I got it, I *just* got it!"

"Got what?" I said.

"Got *what*? Your book, man! Mormon's book. I found it. It wasn't easy, let me tell you. Here, I have it on me."

Shabtai reached into his jacket pocket and produced the tattered book. He instructed me to put it in my bag immediately and take it back to the shop.

"I got it from my guy in Geula," he shouted. Geula: the Hasidic neighborhood. "He made me promise I wouldn't sell it to a Jew, so we'll have to keep it in our secret stash." Shabtai laughed. "He said it's a *Yoshke* book," using the semiaffectionate diminutive that religious East European Jews use for Jesus so as not to utter the name of a false deity. "A *Yoshke* book! Avi! What are you trying to do to me?"

With that, he was swept back into the tumult.

I looked down at Shabtai's copy of *The Book of Mormon*. I was impressed that he, or rather his Hasidic fixer, had found the banned book in Jerusalem. But the joke was on me. For the Lord, in his infinite wisdom and through his Hasidic messenger, saw to it that even this book wouldn't be read by any of his chosen people, and certainly not those in Jerusalem. When I looked down at the book's cover, I saw the words *O le Tusi a Mamona*, in what I would later determine was Samoan.

Jerusalem has always been more about what isn't there than what is. When the women discovered that the tomb was empty, that Jesus' body was not there, *that* was when the story got interesting. It was inevitable, then, that most of *The Book of Mormon*'s Jerusalem chapters had vanished, that the book itself was nowhere to be found in Jerusalem. Without much to go on, we must construct a story to explain mysteriously empty tombs and missing manuscripts. When I thought about what might have been told in those missing 116 pages—the lost backstory of Nephi's family—my own family's Jerusalem-to-America backstory seemed as good a substitute as any.

For as long as anybody can remember, plus about eighteen hundred years, Jewish people, including my family, dreamed of "returning" to Jerusalem, a place they'd never seen and for all they knew didn't actually exist. In typical fashion, this dreaming mostly took the form of endless chatter, and that chatter mostly took the form of exaggerated complaint. The verse from Psalms "If I forget thee, O Jerusalem . . . let my tongue cleave to the roof of my mouth" has always been taken literally: if *Jerusalem*, the word itself, isn't on your tongue at all times, what's the point of having a tongue?

Three times a day we would come together to say prayers that obsessed on the subject. On the Sabbath and holidays, this Jerusalem-talk could go on for hours on end. Even the most common prayers, the blessing over a peanut butter and jelly sandwich, went on at unwarranted length about Jerusalem. People who have experienced mourning or love or addiction are familiar with these kinds of thoughts, in which totally unrelated things are experienced as painfully and undeniably related. When you're preoccupied with loss, even a slice of toast can seem eloquent.

After generations of obsessing over Jerusalem, my family finally moved there. Four years after Israeli paratroopers captured the city—during the heady years between the 1967 and 1973 wars—my parents moved to Jerusalem, the first in their families to live the ancient dream of living in Zion. As young Americans of the '68 generation, they were simultaneously disillusioned with America and deeply illusioned with Israel.

My sister and I were the first in our family to have birth certificates written in the language of the Bible. To my refugee grandparents, these Hebrew documents were as sacred as anything that emerged from a Dead Sea cave. My family is populated by intense religious seekers—to them, moving to Israel was a direct reply to the ancient prophets' call to return to the land, to rebuild the ruined cities, to fulfill the promise. It was a reply to the mystical Song of Solomon, in which the feverish poet bangs on doors and shouts his lovesick demands into the desert night. In 1967 history came knocking, or so believed many young Jews, my parents among them. Hastily they threw the door wide open. And like many starry-eyed people throughout history, they packed up their bags and journeyed across the world to lay claim to holy Jerusalem.

For years they lived that romantic life. My father grew a long beard and studied German philosophy at the university; my mother wore flannel shirts and worked at the zoo. My sister and I chatted away in Hebrew and sat on ancient ruins licking cactus-fruit-flavored Popsicles. On Sabbath mornings, when the stores were shuttered, when the city was empty of traffic and enveloped by a deep, mystical stillness, we played in the middle of the street in our finest clothes.

Thirteen years later, the dream was over. We found ourselves living in Cleveland. Because money was tight, there would be no return visits for almost a decade. My parents became collectors of Jerusalem-themed paintings and prints; the walls of my childhood home were covered with dream images of our once-upon-a-time city. Leaving Jerusalem for Cleveland was a kind of family trauma, a loss of a golden age, a feeling of personal exile deepened by our religion's eloquent harping on that exact narrative. *By the rivers of Ohio, there we sat and wept when we remembered Zion.*

Sometimes I think it was all a dream—that my parents had been living in overcast Cleveland the whole time and all that stuff about Jerusalem, the palm trees and world historical events, Mount Moriah, the Muslim call to prayer ringing out across the desert like a sobbing ghost, all of it was just a stirring hallucination. The stories I was told about this exotic holy city, the place of my birth, mingled with my own surreal kindergartner's recollections, did little to convince me that any of it had actually happened.

The physical evidence, the sun-drenched images in the photos, my passport, my father's army uniform hanging in the closet, suggested that it really did happen, that *something*, anyway, happened to us in Jerusalem. But even those artifacts seemed fanciful, like rocks from the moon.

Thousands of years of obsessing over Jerusalem accustom you to the language of longing; the prayers and stories train you to seek the place. What they don't prepare you for, in the least, is to leave Jerusalem. What comes after Jerusalem? There's no narrative for that—at least, not where I grew up. But as I discovered later, during college, *The Book of Mormon* told precisely that story. It was what first caught my eye.

As a college sophomore, I'd been only dimly aware of the book's existence. During that period of my life, whatever I was aware of,

I was only dimly aware of. These were the blackout years between losing my religion and getting laid.

I had no idea what *The Book of Mormon* was about, what the backstory was. I continued to confuse Joseph Smith with Pocahontas's boyfriend, John Smith. I'd seen, though never heard pronounced, the name of this angel, Moroni, which has the misfortune to be consistently spell-checked as *moronic*. At the time, I was recovering from my own years-long religious bender. I'd had a whole lot of angels swimming around in my head. I wasn't looking for new ones.

Emily was both the first person I'd met who spoke eloquently about *The Book of Mormon* and, perhaps not incidentally, the first who spoke eloquently about *The Book of Mormon* whose pants I was trying to get into. She wasn't a Mormon but had recently become interested in becoming one. Maybe. She wasn't sure yet. At a family reunion she'd somehow realized that her weird religious cousins, the ones who'd converted to Mormonism one summer when she was away at acting camp, really had it all figured out. As someone who had recently been a weird religious cousin himself, I felt vindicated to hear this.

Still, I couldn't see how this hard-drinking, pierced, artsy, punky girl was on the path to embracing what seemed like the squarest religion ever conceived. What about the tattoos she'd planned for the future? Was she down for having ten children?

Emily was the unhappy child of hippies. Once, when she was in kindergarten, they allowed her to go to school wearing only her beloved Mickey Mouse ears and matching Mickey Mouse underwear. That was pretty much how she felt about her life: like she was sent out into the world naked, with only Mickey Mouse ears. She was looking for some order in the universe. The Saints were offering it.

At the beginning of college, I was a fetish object among a rarefied subset of girls who were either religious nutcases or were thinking of becoming religious nutcases. My checkered background as a fresh transfer student from an Orthodox Jewish seminary, which I'd assumed would be a major liability with the ladies, turned out to be an aphrodisiac for a certain kind of occult girl with a taste for self-flagellation.

Emily was one such. Today the events of our first meeting are hazy. It was definitely at a party, one of hundreds. There must have been the usual red plastic cups with vile liquor in them. She attended a neighboring college, where she was majoring in bio—botany, if I remember correctly. But not premed; she was adamant that her study of life was pure and uncompromised by any petty careerist calculations.

Within minutes of her saying "Oh, *really?*" to the disclosure about my years in seminary, we began to make out on a flimsy futon, whose squeaks and creaks sounded, to my ears at least, like the grumbling of disapproving gerbils. Then we stopped. That is, she stopped.

She told me that she was, sort of, Mormon. Such was my curse during that period. Because I attracted girls in the grip of religious mania, I was also doomed to be rejected because of it.

Since it had become painfully clear that I wouldn't be getting any action, I decided I might as well ask her about *The Book of Mormon*, which had always intrigued me. Years earlier, when I was in high school and super-religious, I'd found a copy of *The Book of Mormon* lying around in a subway station, taken it home, and proudly displayed the find to my mother, thoroughly creeping her out. I had no idea what the book was about but knew it was some kind of bizarro bible. That was enough to earn a spot on my bookshelf. But I didn't dare read it.

Now I was finally getting the story. Emily gave me the rundown. Basically the same spiel that the angel Moroni gave to Joseph. *A boat to America?* I asked. *Uh-huh,* she said. *Okay,* I replied, *just wanted to make sure I heard you right.*

It sounded like the backstory to every Jewish American novel of the twentieth century, to the kind of literature that had gotten me interested in literature to begin with.

I was delighted by the sheer weirdness of it, and was especially intrigued by the Jerusalem-to-Great-Lakes saga: that was exactly the story of my family. The idea that this peculiar journey was actually the plot of a 2,400-year-old epic and that this was all going on behind the scenes of the Hebrew Bible I knew—or thought I knew—so well was positively head-spinning.

I don't think I ever saw Emily again. We exchanged some e-mails, which, I seem to recall, eventually petered out into shortish messages that dealt exclusively with the topic of an aged pet dog who still lived with her parents and was like one of the family. Shortly before we lost touch, Emily told me she wasn't destined to be a Mormon after all. Instead she had discovered that she was a lesbian.

Years later, when I walked through the Old City of Jerusalem and visited the wall where Nephi killed Laban, something clicked. In college I'd been interested in *The Book of Mormon* as a reader, but years later, when I was in Jerusalem working on my own book, I saw it with the eyes of a writer. In connecting those ancient Jerusalem ruins with the American story, *The Book of Mormon* was sending a provocative message and changing all the literary rules.

If Nephi really lived here and sneaked around these streets and lived out this whole story here—unknown to the world until Joseph excavated it in 1827—it meant that other such hidden stories may have originated here. Maybe there were thirty other Nephi-like guys hanging around Jerusalem in 586 BCE who also fled to some unexpected destination and wrote a story about it. Maybe there were dozens of works by unknown small-time authors from Jerusalem. Maybe next week there'll be a Joseph Smith in India or Lithuania or Ghana who'll unearth one of these lost books.

For some reason we like to believe that there's always more to the story. Maybe this tendency to make sequels is somehow embedded in how we think. Just as we want and need a story to end, we also want and need a story to never end. We make sequels as a way of bringing our stories closer to life. As a matter of convention and convenience, stories have endings, but if we were to tell them honestly, stories would never end, just like life, whose dramas dip in and out of time and memory, are recalled, shared, stolen, reprised, recovered, revised—anything but neatly concluded. A sequel may well be a deformed kind of story, a pale likeness—as its critics have long charged—but even if it's silly or tragic or nobly deluded or tainted by a shameless profit motive, or, more likely, all of these at once, then all the more is it like life.

This had occurred to me one day in a Jerusalem Laundromat. Because I had no TV in my apartment, I'd adopted the sad habit of slipping away to a Laundromat to watch the *The Simpsons*. I'd watched the program from the very beginning of its run, from when it was a segment on the old *Tracey Ullman Show*. When it first aired, I was the same age as Bart. Now, all these years later, I was an adult embarking on my own projects in the world while Bart remained a ten-year-old punk. At first that made me kind of sad. But then it made me feel weirdly anxious and suffocated.

This, I believed, was why I liked sequels. Sequels don't necessarily believe in progress, but they do insist upon the passing of time, or at the very least a change of place. By contrast, a serial like *The Simpsons* can remain in a state of animated paralysis for eternity.

Critic Terry Castle has described sequels as tragic because they are motivated by a desperate human need to reproduce the original sensation of some pleasurable experience, an impulse, a "mad hope," she says, that is fated to miserable disappointment. But when I saw Bart still throwing spitballs at Springfield Elementary over twenty years later, *that* to me seemed like the tragedy of repetition: Sisyphus on a skateboard. And what made it truly gloomy was Bart's and his family's awareness that they are stuck in this frozen reality. After all these years, the people of Springfield would surely consider themselves lucky if the nuclear power plant finally did them in. This doomed consciousness, this narrative death wish, has become the undercurrent of the show.

But the sequel-y nature of *The Book of Mormon* meant that the old biblical saga wouldn't simply replay forever but somehow, some way, find a way out, maybe even a way forward. *The Book of Mormon* wasn't trying to reproduce the biblical story but rather to escape it by boldly reentering the original and steering it in a different direction. Maybe the sequel isn't subject to the tragedy of repetition: it's a solution to it.

Some people believe that the New Testament, especially the way it was read during the Reformation, helped launch the emerging form of the novel. Because it imagined cultural authority coming in the form of a *book*, and especially in a sequel form of a book, the New Testament opened the door for other sequels and for these new books to command their own kind of cultural authority. Hence the age of the Great European Novel. What *The Book of*

Mormon suggested to me was that the novel could return the favor: if the Bible created novels, maybe it was possible for the novel to create bibles. In Joseph you had someone who was both an old-style biblical prophet and the protagonist of a modern novel. Maybe the Bible could continue to evolve in the modern world—and not just through new readings but through new writings.

I'd always hoped that the Bible was still an open book, still in the process of being written. When I was a child, that was one of my first heretical thoughts. I've long had a special place in my heart for outsider Bible books, starting with those that were almost included in the Bible but at the last minute, and for various reasons, just didn't quite make the cut. Those ancient novellas, known collectively as the Apocrypha—the "hidden books"—were one of my earliest inspirations. As a Bible-reading kid who imagined what it would mean to be a writer, I learned about the Apocrypha—from the *Encyclopedia Judaica* one Sabbath afternoon—and was immediately able to identify. For an aspiring writer, there isn't much to learn from the story of God dictating the text to Moses on Mount Sinai. But the Bible's second-stringers seemed way more approachable as literary heroes.

Later, once I'd experienced my share of rejection, I was able to relate to the crushed feelings of that young scribe who one sunny day in Judea or Babylonia eagerly unfurled the parchment dropped in his mailbox, only to read: "We regret that we cannot include your story in the Bible. While your work was excellent, there were an unprecedented number of submissions this year . . ."

I especially appreciated the rejected writers' literary moxie. When you read a story in which a character is introduced as Tobias, whose father was Tobit and grandfather was Tobiel, and read about how sparrows crapped into a depressed guy's eyes (making him more depressed), and learn about a guy skinny-dipping with an angel, and a woman who's been married seven times, and then watch as the angel-loving skinny-dipper falls in love with the seven-time widow, you can't help but feel that the writer of the Book of Tobit is pulling out all the stops. You also start to understand why an editor might have passed on this one. What, after all, is the timeless meaning of a tale that is resolved by a guy roasting a fish liver, the nauseating odor of which repels a demon named Asmodeus?

But that's why I liked it. He took chances, this writer. He included a dog who follows Tobias and his angel around for no apparent reason. Even if a frisky little mutt had been following Jesus around Galilee—and, let's face it, one probably was—we'd never hear about it, because humorless Matthew wouldn't dare report it. But the author of the Book of Tobit exercised no such restraint, and that's what makes his story great. It's also what makes the *Book of Mormon* lore so compelling. For every account of a shimmery, baritone-voiced angel, there's another in which the prophet Joseph picks up a bugle and throws it at a guy who's threatened his beloved dog.

It's an impressive feat to write a story that's both Bible-like enough to be seriously considered for inclusion in the Bible yet ultimately too gonzo for the canon. That struck me as a killer combination, and an impressive model for any aspiring writer.

To me, *The Book of Mormon* came as an unexpected, much-welcomed addition to this shelf of Bible punk lit. It seemed too good to be true. Some kid from just outside Rochester, New York, just down the road from where I grew up in Cleveland, was making a serious go of it. Who knew that was even possible? How did a regular provincial boy manage to insert himself into the Big Epic?

It never quite made sense to me. And yet when I wandered around Jerusalem, it seemed plausible.

When I walk through Jerusalem, my personal history is all jumbled up with the big narratives, facts are as hazy as myth, and myths are as tangible as street signs. On my way back from the City of David, Nephi's hometown, I walked past Yehuda Halevi Elementary, a state religious school named for the medieval mystical poet who, according to legend, fulfilled his lifelong dream of making a pilgrimage to Jerusalem only to be murdered the moment he arrived. Once upon a time, my sister attended Yehuda Halevi Elementary. Prominently displayed on the wall of the school's auditorium had been a giant mural depicting the biblical story of the binding of Isaac. The dramatic, larger-than-life scene of Abraham tying his beloved son to an altar and raising the slaughterer's knife to the boy's neck was, I suppose, meant as an object lesson for misbehaving kindergarten–fifth graders. Maybe it was some teacher's or principal's idea of gallows humor. Today the motives for placing this macabre image in an elementary school are as mysterious and darkly comic as the biblical story itself.

Whatever the reason, my young mother hadn't been amused. The mural bothered her so much that she initially refused to enroll my sister in the school. But just as Sarah, in the Bible, relents to the sacrifice of her firstborn, so my mother too relented.

The mural after all did make some geographic sense. The binding of Isaac happened a ten-minute bus ride down the road from my sister's elementary school—I'd walked right past the spot in the Old City. Wasn't that why my parents had moved to Jerusalem in the first place, to erase the physical distance between themselves and these stories, to live inside them? You went to Jerusalem because the stories of Abraham and David and Jesus and Muhammad and thousands of saints and prophets weren't exotic tales but neighborhood gossip. You went there because the truth of the story was found neither in its universal message nor in the pages of a book but by encountering it locally and in the flesh.

In the book, the binding of Isaac was the event that marked the site where the city would one day be built. That story is essentially the founding myth of the city of Jerusalem. But unlike the myth of Romulus and Remus, the origin story of Rome, the binding of Isaac is taken as sober history by most of the people who live in Jerusalem today. If someone put a provision on the Jerusalem municipal ballot to declare the binding of Isaac story to be 100 percent factual, it would likely pass. For better or worse, these stories are alive. That's why I can't seem to stay away from the place, why I went there to finish my first book.

There aren't too many cities whose entire being is synonymous with a book, whose existence hinges on the story told in that book. Most great cities grow around a port; very few grow around a text. New York is a literary city because of the bursting diversity of life that has landed on its docks, the fortunes made and lost there.

Jerusalem is not like that at all. In Jerusalem, it isn't city life that generates literature but, oddly—irrationally—the other way around: it is a city sustained by stories. New York is about a hundred million things all at once, Jerusalem just one: the stories that were written in and about it. It's not an accident that New York is associated with the realist novel while the local literary form in Jerusalem is the hallucinatory rant. If no one had written a novel about New York, it would still be New York; but if no one had written the book about Jerusalem, and if people hadn't continued reading that book, the city might not even exist today. In this way,

Jerusalem is more purely—and more perversely—literary than any place I've ever known.

The city was etched onto the map by scribes of the most fanatical poetic bent, literary purists who spent much of their creative energy denouncing the falseness of images and utterly banishing visual representation. It is their second commandment, right behind belief in God. In fact, it's synonymous with belief in God. These writers dedicated their lives to the idea that "the word" was divinity itself.

That's why I go there to write. The scribes of Jerusalem set the lunatic standard for writers, as Joseph Smith well knew. They show us, by example, what it means to live and die by literature. If the written word is threatened, defend it. If it dies, die with it. But most of all, live by it without apologies. They demonstrated all that is beautiful and treacherous about that kind of thinking. Everyone knows that if you want to be a writer, especially in a world dominated by images, you must be kind of crazy. This is made clear to any aspiring writer every single day, sometimes multiple times a day. Those who make a commitment to the written word today are pitied and given a giant complex about it, even from supporters. ("I loved your book—have you ever thought about doing TV or movies?") When an Amazon reviewer—who *liked* your book—gives a higher ranking to a dish towel, what hope is there for a writer?

If you want to write books, you must learn to embrace the very real possibility that what you do isn't totally rational and possibly is even as batty as believing in the virgin birth. You must be a zealot for literature. You must prepare yourself for martyrdom. Jerusalem is an excellent training ground for this.

This is also why I can't live in Jerusalem. Because our world *is* one of images. Whatever can be gotten from Jerusalem must be of the portable variety, not much bigger than a pilgrim's keepsake, compact enough to fit into your bag and lugged back to reality and its shows. To linger in Jerusalem is a kind of romantic sickness.

This sickness has a name. In 1999, in preparation for the millennium, a group of researchers published an article in the *British Journal of Psychiatry* (*BJP*) describing a "Jerusalem syndrome." Upon arrival in the city of Jerusalem, some visitors decompensate, suffer a major mental break, in which the person can become utterly convinced that he (or, in rare cases, she) is a character from the Bible, usually Jesus or David or John the Baptist. Occasionally a guy will think he's Samson, the Gaza strongman. Very rarely will someone call himself Habakkuk or Jehoshaphat or some minor prophet— apparently few people are modest in their delusions. We know of no one who has mistaken himself for Nephi. Yet.

The psychiatric cases followed a similar enough pattern that a local hospital, the Kfar Shaul Mental Health Center, created a special unit for these patients. It also launched a thirteen-year study. Based on its clinical experience, the research team, headed by the hospital's chief, Yair Bar-El, identified three types of Jerusalem syndrome sufferers.

Type I. *Jerusalem Syndrome Superimposed on Previous Psychotic Illness.* This first type comes with four subtypes: (i) psychotic identification with biblical characters, (ii) psychotic identification with an idea, (iii) "magical ideas" concerning connection between health and holy places, and (iv) family problems culminating in psychosis in Jerusalem.

Then there's Type II: *Jerusalem Syndrome Superimposed on and Complicated by Idiosyncratic Ideations.* This one comes with two subtypes.

Now, Type III is where things get really interesting. The authors of the *BJP* article refer to it as "the most fascinating" manifestation of the malady: *Jerusalem Syndrome Discrete Form, Unconfounded by Previous Psychopathology.* In other words, the sudden onset of Jerusalem syndrome in an otherwise healthy person who has no history of mental illness and whose original motive for visiting the city was merely recreational. This unfortunate tourist's holiday in Jerusalem, however, is anything but relaxing. The authors of the study identify seven stages of Type III Jerusalem syndrome. In their words:

1) Anxiety, agitation, nervousness and tension, plus other unspecified reactions.

2) Declaration of the desire to split away from the group or the family and to tour Jerusalem alone. (Tourist guides aware of Jerusalem Syndrome and of the significance of such declarations may at this point refer the tourist to the Kfar Shaul Mental Health Center for psychiatric evaluation in an attempt to pre-empt the subsequent stages of the syndrome. If unattended, these stages are usually unavoidable.)

3) A need to be clean and pure; obsession with taking baths and showers; compulsive fingernail and toenail cutting.

4) Preparation, often with the aid of hotel bed linen, of a long, ankle-length, toga-like gown, which is always white.

5) The need to scream, shout, or sing out loud psalms, verses from the Bible, religious hymns or spirituals. Manifestations of this type serve as a warning to hotel personnel and tour guides, who should then attempt to have the tourist taken for professional treatment. Failing this, the two last stages will develop.

6) A procession or march to one of Jerusalem's holy places.

7) Delivery of a "sermon" in a holy place. The sermon is usually very confused and based on an unrealistic plea to humankind to adopt a more wholesome, moral, simple way of life.

As it turns out, there's only one certain way to be cured of the desire for humankind to adopt a more wholesome, moral, simple way of life: The only effective known remedy for Jerusalem syndrome is to *leave Jerusalem immediately.*

The researchers emphasize the importance of place, the powerful overlap between a person's "inner geography" and actual geography. A regular tourist moves from his home to peripheral places, "vacation sites." A pilgrim, in contrast, moves in the opposite direction: he moves from the periphery, where he actually lives and gets his mail, to his "true home," the holy city, the place that has been the focal point of his mental life. To this person, the arrival in Jerusalem is an arrival home.

For some this homecoming is bliss. For others, though, arriving in modern Jerusalem, not quite the city they'd pictured from reading the Bible, is deeply disillusioning and destabilizing; thus the mind compensates by generating a powerful delusion. At least, that's the theory. Whatever its source, the researchers believe its clinical cure consists of physically removing this poor Bible-quoting, bedsheet-wearing person from Jerusalem posthaste.

Bar-El's research team may have been among the first to study Jerusalem syndrome, but observers have long noticed something seriously strange with Jerusalem's visitors. Isolated descriptions abound. Bar-El cites the example of Nikolai Gogol, who became fixated on visiting Jerusalem in search of a cure for his TB and for help in writing the next installment of *Dead Souls*—a doomed effort, as it turned out. According to the clinicians at Kfar Shaul, Gogol suffered from Jerusalem syndrome, Type I, subtype iii.

For some reason neither Bar-El's team nor subsequent researchers have cited the most vividly documented case study of Jerusalem syndrome: Jesus of Nazareth. The story of his arrival in Jerusalem, as told in the New Testament, can be read as a catalog of the syndrome's clinical criteria. He arrived as a visitor in the city with a book in his hand—the Hebrew Bible—claiming to be a character from this book: the "prince of peace" referred to in the Book of Isaiah, the "anointed one" from the Book of Daniel and Psalms, the direct heir of David's royal lineage as recorded in the books of Samuel and Ruth.

It's easy to forget that before Jesus was himself a character in the Bible, he was just another out-of-towner wearing a white sheet *claiming* to be a character from the Bible. Like any Jerusalem syndrome sufferer, he was a tourist citing passages from a text. Upon arriving in Jerusalem, Jesus cycled through the syndrome's seven clinical steps, as described by Bar-El. There was acute agitation. A fixation with bathing. There was self-segregation from his group. There was the shouting of Psalms, a march to a holy site, and a frenzied sermon delivered at this site. And of course there was that telltale symptom, the "unrealistic plea to humankind to adopt a more wholesome, moral, simple way of life." Like many Jerusalem syndrome sufferers, Jesus committed a few minor criminal acts, and landed in the hands of the authorities. Jesus, in short, has been the inspiration for centuries of Jerusalem syndrome sufferers not because he originated it but because he was one of its most eminent victims.

And it goes back even further than that, to the beginning of the saga, when Abraham, a foreigner overcome by religious fer-

vor, made his pilgrimage to Mount Moriah—the site later identified with Jerusalem—for the sole purpose of committing the truly
insane act of sacrificing an innocent child. Jerusalem was founded
by a psychotic tourist, and the rest is history.

During my walk through the Old City, I'd observed Jerusalem's
pilgrims suffering under the midday sun, weighed down by large
bottles of water and backpacks full of snacks and souvenir nativity
scenes. I watched them wander around the alleys, caressing the city
walls as they walked by, kissing any stone that had a good story
attached to it. The most successful among them would end up
either hanging on crosses or going completely bananas. To make a
pilgrimage to Jerusalem and truly meet it on its own terms would
mean to partner in its delusion. But is that the only way to truly see
it? Is there any other way?

Another team of researchers raised serious objections to Jerusalem syndrome. The data, they claimed, did not point to anything
out of the ordinary. The number of tourists in Jerusalem exhibiting
this form of psychosis was not unusual, and possibly even lower than
might be expected in any tourist city, and according to the researchers the cases always began before the visit to Jerusalem. There is a
well-documented relationship generally between psychotic breaks
and travel (which wouldn't surprise any person who's ever traveled
by airplane). Kfar Shaul's patients probably would have experienced
a similar breakdown if they had visited Milwaukee. The number of
delusional tourists in Jerusalem is therefore nothing to write home
about and certainly nothing to write about in the *British Journal of
Psychiatry*, say the critics.

They may be right. But even so, I believe that Jerusalem syndrome is real. If Jerusalem syndrome doesn't exist, why did it seem so undeniably true to the researchers of Kfar Shaul hospital? Would the editors of the *British Journal of Psychiatry* have accepted an article that posited a Milwaukee syndrome? With Jerusalem syndrome, the misguidedness of the idea—and the acceptance of it, despite its being misguided—is a proof of its existence. The powerful plausibility of illusion is the essence of Jerusalem syndrome. Maybe the researchers themselves became infected by the condition they intended to study: the misattribution of strange and fantastical properties to this dusty hill town in the Judean Hills. Maybe the psychiatric theory of Jerusalem syndrome is itself a type of Jerusalem syndrome, or at least a symptom of it.

In a place like Jerusalem, even perfectly sane people, the researchers themselves, can't help but believe some version of the city's fictions. It's an organic element of the place. It's not a coincidence, for example, that the name of the leading Jerusalem syndrome researcher, Bar-El, translates as "Son of God." It's a common name in Jerusalem—is it common in Milwaukee? Maybe the theory of Jerusalem syndrome doesn't describe a psychiatric condition but rather explains how stories are made, how belief in a story can breathe life into it.

In their 1999 article, the Jerusalem syndrome theorists briefly alluded to the reading habits of their patients. With a few isolated exceptions, every Type III Jerusalem syndrome specimen—those with no background of mental illness—read the Bible intensively from childhood. Although the researchers didn't make much of it, this detail seems to suggest that study subjects had been predisposed to the syndrome by something just as significant as a background of mental illness: a history of obsessive reading.

As the article describes it, Type III Jerusalem syndrome patients

all seem to grow up in homes where "the Bible was the most important book to the family, and they would read it together at least
once a week. The Bible would also serve as a source of answers to
seemingly insoluble problems."

To the researchers, the powerful desire to overidentify with a
story's characters is the result of religious belief. But maybe it says
more about the experience of reading than about religion. Where I
grew up, it was perfectly natural to accept as fact that you and your
family and friends were *literally* among the Israelites who stood at
Mount Sinai, that you were the direct blood relatives of specific
people who lived five thousand years ago. Belief in these doctrines
was generated not necessarily by simplemindedness but rather by
the power of literary suggestion, by having read about it thousands
of times so that it became true. Many of us spent more time with
Moses and Miriam than we did with our own uncles and aunts.
We formed memories of these characters, these places, these stories.
They were as real, as actual, as any memory.

Maybe Jerusalem syndrome isn't really about psychosis or religion. Nor is it necessarily limited to the city of Jerusalem or the
Bible. Maybe it's about reading and writing in general, about the
link between the two, between receiving stories and creating them.
It's about what happens when writing becomes a way of life. When
your life starts to take the form of a book, when books take the
form of life.

It is assumed that people who exhibit Jerusalem syndrome
symptoms suffer a wild, uncanny—but inaccurate—sense that
they are a character in a certain book. But maybe there's a Type
IV Jerusalem syndrome, in which a reader not only imagines himself a character in a book but *has actually become a character in the
book.* What's more, this person became that character because he,

or someone else, put him into that book. In other words: the madness of writing.

The story of Jesus proves that if you are a serious enough reader, your life can take a startling turn. If you believe that you are a character in a book, and if you live your life in accordance with this belief, you may in time literally become a character in that book. For every Old Testament, there's a reader whose radical reading habits and peculiar dedication to the original story will generate a New Testament. Sometimes the obsessive reader will be the new book's author; sometimes, like Jesus, its protagonist; sometimes, like Joseph Smith, both.

It's a theory the prophet Brigham Young may have had in mind when he posed this challenge to early *Book of Mormon* readers: "Do you read the scriptures . . . as though you were writing them?" Joseph certainly did. It has become a cliché in writings about Joseph Smith that he "read little other than the Bible." This observation is usually meant to diminish his literary capacities. But in doing so, it misses something important: reading a book as though one were writing it, this unique way of entering into a book, even just one book, can be enormously powerful. In fact, the reading of "only" one book is exactly where the power lies: this one book holds every story and mystery in it. What other book would one need? To read a single book that closely, and in this kind of enraptured way, is a radical way to read and, as a result, opens up radical literary possibilities.

Joseph appealed to me most because he seemed like a writer anyone could identify with but whose literary ambitions were fantastically peculiar. Unlike me, or anyone I knew, Joseph had set a fairly imposing goal for his first book: to have it stand next to the Bible. But that huge and provocative contrast between him and most writers was precisely the attraction. What was the difference between Joseph and any author? Maybe it was merely one of degree. Was it possible that Joseph simply carried the literary impulse to its logical extreme? (What would that say about the literary impulse?) Was it possible he enacted a kind of *literature ad absurdum*, that he undertook the risky project of completely embracing Jerusalem syndrome? Did he lose himself in it? Did Joseph Smith's life represent what happens if you're really dedicated to literature, like, *really* dedicated? Did Joseph do this so that we don't have to?

From the day he burst onto the literary scene with his debut bible, Joseph was condemned for fostering a cult around his book. But isn't that what literature has always done? Aren't a lot of ambitious books today an attempt to launch a new cult? Is Joseph's crime that he succeeded? That with his shovel and spade he unearthed the ghost of Jerusalem syndrome and unleashed it in America?

For me, it was that piece of the saga, the frame story of Joseph excavating and translating the plates and publishing the book, that came so vividly to mind when I rediscovered *The Book of Mormon* in Jerusalem. With the almost-done manuscript of my first book sitting on my kitchen table, I suddenly saw Joseph in a new light: despite his outrageous literary ambitions, he also was once just a guy with a manuscript sitting on his kitchen table.

As I sat in the Old City, watching Jerusalem's pilgrims struggling to stay sane, or at least hydrated, I finally got it: I had been coming back to Jerusalem in order to figure out how to leave it. I'd been looking for a way to write myself out of the place. But there was no need: the story of leaving Jerusalem for America had already been written. Thanks to Joseph, it had also been translated and published. What I had to do was somehow write myself into that story.

And so I decided to become a pilgrim myself. To take the daunting, heretical jump of going on a pilgrimage *out* of Jerusalem. I would follow Nephi, leave Jerusalem for good, climb aboard the rickety ship, and plunge into the deep. Nor would I come up again, be seen again, until I discovered a new world and set my eyes on sacred Hill Cumorah.

THE LAND OF ZARAHEMLA

After Nephi left Jerusalem, he and his family and some friends wandered for many years in the desert southeast of Jerusalem. Even though they had a magical compass called the Liahona, they were basically lost and directionless. When they reached the coast of the Arabian Sea, probably somewhere around modern-day Oman, Nephi was commanded to build a ship.

I read about this boat as I sat at a gate in the Dallas–Fort Worth airport. I'd intentionally put off reading this chapter of the book until now, saving it for the moment when I was en route to the very place where Nephi's boat made landfall, the new American promised land—or, as we call it, Guatemala.

Some readers are encouraged by evidence, though preliminary, that Mesoamerica is the one *and only* setting for the *Book of Mormon* saga. This is part of a long-standing, ongoing debate about where in the New World Nephi and his family landed and where their thousand-year American story took place. For a long time it was believed that the events described in the book happened over a vast territory spanning North and South America. Among *Book of Mormon* readers, this is called the Hemispheric Theory, or the Heartland or Great Lakes Theory. It has many variants. But all agree that the lands where the Nephites once roamed were vast, and that the Nephites' story concluded in a giant bloody battle in what is today upstate New York. This theory holds that the hill down the road from the Smith farm, where Moroni buried the gold plates, was the same hill where the final battle took place, and where Mormon was killed. This is the view that Joseph Smith seemed to have held. Though it does have vocal adherents among today's *Book of Mormon* readers, this theory is generally disavowed.

These days, the Limited Geography Theory (LGT) is the majority view. The geography of the *Book of Mormon* story, according to this view, does not—cannot possibly—include North America. Mormon never dipped his feet in Lake Superior. Young Moroni never made a snowman. The consensus today is that all of the *Book of Mormon*'s New World action took place in a relatively small region somewhere in Central or South America. Most believe it was Mesoamerica. The story's principal characters, therefore, were Maya or Olmec people. Nephi and his descendants, the first Jewish Americans, were technically Israelite-Maya. Even the ever-cautious, ever-political Church of Jesus Christ of Latter-day Saints, which doesn't take an official position on *Book of Mormon* geography, tacitly nods toward the LGT by consistently giving the story Mesoamerican settings in its official narratives. In its movies, in live productions such as the Hill Cumorah Pageant, and in church paintings and merchandising, the settings and costumes of the characters always have a strong Mesoamerican flavor.

But even within the official storytelling ranks the question remains open. Filmmaker Kieth Merrill, who went with an exclusively Mesoamerican setting for *The Testaments*, the biggest and most popular church-funded *Book of Mormon* film to date, has apparently backtracked on the LGT. He reportedly regrets his earlier decision and now believes the film should have had scenes set in the Great Lakes region. And so the debate goes on and the search continues.

Some of the Mesoamerica proponents consider the archaeological proofs compelling enough for a person, or, say, a busload of people, to make a rather picturesque vacation of the LGT. Even as academic scholars continue to excavate Maya and Olmec sites, groups of *Book of Mormon* readers are traveling down to Guatemala and Mexico to explore the extraordinary ruins and draw their own conclusions.

I'd signed up for one such tour, an intensive sixteen-day exploration run by a mom-and-pop company based in Utah. The trip would begin in Guatemala City/City of Nephi—the first major New World site mentioned in *The Book of Mormon*—then wend its way north, deep into the jungle of Petén, near the border of Belize; then south, down to Lake Atitlán/Waters of Mormon, where Alma was on the lam as a fugitive from King Noah; then northwest along the Pacific coastal plain and into the mountains of southern Mexico, where the notorious Gadianton robbers once dwelled. We would cross into the Chiapas Valley—*The Book of Mormon*'s glorious Land of Zarahemla—then into the Mexican states of Tabasco and Veracruz, known in the story as the Land of Desolation. We'd stop just short of the Land of Moron, aka Oaxaca, Mexico.

Our destination was a mountain in Mexico that is believed to be *The Book of Mormon*'s true Hill Cumorah, the site where the Nephite people met their tragic end and near the spot where Mormon fashioned the gold plates before giving them to Moroni to carry many miles north, to the area now known as upstate New York. There, he was to deposit them in a hill (which in recent years, according to the LGT, mistakenly came to be called Hill Cumorah—more on that later).

Along the route between the City of Nephi and Cumorah, we

would explore ancient Mesoamerican ruins—Maya and Olmec—with our *Book of Mormon* in hand. Over the course of two weeks, we would retrace the entirety of the New World saga of *The Book of Mormon* by examining the physical remains of the story, much like a biblical archaeology tour to Jerusalem and Jericho and the Sea of Galilee. And like America's Holy Land pilgrims, we would stay in luxury hotels, with food and expenses included. We would travel by what our information packets gallantly called a "motor coach," chartered, and would take two short private flights in-country. In all, we'd cover over 1,000 miles. It wasn't a beach vacation, it was a mission—though a high-end one, to be sure.

The Mesoamerican theory of *The Book of Mormon* does not come cheap. But there was no disputing the tour company's claim that this was to be a once-in-a-lifetime opportunity to see the lands where the story really took place, to walk in the footsteps of real *Book of Mormon* characters, to behold the true Hill Cumorah.

As I waited for my flight to board, I struck up a conversation with a fellow member of my tribe, a young Israeli who seemed not the least bit surprised to be chatting in Hebrew with a stranger on a flight from Dallas to Guatemala City. He was fresh out of the army, covered in beads, and preparing to trek across Central and South America with his pals, smoke the local stuff, grow out his hair, and, he believed, with all the certainty of delusion, put his army traumas out of mind.

The young guy nodded toward a third member of our tribe, a Hasidic man who was balancing two massive hatboxes. "That son of a whore has been following me since Tel Aviv," said my friend. "I think he's trailing me." I couldn't tell whether he was joking, and surmised that he'd gotten a jump start on the smoking-grass segment of his journey. He asked me what I was after in Guate-mala. I told him about *The Book of Mormon*, how the events of the story may have taken place in Mesoamerica. I gave him the basic rundown.

"Whoa, no way," he said. "That's amazing. There were Jews from Jerusalem who went there *on a boat* and became Mayan guys, with feather headdresses and stuff? That's some trippy shit."

I felt gratified to imagine this kid in a few weeks' time, wear-ing nothing but a loincloth and leather headband, covered in even more beads, lying half-conscious on a hammock somewhere in the jungle, taking huge bong hits and blowing his pals' minds with tales about how a group of stoner Israelites took a ship to Cen-tral America in ancient times, hung out a lot, and wrote a totally stoned-out bible.

Our conversation was interrupted by an announcement. *"Now boarding: all members of the One Pass Program, Star Travellers, Visa Explorers, executive members and associates, Platinum and Premier Platinum, Star Alliance One and Premier Star Alliance, Gold Star Members, Global Service 1K, and first class."*

Not a single person stepped forward. The flight attendant con-tinued: *"Now seating all Silver Star members."*

This time one guy, out of hundreds waiting around, stepped forward: the Hasid.

I could hear my young Israeli friend mutter, "Sonuva whore."

Our flight was bursting with Judeo-Christian fervor. As I made my way down the aisle, I passed by the Judeo part; the Hasid, a few rows up from me, was rocking lightly in his seat, mumbling psalms from a Hebrew Bible, his long beard curled up on his chest like a napping kitten. The remainder of the plane was packed with non-Mormon Christian missionaries—not the group I'd be trav-eling with in Guatemala—sporting identical blue backpacks and matching ill-fitting caps. Some of the missionaries seemed like missionaries; others struck me as not particularly godly. All of them were fussy and friendly and loud.

I'd been with this group for hours now, having met them way back on the security line, where the mobs of tired men, women, and children wearing pajamas conjured a scene of villagers taken prisoner in an early-morning raid. The missionaries and I had become friends of sorts. I'd agreed to watch their bags; they'd given me crackers. We had a good thing going. I'd overheard and very nearly joined an argument between high schoolers speculating about whether Guatemala would have a Denny's, or at least a Waffle House, and the related question: will this theoretical Guatemalan Denny's/Waffle House be as good as their home Denny's/Waffle House?

At some point during the controversy, as it became personal and involved the tweeting of unflattering instagrams and increasingly sarcastic hashtags, a church elder walked over, overheard what was being discussed, and with a tart Georgia lilt said, "Oh, *hush*." To my astonishment, the kids became instantly silent.

Among those who hadn't been talking of Denny's, it had become a game to listen to the airport PA announcer struggle to pronounce names that really did seem to be getting progressively more complicated, and cheer her on as though she were an underdog contestant plowing through rounds of a quiz show. Among some boys there was a grotesque preboarding gorging on Chicken McNuggets.

Seated next to me on the plane was a sixteen-year-old girl from Tennessee who had the words *Golden Gal* emblazoned in large sequined letters on the ass of her jeggings. Golden Gal brandished a three-and-a-half-foot-long plastic wand filled with M&Ms, which jabbed my neck each time she uncorked it and tipped it back into her mouth—which was often. (To be fair, she did kindly offer me some.) GG chatted frequently with an endless shouting chorus of female family members.

I wasted no time in putting on my headphones, and began to doze off to the sound of an actor's ludicrously deep voice reading from *The Book of Mormon*. As I fell into a dehydrated airplane stupor, a kind of torturous trance, the actor's voice became the distant sound of a voice, and my thoughts morphed into an anxiety carousel of word noise.

Like anyone with a soul, I hate air travel. At the airport, you arrive barefoot and accused, ceding all agency to the control of a remote, faceless tower, like Kafka's unreachable Castle or the indifferent God of the Old Testament. The airplane itself, tightly packed with strangers in various states of unconsciousness, is essentially a mass grave. When you arrive at your destination, you are a ghost of yourself.

A swift, hollow blow rammed my forehead, shaking me out of sleep. I saw Golden Gal reach into the overhead compartment, her candy wand swinging recklessly. But it was just as well. We had arrived in Guatemala City, the ancient City of Nephi.

Nephi and his clan made landfall in America somewhere around 591 BCE, a few years before the Babylonians would lay waste to their hometown and mine, Jerusalem. Nephi's father had foreseen the sack of Jerusalem, the cataclysm that sent the Israelites, Nephi's former neighbors in Jerusalem, into exile and left them heartbroken "by the rivers of Babylon," as the biblical poet famously described them, remembering Zion and weeping and refusing to sing their beautiful hymns. While all that was happening, Nephi and his family were making a fresh start across the globe, in America. In their own way, Nephi and company, like the prophet Jeremiah of the

Hebrew Bible, were among the generation of Jerusalem's dispossessed.

Though there is much dispute over when the Hebrew Bible was edited and compiled—whether before, during, or after the Babylonian exile—much of the story was clearly written to convey a sense of doom. It makes sense that people unsure of their future, who fear imminent extinction, might want to preserve their story, or even reimagine it completely. That was certainly Nephi's experience: on his way out of Jerusalem he'd grabbed the brass plates from Laban, and then, sitting by the rivers of his own Babylon, in the New World, he began writing the next chapters.

He also founded the first Israelite settlement in Guatemala. This city would remain under the sovereignty of the Nephites for roughly the next 450 years, that is, until about 120 years before Jesus. That first New World settlement is known in the story as the City of Nephi; in the Maya archaeological record it is known as Kaminaljuyú; we know it today as Guatemala City.

The opening sections of *The Book of Mormon* are basically the Hebrew Bible told backward. The story of how Nephi's family got to America is a subtle respooling of the biblical yarn: instead of a story about a lifesaving boat (Noah's) followed by wandering in the desert (the exodus of the Hebrew slaves from Egypt) followed by an arrival in the Promised Land, this story *starts* in said Promised Land, moves into the desert wilderness, and then circles back to a boat. It's almost as if we're watching the story rewind back to that original ship and launch forward again, this time in a new and completely different direction. The ship is the vehicle that transports the story from the old biblical saga into a parallel narrative, the American sequel.

As Nephi builds his ship, his brothers Laman and Lemuel, as usual, mock him mercilessly. The number of times Nephi has the crap beat out of him by his brothers in this story makes you want to give the guy a hug and tell him that everything will be all right. I must admit, however, that in this case they were right to laugh. The theme of prophets in boats is a running joke in the Bible.

Unlike classical Greek heroes, the Israelites were not big fans of bodies of water, much less seafaring. The authors of the Hebrew Bible claimed competence neither as sailors nor even as well-behaved passengers. The two major maritime stories in the Hebrew Bible both contain elements of farce. The first involves Noah, whose ship has no navigation, which turns out not to be a problem as it also has no destination. It simply goes up with the flood tide and drifts around aimlessly until it washes up, comically, on top of a mountain. Noah, however, seems heroic compared to the Bible's second major seafarer, Jonah, who insists that the crew of a sinking ship save themselves by tossing him overboard, which they do.

A corollary to these antisailing stories is the famous tale of the parting of the Red Sea, the fantasy of crossing a giant body of water as though it were a stroll in the park. It's as if the Hebrew Bible were warning us: jump overboard or pray for a miraculous reprieve—just do whatever you can to avoid sea voyages.

That's why the idea of Nephi, from landlocked Jerusalem, building a ship for a transoceanic journey—in what would be by far the longest sea voyage in history—gave both Nephi's brothers and me, when I read it, a good laugh. But *The Book of Mormon's* seafaring plot, whether a joke or not, is certainly a signal that this story, like all good sequels, offers some new twists, some surprises.

According to my trip itinerary, the tour guide was supposed to meet me at the airport. Waiting for my luggage, I fumbled through a carry-on bag for my brand-new BOOK OF MORMON LAND TOURS nametag. For months before the trip I'd received many wonderful mailings, which appeared with magical frequency in whimsically shaped boxes: lots of informational packets, a poster-sized map of Nephite/Maya civilization, and a giant, scrupulously detailed textbook with maps and diagrams that illustrated parallels between the *Book of Mormon* saga and Mesoamerican history, literature, culture, language, anthropology, and especially geography. My tour guide was the book's coauthor, Lee Thomas.

Outside the terminal, I immediately identified Lee as the large man standing among a crowd of Guatemalans who was most likely to have descended from the earliest Mormon settlers of Utah. ("Pioneers on both sides," he would later tell me, referring to his own and his wife's families.) The placard in his hand, presumably with my name on it, was drooped over and thus unreadable. This was because Lee was doubled over in laughter, goofing off with two cabbies.

I walked up and tapped him on the shoulder.

"*Hey!*" he said, and deployed a big swooping handshake that was more ranch wrangler than doorbell missionary. "You must be Avi." He pronounced my name with uncommon precision, which came as a relief from an anxiety I hadn't quite realized I'd been feeling.

As the hotel shuttle zigzagged through the streets of Guatemala City, Lee asked, "So, are you a longtime member of the church?" I conceded that I was not and that I was in fact a longtime Jew. Lee seemed to take the news in stride. As it turned out, he had a confession of his own: he had just seen a Hasidic man emerge from the airport terminal and wondered if perhaps this man with the big beard and black hat was the mysterious Steinberg from the East Coast who'd signed up for his tour.

"When I saw that fella," Lee said, "I was thinking, 'Wow, this is gonna be real *neat.*'"

"I hope you're not disappointed."

"Oh no!" he said. "Not *at all.*"

Mormons make regular visits to their local temples to baptize, by proxy, dead people—especially Anne Frank—who didn't have the opportunity to do it for themselves during their living years. This tends to bother Jews—especially Elie Wiesel—though I personally don't mind and actually rather appreciate that someone wants to give my soul a dip. It certainly could use one.

Something about the long lull in my first conversation with Lee gave me the sneaking sense that we were headed toward the big talk, in which Mormons unnecessarily apologize for the misunderstanding regarding Anne Frank.

But that would come later. Instead we got polygamy out of the way. "I know about Jewish people mostly from TV and *Fiddler on the Roof*," Lee was saying as we waited at a red light. "And I'll bet you probably know about us from TV too. You're probably thinking, 'So how many wives does he have?'"

"Yeah—how many *do* you have?"

"Ha, right. Well, I know you're kidding. But as you probably know, that practice was discontinued over a hundred years ago, and it was only instituted for a very brief period, during a time of peril."

I always feel for Mormons when they get defensive about "plural marriage." Isn't every religion entitled to a few youthful indiscretions? God knows Jews were polygamous (God knows because he encouraged it). For another block or two, Lee and I traded a few more jokes and then, thankfully, the van arrived at the hotel.

From the balcony of my sixth-floor hotel room I had a magnificent view of the Land of Nephi. It was exactly as I'd imagined it, exactly as I'd been given to imagine it by *The Book of Mormon's* descriptions. It was a green land of minerals and wood, of lush growth and overgrowth. It was a city that rested luxuriously upon a tropical plateau and received refreshing showers with regularity—it was quite unlike Jerusalem, a desert fortress town that crouched jealously over a tiny creek. Still, through the large and woolly tropical trees I could see small hints of contemporary life in Guatemala's capital that reminded me of the Jerusalem I knew: unsmiling men with rifles standing guard in front of family restaurants.

I watched a spectacular storm drifting toward Guatemala City and the surrounding Land of Nephi. A front of dark gray clouds rolled by overhead and met the surrounding mountains, enclosing the city as if it were a giant terrarium. This was a welcome distraction from the situation in my closet, where I'd discovered a mysterious pair of pants.

It's hard to describe how large these pants were without reference to the number of people who might fit into them at one time. The trousers, I estimated, would comfortably host me and the members of my immediate family, with enough room to allow us to play gin rummy at my Aunt Miriam's fold-up card table. These pants were not just wide but tall, on the order of a giant flag, the kind that inspires people to write national anthems and brings tears to the eyes of grown men. A garment such as this deserves ample space, a stadium, a battlefield. It doesn't belong hanging awkwardly in a hotel room closet—especially not *my* hotel room closet. I found its sudden presence in my living space, its proximity, a distraction and possibly an alarming clue in some mystery I wanted no part of.

Tomorrow I would meet the rest of the tour group. Tonight, though, I was stranded in my room by the rain, left to contemplate either these mysterious, epic trousers or the mysterious, epic map I'd received in the mail along with Lee's tome. The full-color "Proposed Map" of *Book of Mormon* lands had itself been too large—and too much of an objet d'art—to lug around with me in my tour baggage. I'd photocopied a smaller version of the map, which I now unfurled and pinned to my bed with pillows.

It's rare in our day to think about, much less to use, an experimental map. Our maps are packed coast-to-coast with the same predictable, mostly reliable information. But this is a fairly recent development. Only a few hundred years ago, Earth's maps were full of speculation and mystery, outright rumors and bold mythologizing. Maps were used partly for navigation and partly to locate the precise boundaries of experience, the line that marked the exact end of what was known and the beginning of the great Somewhere Else. Outer regions were embellished with little doodles of fantastic creatures, scaly monsters, and Amazon women. *Here Be Dragons*, they'd sometimes write, like a dark analog to our more optimistic *You Are Here*. Modern maps give us the impression we have all things figured out. But the map spread out over my hotel bed did not give this impression at all.

Although the Isthmus of Tehuantepec—the dainty wrist that links the south of Mexico to Central America—is a silhouette of land familiar to me, the place-names that dotted it on this map were not. Or rather, they were familiar from a completely different context: from my reading of *The Book of Mormon*. Here were the Land of Many Waters, the adjoining Lands of Bountiful and Desolation, Zarahemla. The isthmus was identified as *The Book of Mormon*'s "narrow neck of land," one of the story's major geographic markers. It was jarring to see these labels grafted onto a recognizable, real-world landmass, like waking up one day and discovering that all your friends now go by names from *Anna Karenina*. Even more odd and discomfiting were the place-names punctuated with question marks. That isn't a symbol you want to see on a map.

In addition to the question marks, there were trail lines that went in circles with no apparent destination; known cities were omitted. It was almost as if this map's purpose weren't to guide but to visually represent a feeling of disorientation.

The earliest editions of *The Book of Mormon*—those that Joseph himself edited—had no maps or geographical cross-references. They also lacked verse markers, being laid out instead in continuous, unnumbered sentences and paragraphs. The first edition to break up the text into verses, in the 1850s—after Joseph was gone—was also the first to include detailed notes on geography. Maybe the impulse to order a text into neatly measured verses corresponds with the impulse to chart a story numerically on a real map. Both are motivated by a desire to move a story from novelistic fiction into epic history, from the subjectivity of a story to the objectivity of measured quantities. But putting that map to actual use, navigating a real terrain with it, that was bolder still—and possibly a bit daft.

I was well aware that all of this sounded completely nuts. At times it gave me serious pause. I vacillated between thinking it was the good kind of nuts and the bad kind. In darker moments—and my first night in Guatemala City was one—I feared, genuinely feared, that my hasty enrollment on this tour, and this quest in general, were not the actions of a happy, grounded person.

What was this really about? Was I really here to find something, or was I actually avoiding something? Was my quest really just a fancy way of running away from problems on the home front? I'd recently entered into a marriage that was doomed and, worse, doomed largely by my own amorphous sense that it was doomed. My personal hope, or so I'd told myself, was that I might find something genuinely uplifting in witnessing, participating in, a scripture in progress, in seeing how a big story was created from the ground up. It would be like watching the formation of a literary sun: wouldn't that be moving?

So on the one hand, I hoped there might be something inspiring in this journey to Guatemala in search of Zarahemla. On the other hand, *I was in Guatemala in search of Zarahemla*. That just *sounded* nuts. Maybe it was all just a cover. Maybe my quest for Nephite lands was just a means of disappearing into a lala fantasyland, a way to escape the complications of real life. Maybe that's the reason anyone searches for Zarahemla. Maybe that's why Joseph Smith, newly married and facing a tumultuous road ahead, had become enamored with Zarahemla, the idea of Zarahemla, to begin with.

What if I was like that Dutch guy, Jan Dibbets, who once picked at random the coordinates of four spots in Holland and then made an epic search to find them? He claimed that by the time he finally did locate them, the four random spots didn't seem random. The whole thing felt incredibly meaningful, he said. But to me, in my hotel room that night, his project sounded terribly sad. It seemed like a nihilistic satire of life. When Jan Dibbets arrived at one of his meaningless coordinates, he reported seeing "two trees, one with a dog pissing on it." How he hadn't hanged himself from one of those trees seemed remarkable to me.

There were surely many causes of my gloom, all the usual reasons—my failures in life and love—but there was no question that what triggered it was showing up for this tour, sitting in this random hotel room in Guatemala City, a strange, probably hostile man's giant pants lurking in my closet, not totally understanding why I would want to go to a distant country in search of a nonexistent country and with only a half-berserk map covered in question marks as my guide.

As a wild jungle storm lashed the plate-glass windows of my room, I could empathize with those travelers who ended up wrapping themselves in hotel bedsheets and, as the Jerusalem syndrome researchers reported, running into the street and loudly making an "unrealistic plea to humankind to adopt a more wholesome, moral, simple way of life." That's what it feels like to be lost.

At 4:49 a.m. I was jarred awake by a hideous shriek that, after a heart-exploding moment of panic, turned out to be the hotel alarm clock. I hadn't set it. Immediately I looked toward the door of the closet. The giant man. His pants. My suspicions proved correct: the pants had brought about a wicked spirit. I couldn't get back to sleep.

In the bathroom, my face looked all wrong. My mouth seemed misplaced, as though poised to whisper into my own ear. More disturbingly, the slight pinching sensation on my scalp turned out to be little black feathers (which I was hoping had originated in a pillow). The feathers seemed only to confirm the uncanny sense of having woken up mid-metamorphosis—the feeling that if I had slept another hour, I'd have emerged from bed a big black goose.

The morning feathers brought to mind the monsters from my youth, the nocturnal creatures alluded to in the Talmud, who are detected by sprinkling sand around your bedroom. If in the morning light you discover bird tracks in the sand by your bed, said the ancient rabbis, it means you have a little case of demons.

I'd always found it puzzling that Joseph went out of his way to describe Moroni's feet, which were, he confirmed, human and bare. So many other questions were left unanswered by the spirit's appearance—why focus on the guy's feet? Maybe Joseph wanted to emphasize that his midnight visitor did not have bird feet and thus wasn't a demon but an angel. How else would one know the difference?

It was Sunday, the Sabbath. Time for church. I had to admit that I found something comforting in shaking out Saturday night's feathers, putting on a crisp shirt and tie, shaving, forming my hair to look the way a hymn sounds.

From the tour packet I'd received in the mail I knew that thirty-five people were on the tour and that I was the only one from the eastern part of the United States, and also the only person traveling solo.

All of which perhaps explained why my fellow pilgrims gave me a hero's welcome in the hotel lobby. The mad scene was reminiscent of the president entering the chamber of Congress before delivering the State of the Union address. I arrived dramatically late, at which point I was passed around, thoroughly handshaken, back-patted, joshed with, waved to, lovingly embraced. More than once I was on the receiving end of a cross-lobby wink-and-point. In the corner of my eye I spied a large woman clapping—and not a small, mannered gesture but a full-on ovation, complete with whooping. People who hadn't yet introduced themselves were telling me that there were other people who also hadn't yet introduced themselves to whom I absolutely *must* be introduced. These other people, I was told, would be "very excited to *finally* meet you."

People were whispering in my ear, slipping me Snickers bars, inviting me to visit Utah and stay with them for as long as I wanted. With the exception of one elderly woman, they all expressed their heartfelt admiration for the Jewish people. And even the lady who wasn't so into the Jewish people smiled warmly and affirmed the right of the State of Israel to defend its citizens.

As we exited the hotel, a doorman with a well-appointed mullet tapped me on the shoulder and, like a magician, plucked a fluffy goose-butt feather from behind my ear.

"Hey," he said, "joo got fathers in jour hair, dude."

On the bus it became clear that everyone on the trip was enmeshed in complex family dramas. Our tour was chiefly composed of two large clans, one based in Washington State and Utah and the other in Australia. The Americans, the Blackburn family, were a vast and spirited tribe, represented on this trip by possibly six siblings, aged twenty-something to forty-something, each with a spouse. A few cousins or sister-wives may have been somewhere in the mix as well—it was frankly hard to keep track of any given member of the Blackburn family, let alone the sprawling totality of the thing, as they tended to be loud and boisterous and at all times extraordinarily busy. Gleefully did the Blackburns shun the socioautomotive convention of remaining seated. They switched seats as often as mathematically possible, sometimes hopping back and forth in seconds between two seats across the bus aisle. In a related note, they snacked on an inexhaustible supply of candies, purchased wholesale and stored in mammoth zip-lock plastic bags. These sacks of goodies made constant rounds up and down the rows.

The Australian family, by contrast, was a reserved bunch and snacked at reasonable intervals on savory treats. Their humor was more deadpan than that of the screwball Blackburns. Almost immediately the outsized presence of the American Blackburn clan earned the Aussies the reverse nickname, the Whiteburns. The

Whiteburns were represented on this bus by William and Pam and their two twenty-something daughters, Maggie and Tara, the latter accompanied by a husband, Jon, and Pam's two siblings and their spouses.

Standing apart from the tangle of Blackburns and Whiteburns was a Hawaiian-shirted retired couple from a place called Rancho Cucamonga, California, and a smiling elderly gentleman with bulky flip-up sunglasses, accompanied by his seventeen-year-old grandson. Our driver was a local hired hand. At the helm was our guide, Lee Thomas, Lee's wife, Marcia, their college-aged daughter, and her husband, who had an ironic T-shirt for every day of the week.

When Lee finally got us quiet, he offered a few introductory words about himself. We learned that he was "a big microphone guy." As I would later discover, he was rarely without it on the bus. Even in the odd instance that he wasn't speaking, he'd keep the mic on so that we might be lulled to sleep by the melodious sound of his breathing. One of the things he told us, with the help of the bus microphone, was that he didn't need a microphone. His booming voice, he said, was a genetic inheritance from "generations of sheep men." When they were young parents, his wife had told him to speak more softly because he was scaring the kids.

"But I couldn't help it," he told us now. "That's just my regular voice. I got a built-in amp."

Lee's wife tapped his arm and he sat down.

When we arrived at the church, our first stop, the gate was locked and the place seemed to have been abandoned. "I guess everybody's been translated," Lee said, referring to the spiritual process by which a mortal human becomes a cosmic entity. "I guess we're too late. There's no hope for us." Again Lee's wife's hand was seen tapping his arm; again Lee dropped into his seat.

As we waited for the church to open its rusty gates, Lee got on the mic and led the daily devotional, which consisted of an inspirational thought followed by a prayer. He began by reading a poem written by his daughter. When he arrived at the lines "I know this truth / for myself. / I honor him / as a prophet of God," he choked up, paused, and took a deep breath.

Lee's tour company was a family business, passed down to him from his father. Over the course of his life, Lee had been in Mesoamerica too many times to count. Years ago, when his father was busy at work on a Ph.D. about Quetzalcoatl, the great feathered serpent god of the Maya, he would let Lee wander around the National Museum of Anthropology in Mexico City. At the end of each day his father would find little Lee curled up asleep on a bench in one of the museum galleries. For Lee, Mesoamerican/Nephite archaeology is home.

Lee's thought that morning was a word of caution. "I have a strong testimony for *The Book of Mormon*," he told us. "I *know* the book is true. And I *know* Joseph Smith was a prophet. What I don't have yet is a testimony for the archaeology." Lee wanted us to understand that the full truth of *The Book of Mormon* isn't known, that much is yet to be revealed. We couldn't be certain where Nephi lived exactly. "We're still working on that. It's a process, you see. But we know these places are real and we're slowly getting there, finding little hints along the way. Every hint we find means something. Everything we see in the world *means* something." As far as the archaeology went, Lee continued, it could sharpen our knowledge of the story told in *The Book of Mormon*, and it could strengthen our faith, even though faith isn't dependent on any findings or lack of findings. "The main thing," Lee concluded, "is to have some fun with it." As he said this, I looked up in surprise as everyone else bent their heads in prayer.

———

Later that afternoon, in the Guatemala National Museum, Lee was outfitted with a portable mic, whose signal was piped into the 1990-era Walkmen—the kinds outfitted for tape cassettes—that we'd been issued on the bus. In the museum, Lee was all business. With a laser pointer he traced our journey on a giant wall map. He highlighted a giant Guatemalan mountain range which, in *The Book of Mormon*, separated the people of Nephi from the wicked Lamanites. Geographically, everything hinges on this mountain range. We'd get a good view of everything tomorrow from the plane, he said, then lasered our attention to a northern river. "Some people propose this as the River Sidon," the only named river in *The Book of Mormon*. "But we do not."

I noticed some other tourists, not from our group, eavesdropping on Lee's presentation. The looks on their faces were of utter confusion.

As Lee continued, I was beginning to detect which of my fellow travelers had a taste for Nephite geography. Uncle Hugh, a handsome Aussie in his fifties, wasn't interested in the mountain range or the possible location of the River Sidon. Well, actually, that's not quite true. Uncle Hugh was very interested in the river and mountain range but was also very interested in about five other things at once. His attention span was as boundless as it was omnivorous; typically his curiosity culminated in the touching of things. He had adopted the controversial practice of laying hands on museum artifacts, which he did often and with great relish. When he couldn't actually touch an ancient column or altar, he'd press his palms against the display case that separated him from the object of desire and gaze at it forlornly.

As I studiously set out to grasp Lee's critique of the misguided people who argued for a northern location of the River Sidon,

Uncle Hugh was whispering in my ear about lasers. He was big-time into lasers, he told me. No, seriously, he said, he harbored an outsized *love* of lasers and—and this was the upshot—so did his people. Laser pointers were outlawed in Australia, because his countrymen hadn't been responsible with the technology. "We love gadgets more than . . ." Uncle Hugh shook his head, unable to come up with one thing under the heavens that might possibly serve as a comparison. "I don't even know," he said. But, he assured me, people in Australia are constantly getting killed playing with gadgets. Standing nearby, one of our fellow travelers, from the American side, took note of this dark premonition.

Having spent a few hours now with my fellow tourists, it was time to ask the three-thousand-year-old question: who in the group had the highest risk of contracting a Jerusalem syndrome–like syndrome on this once-in-a-lifetime tour of the lost Central American cities of the Nephite people?

From the first moment, most of my fellow travelers were eliminated from the pool of candidates. The friendly folks who told heartwarming anecdotes about church potlucks back in Orem, Utah, for example. People who showed pictures of the grandkids. These people were way too grounded, way too healthy for Jerusalem syndromes of any kind.

At the other end of the spectrum were the people who spent a suspicious amount of time examining the archaeological/historical/ spiritual issues related to our expedition into Nephite lands. Like me, these people seemed to harbor an unstated, emotionally risky, personal investment in finding Zarahemla. To wit, Uncles Ian and Hugh. From my first conversation with them, I placed the Aussie uncles into the "maybe" category regarding Jerusalem syndrome.

The three of us immediately opened up a conversation about the contentious academic arguments surrounding the Mesoamerica theory of *Book of Mormon* geography. We also confessed to the personal thrill of walking in the same lands where Nephi once walked. I'm pretty sure I heard Uncle Hugh sitting alone on the bus mumbling verses, but it's also possible he was humming Australian pop hits from the late sixties. Needless to say, his hands-on approach to artifacts could certainly be construed as syndromic.

The last major candidate for Jerusalem syndrome was the youngest Aussie, Maggie. Her symptoms presented in a less obvious way. She wasn't infatuated with things Maya/Nephite per se. She was twenty years old and had other things on her mind. Namely, fretting over an imminent and dreaded missionary posting in Japan—"and not even in the city," she told me, "but in, like, a little village *close to Russia*." Maggie was a gloomy insomniac, artistic and accident-prone and apparently also a savant in the history of cinema. Her dream was to be a film critic and/or a filmmaker. She feared that having to abstain from movies and secular books during her mission might make her "*literally* insane." Should Maggie's fervent, sleep-deprived imagination latch onto the Nephite saga during this tour, she could fall hard. I put her on the "maybe" list.

As *Book of Mormon* pilgrims, we were most interested in Preclassic Maya Mesoamerica, specifically the Late Formative period (roughly the same era as the golden age of the Roman Republic). The start of the great Classic period of the Maya, in other words, corresponded with the years when the Nephite saga was ending. In fact, it was precisely the rise of the social and political forces that historians associate with the flourishing of Mesoamerican civilization—the consolidation of powerful and wealthy rulers—that people like Lee identify with the sad and bloody conclusion to *The Book of Mormon*. The artifacts that attested to a thriving culture in the Mesoamerican Classic period are, to readers of *The Book of Mormon*, signs of a culture that had become decadent, deeply corrupt. The beautiful jewelry and sculptures of the Maya, the monumental architecture, all of it belonged to a culture of profligate, materialistic, pagan sensuality.

Our trip to the National Museum was something of an opening argument in Lee's case for Mesoamerica as the true land of *The Book of Mormon*. In a walk through the galleries we touched on some of the main subjects and artifacts—in Uncle Hugh's case, literally touched—which we'd be exploring in their original locations in the coming weeks.

In my headphones I heard Lee's voice summoning us to a painting. It depicted an elaborately arrayed Maya priest standing with arms aloft at the apex of a grand temple, a massive terraced structure built to resemble a sacred mountain. Bonfires blazed on each level of the structure, cloaking the holy man in layers upon layers of smoke. Onlookers were depicted standing far below, at the foot of the building, gaping—as we were—at the impressive spectacle taking place atop the temple, in the space between the earth and heaven. This portrait, Lee said, should be very familiar to readers of *The Book of Mormon*. It was the image of the decline of the Nephites, when corrupt royal priests rose to undue prominence and literally elevated themselves, and their political cronies, to an untouchable class above the regular people.

As we contemplated the image of the (corrupt) Maya priest, Lee opened up his well-worn *Book of Mormon* and read passages to us. This approach was similar to what I'd seen at official Mormon sites, where you'd be seated in front of a giant painting of Joseph dictating his translation of *The Book of Mormon* to a scribe as a missionary read passages to you from that very book. But those missionaries had been working from a tight script, while this Meso-american version of it was not official; there was no approved script for our journey. This perhaps was why Lee had given us the dis-claimer that *Book of Mormon* archaeology, his life's work, was about "just having fun."

After many tantalizing introductions, the time had finally come for our very first true *Book of Mormon* treasure: the "and it came to pass" glyph. The story is littered with the phrase "and it came to pass." It occurs, according to Lee's count, no fewer than 1,381 times in *The Book of Mormon*. No plot twist worth a hill of beans hap-pens unless it has first come to pass. Since the day the book was published, the phrase "and it came to pass" has been catnip for debunkers, strongly suggestive, so they say, of the book's weak ven-triloquism of biblical idiom. But that's not how the book's devoted readers tend to see it. Like a charming quirk of one's beloved, the compulsively repeated phrase holds a special place in their hearts. It was thus with great pride and much ado that Lee now summoned us to another museum gallery, to examine a Maya altar inscription that some scholars have translated as none other than "and it came to pass."

There had been a great deal of premuseum buzz about this relic. An image of it occupied a prominent spot on the back of our tour booklets. On the bus, in the parking lot of the museum, Lee had gotten us fired up about it. Now we would see it. Some of us would be touching it. I could hear Lee's voice streaming through my head-set, telling us to savor the moment, to take pictures, to just have fun with it. Later we'd discuss the historical context of this find. But now it was just about being in the moment.

And it came to pass that we reached the gallery, wherein we did rush en masse and fall upon the altar, alarming fellow museum-goers and security personnel alike. I was as excited as anyone to see it, and curious how this little gargoyle, which looked like a cross-eyed version of a monster from *Where the Wild Things Are*, could be translated as "and it came to pass"—or as anything at all—when suddenly Uncle Hugh squirmed to the front. I quickly dispensed with the notion—the hope, really—that he was trying to touch the glyph *with a hand*. No, Uncle Hugh, it seemed, was leading with his head, leaning in for a full lip-lock. At the last second, though, he turned his head and mugged widely. He wasn't trying to French the "and it came to pass" glyph, or had changed his mind and settled for a cheek-to-cheek buddy pic with it.

Like crazed paparazzi, we pilgrims jostled for photos of the altar. I suddenly found myself at the back of a surging mass of smiling people and of squinting people photographing the smiling people. From where I was standing, I could see a tangle of cameras, each with the little crocodilelike "and it came to pass" glyph grinning back at me from the photo screen. In the presence of this altar, we as a group had morphed into a single gargoylelike creature with many eyes and seventy swinging arms.

On our way out of the National Museum we walked under a giant mural that narrated the entire history of religious tumult in Mesoamerica, from the early Maya and their corn-based creation myth, to the coming of bearded, armor-clad Spanish, who converted the natives at the ends of their swords, and on through the present. Standing at the very end of this long epic were two colossal figures, expressionless blond Frankensteins, a pair of Mormon missionaries positively bursting out of their short-sleeved white shirts and dark slacks. Unlike the other figures on the mural, these men had no accouterments, no religious symbols or flashy clothes or weapons, or even distinguishable faces. They were identified mostly by their massive steroidy upper bodies. Pictured at the end of the

Guatemalan epic mural, they appeared not to round off the history so much as to have swallowed it whole. My fellow pilgrims were alternately amused and appalled.

Later that day I caught up with Lee in the lobby of our hotel and asked him why he thought the phrase "and it came to pass" was repeated so often in *The Book of Mormon*. "Well, we don't know for certain, of course," he said. "But, I dunno, maybe it was put there to bring it to our attention. You know, to really highlight it, to make a big deal of it, in a way, so when the time came, we'd be able to make the connection to the ancient inscriptions. It was as if the old prophets were telling us, 'Hey, pay attention to this phrase 'cause it's gonna come in handy when the time comes to search the archaeological record.'"

He conceded that some readers of *The Book of Mormon* regarded the crazy repetition of this phrase as superfluous—but now we're beginning to recognize the prophetic reason for it. Everything, every mystery, every slightly odd detail, would eventually reveal something. Before I could ask one of the million follow-up questions to this theory, Lee, scion of sheep men, was herding us out the door to dinner.

Sitting at the head of a long restaurant table, young Sam Blackburn, of Provo, Utah, one of the more animated members of his unusually animated family, was getting himself so worked up about the imminent steak feast—becoming even more emphatic than usual, even more windily vehement—that he'd unintentionally, and without realizing it, blown out a candle on the table. The arm of a busboy immediately materialized and reignited it.

I suddenly noticed Uncle Hugh looking at me in a way that strongly suggested he was about to bring up Anne Frank. And so he did, by way of preface, to tell me that while he was sympathetic to people who wanted to proxy-baptize the famous dead, he himself didn't quite endorse it.

When he was a teenager, Uncle Hugh had come to believe that *The Book of Mormon* was true. Missionaries a few years older than he had come to his house with a board overlaid with velvet, on which they'd used paper dolls to dramatize Joseph Smith's story. With these simple, flat puppets, the missionaries narrated the story of young Joseph's discovery of the gold plates, his translation of *The Book of Mormon*.

(Out of the corner of my eye, I noticed Sam Blackburn getting worked up again, and again accidentally blowing out a candle.)

As the steaks began to arrive, Uncle Hugh filled me in on the details of his conversion moment. It had happened during the puppet show, when the paper doll Joseph was in the forest, paper doll angels floating overhead. "*That* was my moment," he said. "Exactly then. It hit me: This is *real*. This happened. That was when my blood began to boil."

For many years it was the tale of Joseph's excavation of the gold plates, *The Book of Mormon*'s frame story, that most appealed to readers, even to the exclusion of the Nephite story. When Lee first spoke to our group, he asked us to raise our hands if we'd read *The Book of Mormon* all the way through. Almost every hand went up—but in the old days, he told us, the count was consistently less than half. The drama of authorship, of the book's discovery and its translation, was for many years *the* story, the thing that bewitched readers, the thing that made people's blood boil. It was at a surprisingly late date that a prophet commanded people to read *The Book of Mormon* closely and thoroughly. That was in *1986*.

I had to admit that the story of Joseph and the gold plates, the frame story, was still the piece that most appealed to me on a personal level. The story of Joseph, the writer. Even now that I was in Mesoamerica, the land where Nephi and Alma once roamed, I still found myself thinking of how it related back to Joseph. Those questions, about writing and how to live, were still the things that made *my* blood boil.

Those questions were certainly foremost on my mind when I sat at my hotel room desk that night and tried to write an already overdue magazine article on ventriloquism. I'd made the tactical error of taking on a deadline during this trip. But I couldn't resist. Ventriloquism was a subject I considered deep and broad, touching on fields as varied as audiovisual technology, human psychology, religion, and the history of the Enlightenment in France. I'd planned to dedicate a great deal of time researching the history of ventriloquism and had in fact been doing just that, and thus missed two deadlines. My editor was growing anxious, and so I was obliged to bring it together on the road.

In what was to become a regular occurrence on this trip, I sat down to write about ventriloquism but inevitably veered into thoughts of Joseph Smith and the Maya, which blended into questions about life and art and love and my struggles in those respective categories. My attempt to write an entertaining essay on the art of ventriloquism was turning into a series of long confessional letters addressed to my editor—an epistolary novel—that ruminated on the nature of human communication, on the relationship between "throwing your voice" and "finding your voice," and on the deeper meanings of the old comedy bit in which the ventriloquist and his dummy argue over who's "the real dummy." *Who, in fact, is the dummy,* I chanced in one missive to my editor, *is a basic—though deceptively simple—question; it happens also to be*

the ambiguity underlying Joseph Smith's translation of The Book of
Mormon. *The Dummy Conundrum is the question every writer must
confront. It's the question I myself have been trying to face.*

I made the wise decision not to send my editor that particular
installment of the ventriloquism article in progress. If my copy was
any indication, I was still feeling somewhat lost. But I also felt more
hopeful than I'd been that first night, during the storm. I was starting to really like the other people on the tour. Actually, I'd liked
them from the moment they'd welcomed me in the hotel lobby as
though I were homecoming king. But their enthusiasm for the "and
it came to pass" glyph had clinched it. If I was lost here in Guatemala, in search of Zarahemla, if I had indeed kidnapped myself
onto a high-end trip to nowhere, at least I had some pretty great
fellow travelers—and it was still early: there was always the hope
that one of us would go wild with Jerusalem syndrome.

As we sat waiting in the terminal of a tiny Guatemala City airfield early that morning, most of the group caught a few more minutes of sleep. Sandwiched between his dozing wife and sister, Uncle Ian, however, was wide awake.

"I'm a hunter," he was telling me. "This isn't early to me. In the field, I wake up at four a.m., three a.m. if I have to."

"Two a.m.?" I asked.

"No."

We paused for a moment to contemplate the odd spectacle visible through the airport window: set against a blue-black sky, a giant volcano, a perfect cone, shadowed purple by the early morning light, was capped by a smooth ring of clouds shaped like the Platonic ideal of Doughnut.

Uncle Ian was telling me that killing deer is an interesting thing to do. You have to use your wits. Before you go into the field you take a shower without soap, to remove all scents, then you anoint yourself all over with eucalyptus oil. I wished he hadn't used the word *anoint*, but he did, and there was nothing to be done about it now.

He produced his Australian passport and pointed to the little line-drawn figures on the cover.

"Know what these are?" he asked.

"That's definitely a kangaroo," I said, "and that is . . . an ostrich?"

"Emu."

These animals are physically incapable of walking backward, he told me, and thus "do not retreat *ever*," which is why they're symbols of the fearless Australian people.

I recalled a conversation from last night's banquet, when I'd overheard this very same Uncle Ian debunking American notions regarding the alleged cuddliness of Australian fauna. Chewing on a mouthful of medium-rare steak, he made stinging remarks about wallabies and strong insinuations about koalas. He disparaged wombats. Kangaroos he denounced in the harshest of terms. "They're vermin," he said, patting his mouth with a napkin. "We shoot 'em wherever we can, often as we can." And, he added, kangaroos were easy prey because they aren't able to retreat.

As we waited in the terminal, I asked Uncle Ian why he thought *The Book of Mormon* was so violent, why there was so much war in the story—much more bloodshed than in the stories of Jesus, which, with some exceptions, seem to center around dinner parties, long chatty walks, and fishing. Wasn't that what made the bloodiness of the crucifixion so shocking?

"Look around you—" Uncle Ian began to say. But before he could continue, Lee was ushering us onto the tarmac.

Lee apologized for the delay and tried to lighten the mood by telling us of a flight delay on a previous *Book of Mormon* tour. In that instance there had been a technical problem with the plane and the pilot had refused to fly. After a long wait, the plane finally took off. Once airborne, Lee asked the flight attendant how the problem had been resolved. "Oh, no," she replied, "the problem wasn't resolved. We just got a new pilot." Half of our group laughed. Actually, it was mostly just Uncle Ian laughing.

Our chartered plane, a thirty-five-seat Saab 340A, vaulted us over a volcanic land, dark brown, black, very green, very mountainous, twisted and dizzying, gnarled by geologic upheaval and softened under layers of vegetation and a heavy, shifting mist. It was a short trip. Uncle Ian had barely enough time to point out the difficulty of maneuvering large armies through this terrain before a tiny, courtly bald man, who looked somber in his unfashionable tie, emerged from a tiny cupboard in the flight deck and mutely distributed tiny bottles of water and ranch-flavored potato chips. Uncle Hugh, awake now and refreshed, praised the plastic lining of the barf bags. I noticed that our airline safety card depicted a faceless man, doomed no doubt to a watery grave, and that I was dressed in exactly the same outfit as this faceless man. We even had similar hair.

The bus ride from the airfield to ancient Tikal was our first glimpse at the interior of the country. We had traveled from Guatemala City to the jungle of Petén, near the border of Belize. *Book of Mormon*–wise, we had traveled from the Land of Nephi to the East Wilderness. Unlike the temperate capital—average temp 73 degrees Fahrenheit—the lowlands of the Petén were tropical, thick in vegetation and humidity. Our guide through the jungle was Benecio, a good-humored man who spent much of the forty-five-minute bus ride telling us how the cocaine trade worked. The cartels had better weapons than the police, he explained, and the army was on high alert. Sensing the discomfort of his foreign visitors, he concluded by saying, "But it's not so bad, really."

In order to put us in better spirits, Benecio decided to focus on details of the passing green landscape. He pointed out the wild boars and tropical turkeys. As we drove by a basketball court, Benecio told us that in his village basketball is considered a "girls' game." This news seemed to upset the American men. It did, however, confirm Uncle Ian's suspicions, and he spent the remainder of the trip singing the praises of rugby. In the blur of driving, the faces we encountered looking back at us along the side of the road, the countenances of man, woman, boar, child, and turkey alike, all began to blend together into one inquisitive gaze.

No matter how much you dig out cities abandoned in the middle of jungles, they always feel buried, saturated by the thick flora. Wandering through the ruins feels like scuba diving through a shipwreck. When at last you climb a giant temple tower and look down over the waving jungle canopy, the weatherworn stone buildings peek back like distant gray boats on a vast green sea.

For the two-mile walk through the once-glorious city, now glorious ruin, of Tikal, our group was split in two, the American Blackburn clan and the Aussie "Whiteburns." I was roped into the American group, which had split in two: those who skipped through the jungle with childlike glee and those who walked at a contemplative, sheeplike pace. For the first mile or so, until I grew weary, I ran with the fast-moving Blackburns. There were enough family members to conduct an entire track-and-field tournament around Tikal's ancient tiered temples. Blackburns raced each other up and down the giant stairways. They tried to beat their own times. They played hide-and-seek. They swung on the vines of the sacred ceiba tree and made George of the Jungle/Tarzan jokes. As a family choir, they sang "Eye of the Tiger" as members of the clan took turns mimicking the scene from *Rocky* in which the champ-in-training runs up the giant steps and throws his arms in the air triumphantly at the top.

Tikal was lousy with Blackburns and their games. They ran continuously, shouted continuously. When a Blackburn reached the top of a Maya temple, he would shout taunts to those below. When he reached the bottom, he would shout taunts back to those on top.

A day earlier, at the museum, we'd huddled around a model replica of Tikal. The history of the city spanned the entire Nephite period. Lee said that we didn't yet have enough information to link Tikal to any particular *Book of Mormon* city but that there must be *something* there connected to the story. For a moment we sat quietly as group, collectively wondering what that something might be; some of us began to flip through our *Book of Mormon* for clues.

That's when Maggie raised her hand. It was the first time she'd spoken in front of the whole group. She wanted us to know that Tikal was the site of the Rebel base on Planet Yavin, as depicted in *Star Wars IV.* (I immediately, though vaguely, recalled a scene of ships flying over a lushly green landscape dotted with Maya temples.) Standing next to me, Maggie's older sister, holding her husband's hand, quietly sighed, "Oh, Maggie." Her husband, Jon, squeezed her hand, shushing her.

But Lee was rolling with it. "Sure, sure, thanks for mentioning that, Maggie," he said. "People love putting science fiction in Maya cities 'cause they've got that, you know, otherworldly, mysterious look."

The American Maya fetish goes back to about the time of Joseph Smith. Ten years after the publication of *The Book of Mormon,* bearded adventure writer John Lloyd Stephens's lavishly illustrated Mesoamerica travelogue became a bestseller in the United States, influencing writers such as Melville and Poe—and introducing the public to the great civilizations to their south. Stephens's narrative, which still makes great reading, was full of enchanting stories, such as the one about the night in Palenque when he reclined inside a snake-infested Maya temple and read a newspaper by the light of magi-

Wandering through the ruins feels like scuba diving through a shipwreck.

cally luminescent jungle beetles. When Stephens's book came out, Joseph's deputies wrote a series of ecstatic essays on it. Joseph himself encouraged exploration of the cities that Stephens described. How could this magnificent civilization be anything other than Nephite?

As pilgrims, we were heeding that call, helping document, and in some ways shape, the story by going there, like Stephens, and bringing back stories of our own. I thought back to the hotel lobby the night before, where some of the Blackburn clan had enlisted my help in selecting which of the many "and it came to pass" glyph pics to post online. That had been about more than just fun and games.

If my fellow travelers each posted an image to their various feeds, which reached an average of say, 350 people, that would instantly put the glyph before a conservative count of about 12,000 pairs of eyes—and that was only the beginning. The sum total of "and it came to pass" glyphs that day alone would far outpace the already formidable number of "and it came to pass" phrases in *The Book of Mormon* text. Maybe Lee was right about the nature of prophetic texts: they work virally.

First, as Lee had theorized, the text replicates this phrase so often that it sticks in readers' minds and eventually leads them to find it engraved on an ancient altar, which is itself then reproduced with photos, endlessly, and beamed out into the world. The job of the pilgrim is to visit the land that gave rise to the text, to photograph it—or buy a postcard, or draw it or write about it—and share it with others, to tell the story to others. Unlike Catholic sites, which tend to be associated with ongoing miracle-making powers, these sites are linked to narrative. Hill Cumorah in New York State is sacred not for its healing power but rather because a visit there proves that it *exists*—and if it exists, the text is authentic, and if the text is authentic, Joseph, who discovered and translated that text, was a real prophet. The text creates a map that leads to a specific spot, and the arrival there thus vindicates the reliability of both the map and the text.

The process of finding and sharing is greatly enhanced by the placement of monuments. Consider the hill in upstate New York, which is outfitted with a giant monument inscribed with a verse from the Book of Moroni. Moroni's own words are engraved in the very place where Moroni buried the book and where, as a spirit, he revealed it to Joseph in 1823. With this monument, the site and the text have become one physical entity.

That's where my fellow pilgrims and I came into play. This was our bigger mission here. Knowingly or not, we were working as pioneers. Our job was to blaze the trail, to help *create* the pilgrim circuit in Mesoamerica by walking around the sites, studying them, picnicking around them, taking pictures of them, and, most importantly, sharing the whole experience with others.

Perhaps one day there would be a stone monument that completed the process by inscribing the verses back into the Mesoamerican lands from which they came. Perhaps in two hundred years there'll be an official *Book of Mormon* "and it came to pass" monument on the site where these words were written. Perhaps the Maya capital of Kaminaljuyú will have a sign, with the official brand fonts on it, identifying it as the City of Nephi. These things take time. The trail of the Stations of the Cross in Jerusalem wasn't officially marked off for over a thousand years. *The Book of Mormon* has been around for less than two hundred. The tradition of pilgrimage to the true *Book of Mormon* lands of Mesoamerica is barely decades old, and only getting started.

In the meantime, for those of us on the road in Tikal, it was time for lunch. After a long day in the East Wilderness, I took my seat at a jungle hut with the young crowd. I arrived just in time to hear Maggie's sister, Tara, recounting the day's major event: Maggie had been crapped upon by a spider monkey, an incident Tara dramatized by making her eyes bulge and slamming her hand down on our lunch table, thus causing everyone to groan. Seated silently in her slightly too small *Star Wars* T-shirt, Maggie looked miserable and indeed shit-upon. I was beginning to realize that Maggie was a bit of the unlucky type. With a heavy heart, she quietly said, "I thought it was an orange frog falling out of the sky." Maggie's brother-in-law, Jon, nodded empathetically.

As we headed back to the bus, it was noted that Uncle Ian had gone missing. He'd last been seen heading back into the jungle. I volunteered to retrieve him or, I suppose, whatever remained of him. After ten minutes on the path, I heard a fantastic shriek, which pierced my soul and froze me in my tracks. Howler monkey? I made a quick look around, and especially above me.

The desolate cry of a monkey in the jungle is, in traditional Chinese poetry, a conventional metaphor for solitude. What, I wondered, would the Chinese bards have made of what I saw before me in the jungle of Tikal: an Australian retiree with a big potbelly, khaki shorts, and black dress socks pulled up almost to his knees, producing a hideous yelp? What was the poetic significance of a man alone in the forest imitating a monkey call? Was this not an even deeper kind of solitude? Was Uncle Ian finally sliding into full-blown Jerusalem syndrome?

I didn't dare disturb him on the hunt. For a moment I observed Uncle Ian alone in the state of nature, stalking around like a large, flightless bird—the noble emu, perhaps—eyes wide, nostrils flaring, scowling, and showing no signs of retreat. He repeated the desolate monkey call. Finally he noticed my presence, snapped to attention, and walked over to me, shaking his head.

"Almost drew the little bugger out, too," he said as he tapped me on the back and walked toward the parking lot.

On the bus, almost all my fellow pilgrims were asleep, suffering from jungle hangover. Maggie was passed out, sunburned and openmouthed, against the bus window, clutching a sketchbook. She'd drawn a lovely illustration of a Tikal temple structure. Floating over the tower, in a looping calligraphy, she had inscribed the opening words of the *Star Wars* saga: *A long time ago, in a galaxy far, far away . . .* The sketchbook was wedged into her copy of *The Book of Mormon*, one story enveloping the other.

Uncle Hugh, seated a few rows up, was also asleep. What was he dreaming? Who can say? In Tikal, I'd found him alone in a large plaza, surrounded by temple towers, a kind of city center, sitting on a ruin, deeply absorbed, scribbling into his notebook. He had separated from the group, as was his wont, and gone off to have, then record, a personal adventure. I'd seen him out there, digging and rooting around the temples, then noting his thoughts in a journal.

And Uncle Ian? He was wide awake, as was his wont, gazing from his window deep into the jungle.

It was the Yanks' turn to deliver the daily devotional. In a scene reminiscent of *Family Feud*, Don, a contestant representing the Blackburn family, was sent to the front of the bus, amid much fraternal cheerleading, high-fiving, and back-patting.

Don spoke of the repetition of names in *The Book of Mormon*. For example, there are multiple characters named Nephi, which gets terribly confusing. But the takeaway from these name sequels, he suggested, is that history unfolds very slowly—very, very slowly. "Sometimes it takes three Nephis, spread out over a thousand years, just to get something small done." This struck me as a wise interpretation, the kind earned the hard way by a guy who comes from a big, unruly family.

After we finished the daily prayer, Don quietly returned to his seat. For a brief moment our group fell into silent meditation. This was rare for us. We could hear raindrops gently falling on the roof of the bus. But the quiet was immediately broken when one of Don's numerous beefy brothers catapulted him back to the front. "*Do* it!" the brother shouted. This was all it took for the entire Blackburn clan to begin chanting "Do *it*, do *it*, do *it!*"

"Okay, fine," said Don, standing again at the head of the bus.

He took a deep breath. "Rencerella," he began. "Murdy ugler sad twine bad blisters . . . and they rell in fur . . ."

"It's a pig latin version of Cinderella," one of the Utah Blackburns was whispering to me.

It was odd and somewhat disillusioning to hear the man who'd just led us in solemn prayer now spouting absolute gibberish—but that's how life is sometimes. As it turned out, Don was doing the long version of *Rencerella;* it went on for upwards of four traffic lights and two left turns. As we pulled into our destination, the ruins of the ancient City of Nephi, located on the outskirts of Guatemala City, he was reaching the finale. Even as we exited the bus, Don was saying into the microphone, "Okay, guys, so the lesson is, *before you baney fill, don't forget to slop your dripper!"*

The one thing the great City of Nephi didn't resemble was a city. The most immediate impression was of an off-kilter golf course. The site of the great Maya capital, Kaminaljuyú, was now a large field of bright, freshly cut grass that rose and fell every few feet in steep groundswells created by centuries of collected soil deposited around the city buildings. Today only the rounded green silhouettes of the towers' tops are visible, like toes under a blanket.

As we stood next to one of these mounds, Lee read to us from *The Book of Mormon.* Some of us were stirred by this recitation. Others were beginning to feel sunburned and dehydrated. The clouds looked succulent and deliciously chilly. A cloud shaped exactly like a human brain, complete with cerebellum and medulla, was slowly but steadily floating away. Suddenly the whole group was looking at the sky. For a moment the heavens darkened and swarmed.

"Vultures," whispered Uncle Ian.

"Oh gee, would ya look at that?" said Lee, using his tattered copy of *The Book of Mormon* to shield his eyes. "Everyone make sure to drink some water."

We entered one of the mounds through a tunnel. Most of the ancient buildings had already been excavated, but the archaeologists had since resealed the dig and allowed the soil and grass to grow in order to preserve the site. Since they'd also built a large shelter over the dig site, a strange darkness prevailed within—it was as if we'd walked into the City of Nephi in the middle of the night. The effect was of an atmospherically lit stage set of a city alley. To the untrained eye, the ancient city didn't look all that different from Bible-era Jerusalem. It wasn't hard to imagine Nephi hanging out here. Through cracks overhead, shafts of light illumined isolated spots of the ancient street—a set of large, stunningly well preserved steps, a small tub of some sort, the outer walls of buildings, windows, exposed rooms, more stairs leading down to even deeper chambers. Assorted statue heads lay on the curb, as though awaiting a garbage collection. Lee suddenly materialized on a balcony structure overhead and explained that Nephi completed his temple in America around 570 BCE, the same period as Preclassic Maya temples discovered here.

All over the ruin, the pilgrims busily created personal records, capturing the painterly contours of light pouring in, the odd insects crawling around, or the architectural markers that Lee was relating to *The Book of Mormon*. Each person was collecting the information differently, interpreting it differently, presenting it to others differently. Even if our job was to blaze *The Book of Mormon* trail, people were finding their own ways of doing it. The power of the pilgrimage was exactly that: both in documenting the big official narrative and in finding a way to make that narrative personal.

Back on the bus, the Aussies compared sunburns. Maggie took a seat next to me, pulled out her sketchbook, and began making some touch-ups. She had elaborated on her drawings from our jungle excursion yesterday in Tikal, adding little figures, *Star Wars* guys, battling each other. Sitting in front of us, Uncle Hugh had also spied out Maggie's sketches and had, in his fashion, run a finger over one of the pages.

"Love that paper," he said. "High quality."

Underneath the cartoon panels Maggie had carefully inscribed, in an elegant lettering, verses from *The Book of Mormon*: "And I, Nephi, did take the sword of Laban, and after the manner of it did make many swords . . ."

Among *Book of Mormon* readers, I most enjoyed talking to the sci-fi obsessives, the gamers and fantasy role-players. They, the nerds, not the jocks or preppies, seemed to really get it. In their dweebish intensity, they seemed to understand what this journey was all about. Intuitively Maggie knew why both *Star Wars* and *Book of Mormon* stories played out on the temple structures built by Maya kings with names like Spear-Thrower Owl.

Benjamin Nugent, author of *American Nerd*, explains why tech nerds often gravitate to certain modes of storytelling, namely sci-fi and fantasy fiction. Science fiction and fantasy stories are, at their core, a type of experimental technology, he says. These kinds of stories are animated by "the mechanics of the situation." Writes Nugent: "A large part of the fun of reading a sci-fi series is about inputting a particular set of variables (dragon-on-dragon without magic) into a model (the Napoleonic Wars) and seeing what kind of output you get."

Maybe something similar was happening here on the Nephite lands tour. We were proposing an earnest experiment, the creation of a narrative made out of existing pieces that offered the kind of satisfaction a DIY techie gets from fashioning a functioning system, from tooling around, taking something apart and putting it back together in a new way, then watching it do something new and exciting. If you work out the technical details and the thing really does function, it means it's a good system, no matter how weird the premise. Were the gold plates inscribed in Egyptian hieroglyphs by Preclassic Maya people? *Why not?* Was it possible that they were edited by one of those men, Mormon, the scion of an ancient Israelite family from Jerusalem, in Veracruz, Mexico, and given to his son, Moroni, to bury in what would eventually be known as the greater Rochester area? *Let's make it happen.*

Why be biased? We were simply inputting a set of variables (ancient sea voyage from Middle East to Mesoamerica, Israelites inhabiting Maya civilization, seer stones, angels) into a model (the biblical narrative and American history) and observing the output.

At the moment, from the window of our tour bus, this output looked like a magnificent fertile valley, with waterfalls and deep, mysterious caverns and a jungle fog thick enough to sustain any idea you might imagine. Which was why we, *Book of Mormon* readers, dove into our backpacks to retrieve our cameras the moment Lee got on the mic and excitedly told us to look out our windows and behold the valley that lay before us, for it was none other than the Land of Mormon.

A few hours before sundown we arrived at the Waters of Mormon, more commonly known as Lake Atitlán. The dark green-black, black-purple light of the surrounding country permeated the lake, making the water look silken and regal. Three steeplelike volcanoes, perfectly spaced along its sides, gave the landscape an elegant symmetry. You took one look at those volcanoes and you knew immediately that they have been considered sacred for as long as people have set eyes on them, that they probably *created* the concept of sacredness in the minds of those who first saw them.

The landscape here was wide open; you could tell it your own way. There were endless ways to spin the story of walking into Maya Kaminaljuyú and finding the City of Nephi in it, of arriving at Lake Atitlán and seeing the Waters of Mormon there—and we were still among the first ones to give it a try.

According to Gershom Scholem, the great scholar of the Kabbalah, that openness, in fact, is the definition of a prophetic text: a story that can generate endless meanings, endless interpretations, a story that isn't limited in time or place to one particular interpretation and that is frankly weird and plastic and unrealistic enough—yet also plausible enough—for all readings of it to be simultaneously true. (His modern example was Kafka.) Despite a history of dogmatic readings, prophetic stories are those that actually push against dogmatic reading. That's what makes them perpetually relevant.

As the days went by, as we continued to trace out our map and examine artifacts, and as I watched different kinds of readings happening all around me—many of which were also being simultaneously recorded—I felt as though I really were watching a prophetic text in the making, that we really were traveling through the lands of Joseph's book, the places he'd seen so vividly, though never actually visited. The process that Joseph began was still evolving, and seemed, actually, to be just getting interesting.

As we sat aboard our idling bus, it became clear that Uncle Hugh was nowhere to be found. Finally, after a few minutes, Maggie discovered him on a grassy spot behind the bus; we all turned to see him lounging on a picnic blanket, sandals off, sipping a tall glass of orange juice while he read the newspaper, his brows arching philosophically over his bifocals as if he were a diplomat on holiday.

"Oh, good *heavens*," said his wife as she marched out to retrieve him.

Having spent breakfast gazing longingly at coffee, which I'd forsworn in solidarity with my fellow pilgrims, I was drowsy and in no mood for the uncles' shenanigans, no matter how avuncular they might be. Even so, Uncle Hugh continued to captivate, like a hard-to-put-down book. At some earlier point his nieces had approached me with a question: which member of their group, in my opinion, had an accent closest to that of Crocodile Dundee? When, after some deliberation, I replied, "Uncle Hugh," the young Aussies exchanged worried looks. "You must never tell him that," said Maggie's sister, turning grim.

Uncle Hugh wasn't the only source of intrigue. As we boarded the bus that morning, one of the Utah women stood by the bus door, jiggling an orange prescription pill bottle and asking each person, "Want some?" The bus itself had gotten weird: yesterday it had been painted like a regular bus, but now it was painted from head to tail in an intense leopard print.

Once Uncle Hugh had drained his OJ, reluctantly put on his sandals, and rejoined us on the bus, we began our day trip to the remote hill village of Almolonga, where we would be investigating *Book of Mormon* parallels at the large outdoor market. Some people believe that the *Almo* of *Almolonga* is connected to the *Book of Mormon* hero Alma. Lee dismissed this as a "cute idea."

The region around the village was fantastically fertile, which was why Lee identified it as *The Book of Mormon*'s Land of Pure Water, the spot where Alma met up with Helam after an "eight days' journey into the wilderness." Assuming that Alma hiked at a rate of eight miles per day—the standard local rate for overland travel—the Land of Pure Water would be roughly sixty-four miles from the Waters of Mormon, the same distance that separated the village of Almolonga and Lake Atitlán. Even if *The Book of Mormon* had nothing to do with Mesoamerica, there was still something satisfying in finding these small, elegant correspondences.

But at times Lee seemed preoccupied by the conjectural nature of his calculations. During our drive to Almolonga, he pointed to a waterfall and announced, "That's the *exact* waterfall from the Book of Mosiah." Then he paused and said, "Just kidding."

In past years, he explained, someone on the tour hadn't realized that he'd been kidding about the waterfall. That person had taken a picture and published it in a paper. It still made Lee wince to think of it.

But nobody on our bus was awake to hear Lee's cautionary tale, except me and Uncle Hugh, who was too busy immersed in Lee's textbook. Noticing that he had no audience, Lee cut off the mic and sat down.

As we drove on, following the route of Alma's eight-day journey into the wilderness—and passing what surely was not the waterfall of Mosiah—country folk at the side of the road pointed and laughed or else gazed in mute astonishment at our giant leopard-print bus. Children chased us.

I must have fallen asleep myself, because the next thing I knew one of the Utah women was shaking me awake. I was very groggy and confused but immediately noticed that our bus had stopped and was wedged into a distressingly snug alley. "They need males," she was now saying, possibly, I surmised, in order to explain why she was shaking me. I wandered outside, where confusion reigned. I saw nine Saints rocking a small car parked on the curb next to our bus; Uncle Hugh waved me over to join them. At that same moment, I saw a cop jogging up the street toward us and then I heard someone yell, "Everyone! Back on the bus!" When we returned to our seats, the men exchanged high fives. Uncle Ian briefed me on the operation. "Road too narrow," he said, trying to catch his breath. "Car had to go."

Almolonga's buildings seemed to be made of faded candy, with a faded birthday-cake cathedral at their center. The outdoor market, though, was a kaleidoscope of vibrant colors, wafts of grilled corn smoke, and old guys with giant cowboy hats grumbling into bullhorns. The produce was piled higher than a taller-than-average Almolongan. It was the season of the scallion and the market was permeated by its sweet, acidic aroma.

As we browsed among the stalls, I heard Lee tell one of the cornmongers that members of his group were from Australia. She'd never heard of it. He described it as "a large land on the other side of the world inhabited by a very strange animal that is like a giant bunny," which he illustrated by hopping. The woman was unsure how to reply to this.

To be fair, the ways of the Aussie pilgrims remained mysterious, even to us, their fellow travelers. Just a day earlier, during a cruise on the Waters of Mormon, Jon had confided in me that he wanted to become famous.

"So there's this guy back home, right?" he'd told me. "A surfer. Got his arm properly bitten off by a shark. His whole arm, like. Right off. Wrote this amazing book about it . . . everyone knows him. He's on all the shows."

"He wrote the book with one arm?" I asked.

"One arm," said Jon. "Young guy, too. Just like me."

"Wow," I said. "But what's your plan? I mean, you aren't planning to lose an arm in a shark attack and then write a book about it with your one remaining arm, are you?"

"Yeah," he said, "that's what I'm saying."

"But don't you like your arm? I mean, it's your *arm*."

"Yeah, right. But being famous, you know? You get everything easy, everything taken care of. You don't need the arm."

That was yesterday. Today, unfortunately, Jon was busy buying chocolate in the Almolonga market and missed a critical, potentially life-changing conversation taking place between Uncle Ian and Lee concerning a scene in *The Book of Mormon* in which a guy named Ammon fights off a group of Lamanites by systematically slashing them down with a sword, kung fu–style. As Alma admiringly reports, Ammon "smote off as many of their arms as were lifted against him, and they were not a few." He took this sizable collection of severed limbs to the king as proof of his valor. From tapestries and other sources, Lee was now explaining, we know that Mesoamerican warriors indeed used to present the ruler with severed-arm trophies. It was a pity Jon didn't receive this key teaching from *The Book of Mormon* and the Maya: if you want to be famous, cut off *someone else's* arm.

But we'd come to Almolonga to investigate nondismemberment-related parallels between Maya and Nephite customs. The main examples were the story's reference to "weights and measures" and "burdens on their backs," which may match the local use of little iron weights for weighing produce and of porters who haul goods on their backs. As we stood in a traffic jam created by the collective girth of our group—we never did succeed at physically reconciling ourselves to the village of Almolonga—I pulled out my *Book of Mormon* to examine the source.

"Now they [the Lamanites] durst not slay them," reads the Book of Mosiah, "because of the oath which their king had made unto Limhi; but they would smite them on their cheeks and exercise authority over them; and began to put heavy burdens upon their backs, and drive them as they would a dumb ass."

The villagers were all superfriendly and welcoming, so it seemed unfortunate that we were visiting them because of a line in a book that connected their practice of carrying things on their backs to their ancestors' alleged servility and forced dumb-assedness. This awkward feeling was perhaps inevitable during this portion of the tour, when our *Book of Mormon* parallels concerned real, live humans and not simply ruins and natural landforms.

And who can tell what these burden-bearing descendants of King Limhi's people really thought of our group? What did they make of this tribe from across the ocean that had grown large and bold on the flesh of gigantic bunnies, who yearned for shark attacks, and who'd forcibly entered their village in a massive leopard-print bus? Perhaps there was a hint in the drunk guy following us through the market, who alternated between heaping elaborate curses on Lee and snacking on a raw plantain. He seemed to be on to us.

Maggie hadn't been paying attention to any of this, nor to the discussions of severed arms and smitten cheeks. She was more concerned with her own physical trials, having injured herself in a series of freak accidents. She showed up to lunch in Almolonga with a giant bag of ice on her arm, which she thought might be broken. She also had a bandage on her knee from when she had fallen trying to pick up her bag. In a separate incident, a cascade of bags had fallen on her. After the injury had weakened her knee—and her morale—she'd slipped on a washcloth and twisted her ankle. This was in addition to the spider monkey flop that had dropped on her the week before, the rash acquired in Tikal, an ever-deepening sunburn, and the plague of motion sickness for which no end was in sight. Her only solace was the delicious-looking flan that was being served for dessert. So when Uncle Ian announced that the flan was topped with a sauce derived from the illicit coffee bean, Maggie's expression went sour and she brought a napkin to her lips, from which a particularly sad mouthful of flan issued sluggishly forth.

Later, in our hotel lobby, Jon told me about how close he'd once come to getting shark-attacked. The shark had just kind of bumped him, given him a little head butt but nothing more. These encounters were not uncommon among serious surfers, he told me. Still, Jon knew the odds were against him. He sighed. "That may be the closest I'll ever get."

With some rare downtime to kill, I wandered over to the front desk and asked to see the Mel Gibson suite. To my dismay, the request was denied. But as I returned to my room on the third floor, downcast and cursing my fortune, I came upon Miguel, a friendly bellhop, just a few paces from my intended destination. I mustered up the courage and pointed to the plaque on the suite's door and, in a Spanish-sounding dialect of my own making, asked if he might show me in. I produced whatever amount of currency seemed appropriate, then added some more, and conveyed it to Miguel, attempting a nonsleazy nonchalance which might suggest that bribery was just part of my normal, gentlemanly modus operandi. Everything about his swift reciprocity indicated that Miguel had done this before.

Mel Gibson had apparently camped out at our hotel during the months he was on location filming his Maya slasher flick, *Apocalypto*. As it turned out, the movie was of special interest to *Book of Mormon* buffs. Many bloggers, especially the cinematically inclined, regarded the film as an unofficial *Book of Mormon* movie—and what's more, the best one out there. (*Corianton: A Story of Unholy Love*, a very racy *Book of Mormon* movie from the 1930s, before Hollywood standards existed, is hard to find and arguably not very good.) For today's fans, Gibson's aesthetic has exactly what *Book of Mormon* films sorely need. A post on an online discussion forum summed up this view in its subject line: *Why Does the Church Always Produce Crappy Films?* "As missionaries," the contributor wrote, "we used to have only about three or four God-awful VHS movies to show . . . I was always embarrassed to show those to anybody. They sucked ass."

Why, he asked, couldn't there be a good *Book of Mormon* film like Mel Gibson's *The Passion?*

Another guy, identified only by an avatar of Darth Vader, concurred that *The Passion of the Christ* was a great film. "I know it was anti-Semitic at times," he conceded, "and Mel Gibson is a total prick, but that film moved me like no other religious movie has. But there is no way an active Mormon could have made that film." But *Apocalypto*, which he described as a movie "about the Lamanites in Mesoamerica," that was a brilliant movie. "But once again, there is no way a Mormon could make a *Book of Mormon*–themed film as good as *Apocalypto.*" The consensus among *Book of Mormon* film geeks seemed to be that Mel Gibson had come as close as anyone to making a believable film about *Book of Mormon* people. This had certainly been Maggie's view when I'd asked her about it the day before.

Now, thanks to Miguel, I had the privilege of standing in the very room that Mel Gibson had inhabited when he was unintentionally making arguably the greatest big-screen *Book of Mormon* epic yet. This was the place where Mel returned exhausted after a long day of filming Lamanites hacking at each other's heads.

I got to work at once, scanning the spacious room for any nefarious traces of satanism, of some bloodbath or orgy, something viscerally horrifying and Mel Gibsonish. But all traces of Mel's residence had long been scrubbed away. I walked around, inspecting the premises and nodding decisively, as if to express to Miguel that my suspicions, whatever they might have been, had all been terribly confirmed. Standing by the door, Miguel too nodded decisively.

Suddenly, as though remembering something important, he became animated by a thought, which he communicated through emphatic sign language. Did I want to lie down on Mel Gibson's bed for a moment?

"Oh," I said. "No. That's cool. Thanks, though."

There was nothing in the world I wanted to do less than climb into Mel Gibson's bed. But Miguel seemed disappointed with my answer, and so I halfheartedly slouched on it. It was a good mattress, no question about that, better than the one in my room and, I noted, certainly large and sturdy enough to accommodate whatever kinds of uses Mel might put it to. It was covered with an abnormally large quantity of pillows. I now noticed the presence of an objectively outrageous number of pillows stashed in every corner of the room. This, and the correspondingly outrageous number of little shampoo bottles stashed in the bathroom, surely testified to the depravity committed in this suite overlooking the Waters of Mormon. Nevertheless, it was circumstantial evidence.

"Mel Gibson," I said, turning to Miguel. "Señor Gibson? He likes pillows, huh?"

As a visual aid to my insinuation, I picked up a pillow and sort of hugged it.

"Yes, yes," said Miguel. "Señor Gibson."

I dropped the pillow. Miguel, perhaps interpreting the gesture as disappointment in my visit, jumped into action. He marched over to the window, opened it, and made a vomiting hand motion out of it, then pantomimed mopping the floor. He laughed at the memory or, more likely, was amused by the grossed-out expression I was making. In either case, Miguel seemed satisfied that he'd given me my money's worth. He nodded to the door. The tour was over.

Later I wandered down to the deck overlooking Lake Atitlán, the Waters of Mormon, the lake that had given its name to the book's editor, who in turn passed his name to that book and, through it, to its most devoted readers. I took out my copy and indulged in the rare treat of reading *The Book of Mormon* as I sat next to the Waters of Mormon.

During our drive down through the Land of Mormon, Lee had told us that he was "pretty comfortable" in his identification of Mormon as a man of the late Preclassic Maya period. Leaning against the back of a seat, with the microphone nestled between his crossed arms, Lee had indeed appeared rather comfortable while making this assertion.

He believed that the word *Mormon* may be related to the Maya words meaning "jaguar mountain." In the Chorti Maya dialect, *mor* means "hill" or "mountain crest" and *mon* means "ferocious beast." This accords elegantly with the line from the Book of Mosiah that characterizes this land of Mormon as "infested, by times or at seasons, by wild beasts." Given the prevalence of jaguars in the region, Lee felt comfortable identifying the wild beasts mentioned in the book as jaguars, hence his translation of *Mormon* as "jaguar mountain."

The Waters of Mormon were the site of some important events in the story. Alma fled to the lake after becoming persona non grata in the court of King Noah (whose seat of power was north, in the City of Nephi). One of the book's great heroes, Alma had been a trusted member of the court's wicked priests, a cabal of lecherous fat cats. When he publicly questioned the king's decision to execute a dissenter, Alma himself became a dissenter. Barely escaping execution, he and some allies fled into the wilderness. Alma's path of escape was the very same route we'd taken the day before, from the royal City of Nephi down into the forested Land of Mormon and finally to the Waters of Mormon.

Alma's journey in the wilderness was one of the geographical lodestars of the story: it gave us all kinds of orientation clues, the names and distances between key cities and waterways. Lee also posited some cultural parallels in Alma's retreat to the Waters of Mormon. The highlands around Lake Atitlán, with their access to water and remote places, had long been a prime spot for Guatemalan guerrillas. Alma and his band of 450 men were, in other words, an early version of a Central American insurgency. It was here that Alma promised his men that a man, a godlike man, would eventually come to save them. It was along these very shores that they'd organized their group and sworn allegiance to each other.

The lake, I read, was originally given its name by the notorious

King Noah. I was surprised that the name Mormon had originated with one of the story's most despicable characters. But it was fitting, in a way. Most of what we'd encountered so far—the weapons and jewelry and palaces and temples—had belonged to the bad guys in *The Book of Mormon*. Everything about the finely crafted Maya artifacts—the paintings and reliefs of fearsome, nearly nude warriors, the bug eyes and dangling tongues on the altarpieces— silently screamed out *Heathen!* Even the beloved "and it came to pass" glyph was made by the bad guys. Who else would make such vain, expensive engravings in stone?

But wasn't that the allure of our journey? Wasn't that the unspoken selling point of this tour? Like *The Book of Mormon* film buffs who were drawn to *Apocalypto* for its flamboyantly bloody version of realism, we on this trip were drawn to the dark side of the story: it was more picturesque. Even if *The Book of Mormon* did indeed happen in Mesoamerica, would it have been worth the high-end prices if we had not been able to take pictures in front of those one-of-a-kind structures that also just happen to represent the worst kind of decadence and corruption, or to have fun climbing the "monuments to false gods" built by the very people who slaughtered the Nephites, to picnic in the mighty cities of the people who killed Mormon himself? Would it have been worth the money if we had not been able to feast our eyes on the excavated jewels of the "wicked and powerful rulers"?

Maybe that's how pilgrimages always go: you have to give your pilgrims their money's worth—a little blood, or maybe a lot of blood, mixed in with some voyeurism and sin. Shouldn't an encounter with the divine be at least as exciting as a summer blockbuster?

When I tried to track down Lee before breakfast, the clerk at the hotel desk told me that the "señor" was busy "talking to his phone." Rumors had been circulating that Lee was unhappy with the performance of our leopard-print motor coach. But there was no turning back now. We still had big things to see. Our day's destination, Izapa, was the site of a major relic, the Tree of Life engraving.

First, though, we had to cross into Mexico. Guatemala had been kind to us; it had offered us many stunning *Book of Mormon* remnants to explore and given Uncle Hugh many priceless artifacts with which to canoodle, but we took comfort in the promise that Mexico would give us more opportunities to eat at McDonald's.

At the border crossing we stood in a long, winding line that had all the trappings of waiting for an amusement park ride, with one difference: when you reached the front, there was no roller coaster, just a heavy door that opened to reveal a four-foot-tall, five-hundred-year-old Mexican lady grilling corn and a group of men dressed in assassin casual flipping wads of cash at flimsy plastic card tables as they conducted currency exchanges. As we waited, we had a clear view of a nearby creek, over which people brazenly crossed the border on a zip line.

Once processed into Mexico, we made a mad dash for burgers.

Seeing Americans find a McDonald's in a foreign country is almost moving, like witnessing a reunion between long-lost relatives. Back on the bus, an eerie quiet prevailed. I popped my head up over the seats to investigate and beheld a busload of pilgrims clutching McFlurries, each mouth contentedly plugged with a straw. We carried on in wintry silence until Maggie began to suffer loudly the pangs of an ice cream headache.

Izapa, located on the Pacific coast, is one of the most extensive archaeological digs in the region. It may have been the site of the first-century Nephite city called Judea, made famous by one General Helaman, commander of an elite unit of two thousand young men known as the stripling warriors, who are very popular among today's *Book of Mormon* readers, especially the striplings among them. (Stripling warrior action figures, cards, T-shirts, mugs, costumes, and a video game are widely available.)

Helaman also played a critical role in the writing of *The Book of Mormon*. His father, Alma the Younger, entrusted him with plates and the very seer stones Joseph Smith would eventually unearth from his hill.

The big money draw at the Izapa site, the Tree of Life stone, is one of the most important artifacts in *Book of Mormon* archaeology. This is no secret to those living nearby: all along the route of our travels, local artists, tipped off to our arrival, presented us with Tree of Life souvenirs, from key chains and oil paintings to a five-hundred-buck engraved jade replica at a fancy shop.

Izapa itself was a mowed-grass clearing on the tropical coastal plain. A tall chain-link fence separated the archaeological park from a few shanty homes that were built right up to the property line. In the yard of one of these homes, a bright-pink pig, a real sweetheart, lay curled up with a contented smile, napping in the plush grass while the usual chickens regarded us with bloodshot, paranoid eyes.

Inside the fence, stone slab monuments protruded from the grass at irregular intervals. These were Izapa's famous stelae. A squat shelter built over every six-foot-tall stela gave each the look of a cave-dwelling oracle. We made a beeline for Stela 5, the engraved stone that Wells Jakeman, the first chair of BYU's Archaeology Department, had proposed as a direct graphic depiction of the Tree of Life vision that Lehi had had shortly after he fled Jerusalem, when he and his family were marooned in the desert wilderness, unsure of their next move.

The connection between Lehi and Stela 5 is supported by the theory that the coastal area near Izapa was the spot where Lehi and Nephi's ship made landfall, *The Book of Mormon*'s "land of first inheritance." Lehi died soon after his arrival in the New World and may be buried near the coast, which has led some people to believe that Stela 5 was a memorial monument to him. If it indeed records Lehi's famous dream, Stela 5 would be a rare Mesoamerican depiction of a scene directly from *The Book of Mormon*.

Which was why finally seeing it in person was so horribly disappointing. Alas, the badly weathered Tree of Life was not as lifelike as one would hope. But with Lee's laser pointer, Uncle Hugh made a valiant effort to trace the contours of the engraving, which to any outsider were invisible. We, however, had become well acquainted with the lines of the stela.

They were all there: Nephi, the writer, making engravings with a stylus. Lehi, wearing a conical wizard's cap. Lehi's wife, Sariah, with a good-humored smile. The wicked brothers, their hands busy with mischief. Angels, with bird heads and human feet. The allegorical Blind Person, depicted on the stela with a sack over his head, and the Ashamed Person, wearing a little Santa Claus cap and humbly offering up a piece of fruit. Uncle Ian was even able to locate the celebrated upside-down fish, symbol of eternal life.

There, firmly planted in the soil of Mesoamerica, etched into stone, was *The Book of Mormon*'s very first illustration. Unlike the later depictions of these characters, the iconic musclemen of twentieth-century *Book of Mormon* illustrations, these guys were charming little elves with gnomic headgear.

At the center of the composition, of course, was the star of the show, the blossoming Tree of Life, depicted as the sacred Maya ceiba tree, with its white fruit—exactly like Lehi's dream fruit!—its branches fanning out like jazz hands, its roots reaching far into the soil, a bridge between the heavens and the earth.

We could even make out the "fountain of filthy waters" that had given Lehi's dream a sour aftertaste. Barely visible as they were, the whole array of dream glyphs were all there, piled onto Stela 5 in overlaid tiers of complexity, exactly as in his vision.

The Book of Mormon is surprisingly devoid of dreams. The word *dream* appears a mere thirteen times in the story, as opposed to the eighty-three times it appears in the Bible. In the Hebrew Bible in particular, prophecy often comes by way of fantastic sleep visions. Of *The Book of Mormon*'s thirteen mentions of *dream*, nine refer to Lehi's visions. The one and only serious dreamer in the entire *Book of Mormon* is Nephi's father, Lehi.

This might not be an accident. Joseph's father, like Nephi's, was also his family's main dreamer. (Joseph Junior invariably received his revelations in waking visions.) Joe Senior's dreams, as recorded in family oral histories, were also clear echoes of Lehi's: both dreams featured a barren land, a beautiful tree whose fruit he wants to share with his family, a building full of rich people mocking him.

At Izapa, I watched the little red laser work arabesques over the dark, nearly smooth stone and listened to the assembled pilgrims continue excavating entire sagas from its nearly blank surface. By the wild, dreamlike logic of this entire journey I found myself looking deep into this Mesoamerican monument, darkly, as though into a seer stone, and witnessing the ancient dreams of Lehi and, through those, the modern complexities of Joseph Smith's relationship with his father, Joseph Smith.

Enough was going on with Stela 5 that I hardly noticed the giant spider that had perched on the back of my hat—I didn't notice it, that is, until one of the women let out a bloodcurdling cry and, in that same confused moment, as I turned around, I saw Uncle Ian ambushing me, eyes popping, lips curled in an appalling sneer, hand cocked like a tomahawk. The slaughterous blow that came to my head succeeded both in dislodging the invader and sending me, lightheaded and chastened, to my knees. But I was not too dazed to see the spider land on one of the Utah ladies' fanny packs and spread panic through our entire group.

That night, for the first time in days—weeks, really—I made progress on my ventriloquism article, a small breakthrough I attributed to our encounter with the mystical Tree of Life stone. Namely, to the moment when we collectively gazed into its nearly blank seer stone–like surface and, as Uncle Hugh worked the laser, listened to Lee read, "Your voice will also be like that of a spirit from the ground, and your speech will whisper from the dust." Sometimes it's hard to tell a prophetic performance from a ventriloquist act. Prophecy, like ventriloquism, is only convincing if the performance convinces. Or, as they say, seeing is believing.

The next morning on the bus, I thanked Uncle Ian for saving me from the Izapa spider with his quick, warlike reflexes. Gallantly he deflected all credit to his wife for her conscientious shrieking. After the day's prayer, we sang "Let Us All Press On," a hymn that has a surprisingly upbeat melody considering lines like "Fear not / though the enemy deride . . . we will not retreat, though our numbers may be few / when compared with the opposite host in view."

This day we would enter the mountains and make our way to the Chiapas Valley, aka Zarahemla, that most celebrated of all lands, site of the Nephite golden age.

But first we made a quick stop at a dingy volcanic sand beach inhabited by sleeping drunks, burned-out hippie trekkers, stray dogs of Christ-like pathos, and guys on ATVs trying to hustle tourists into paying for joyrides. We scavenged a lunch of potato chips and gum. A storm on the horizon darkened the water and further shadowed the black post-apocalyptic sand. This spot was, Lee said, "more or less" where Nephi's ship landed.

As we walked to the shore, Lee's wife told me that they used to visit another part of the beach but stopped going there because the rank fish stench offended some of the pilgrims. I was disappointed, because, fish reek notwithstanding, it was the spot where a ruin of an ancient wall had been identified as a fortification built by Captain Moroni, namesake of the man who would eventually bury the plates and whose ghost would appear to Joseph. Needless to say, this first Moroni, the swashbuckling captain, is one of the best characters in *The Book of Mormon*. During a battle he ran up to the front line, raised a giant flag, proclaimed liberty, and buoyed his underdog troops to victory. Captain Moroni was a spirited patriot, a legend like those from the Revolutionary War generation of Joseph Smith's parents.

But today we had to cover a lot of ground. The long ride meant we'd be treated to *Book of Mormon* movies, starting with a documentary in which an old lady, a devout reader of *The Book of Mormon*, said things like "He was a prophet. A colonizer. A leader. He was *irresistible*." At a later point in that same film, *The New World*, another old lady observed that "every woman *in the world* wants a man like Moroni." As the erotic undercurrent of the film, set to a soundtrack of heavy Celtic drumbeats, grew more insistent, our bus climbed deeper into the mountains, deeper and deeper into the thick fog, until we were enveloped.

After a night of heavy rains, which continued into the morning, the roads had become slippery and beset by mudslides. A certain kind of bonding inevitably happens on a bus that might at any moment fly off a grotesquely steep, muddy mountain pass. In our case, this took the form of people walking to the front of the bus and telling stories, *Canterbury Tales*–style. Instead of hearing about the Knight and the Miller and the bawdy Wife of Bath, we heard tales of the Hairdresser, the Insulated Window Salesman, the Caterer, Pharmacist, Gift Shop Proprietor, Exterminator, Coach, and Human Resources Director for a Blueberry Farm.

Everyone who stood up to tell a story introduced him- or herself by reference to vast numbers of children and grandchildren and siblings, along with full recitations of their invariably alliterative names, dizzying litanies of Baylees, Blakes, Brookes, Brittanys, Braydons, Bries, and Brians. There were some emotional stories. One of the women spoke of an angel who had conveyed a message "from beyond the veil" that her dead father had approved of her decision to become a Mormon. This story brought tears to the eyes of almost every pilgrim on the bus. But the spell was broken by her husband. As soon as she'd concluded, he grabbed the mic and launched into a comedy shtick that he prefaced by asking, "So . . . anyone here ever been on a hijacked plane?" When no hands went up, he said, "Okay, good . . ."

Later my peaceful nap was brought to a shattering end by Maggie's belting-out of a song from the hit musical *Wicked* at a deafening pitch that neither the bus sound system nor the human ear was equipped to handle. I noticed our bus driver squirming in his seat and was certain that this rendition of "I'm Not That Girl" was going to be the last thing I heard before our bus catapulted a couple thousand feet off the side of a mountain.

Road conditions had worsened. At one point the bus tilted precipitously, throwing everything—people, bags, bottles, and snacks—to one side. Our luggage scraped loudly and wretchedly below us, like souls trying to claw their way out of hell. People clutched whatever they could. Some screamed. In dreams and waking nightmares, I've often imagined Death coming to me in the form of a bus driver.

To divert us from our fears, Lee worked the mic. "You can really get a sense of the [*Book of Mormon*–era] destruction that happened here," he remarked as we watched a family pulled from a car that had been pushed almost to the edge of the road. "In this area, mud can destroy a village in an instant." He snapped his fingers just as his wife's hand popped up and tapped him on the arm. Immediately he changed the subject to the fantastic wooden tables at the restaurant where we'd be having lunch. He also spoke of the Kingdom of Zarahemla. We were just a few miles away.

Zarahemla presents a plot twist in *The Book of Mormon*. As Nephites began to migrate northwest, into the Chiapas Valley, they made a remarkable discovery: some of the people who lived there were Hebrews just like them, former neighbors from the old country. It turned out that Nephi wasn't the only Israelite to have sailed from the Middle East to America. In this sequel-within-a-sequel, a prince named Mulek, a son of the Hebrew Bible's King Zedekiah, had also escaped Jerusalem's destruction with a large entourage and sailed to America. Nephi and Mulek must have barely missed each other.

For the next four hundred years, as each tribe settled in America, they remained unknown to each other—until, that is, the Nephites began moving north. At that point the Zarahemlan plains were heavily populated with the descendants of their Israelite cousins, the people of Mulek.

The Jewish family reunion that occurred in Chiapas, in about 180 BCE, was a joyous event, to say the least. The loosely organized Mulekites embraced the king of the Nephites, Mosiah, as their leader, and the two peoples began hanging out together a lot. They also exchanged notes. The Nephites shared their growing library with the Mulekites, who possessed no records from Jerusalem and had, in the course of four centuries, forgotten many of the old tribal myths. (Mulek had escaped Jerusalem in a rush and, unlike Nephi, wasn't able to grab any books.) Whatever oral history the Mulekites had managed to preserve they dictated to Mosiah, who carefully wrote everything down on plates.

The Mulekites also presented the Nephites with a giant stone covered in mysterious engravings. Like Joseph Smith almost two thousand years later, King Mosiah was able to translate these engravings by supernatural means, and in the process discovered an additional wild twist in the saga: according to the engravings, yet another group of Bible guys had come to Mesoamerica on a ship. That group, however, had arrived much, much earlier, thousands of years before Nephi and Mulek. They'd departed from the Middle East shortly after the Tower of Babel had fallen. Named after their leader, Jared, these ancient distant relatives had established a mighty kingdom in Veracruz, Mexico, but had since died out.

All of this Israelite reminiscing brought the Nephites and Mulekites closer together. They hung out more and eventually fell in love and became one people. Thus commenced a five-hundred-year golden age of Hebrew settlement in Zarahemla/Chiapas. Which was really great until it became really horrible and ended in their annihilation.

As we inched closer to the storied land of Zarahemla, we hit a giant traffic jam—which, given the lack of a rush hour in rural Chiapas, struck us as ominous. As we slowly approached the scene of the blockage, it became clear that we were right to be nervous. A group of men with machetes and rifles had set up a roadblock. Our usually unflappable bus driver advised us to pull down our shades. In the mirror, I observed him worry-stroking his mustache. Lee used the moment to tell us the *Book of Mormon* story about the notorious Gadianton robbers, the secret society of outlaws who eventually became powerful enough to overthrow the Nephite state. (Skeptical readers believe that the Gadianton robbers are a thinly veiled stand-in for the Masons, who were extremely unpopular in America during the late 1820s.) As it turned out, the Gadianton clan had lived right here in these mountains.

As our shiny bus full of American luxury tourists was about to pass into guerrilla/Gadianton robber hands, Lee's wife once again reached up to tap his arm, and he immediately switched topics, turning his attention to the lay of the land. In *Book of Mormon* geography, he said, "Desolation bordered on Bountiful." I pulled out my maps and followed along.

But what if these latter-day Gadiantons really were hostile? What, for that matter, if our bus were to plunge off a cliff? I imagined how these things would play with my friends and family back home. Some would want to interpret it as a freak accident. Others would take a more critical line. Why, they'd ask each other, had he risked his life with a busload of zealots in search of the Land of Whatchamahoozit?

As we inched closer to the roadblock, I made a resolution: should it be my fate, I would be proud to go down on this pilgrimage in search of the lost cities of the Nephite people and their cousins, the Mulekites. It would be an honorable end. Somewhere down in the valley, in the wreckage, they'd find me still clutching my charred notebooks and charts of Zarahemla. I was weirdly okay with that. I believed in the quest. It felt good to feel that way. Putting aside my fears, I turned once again to my annotated map, added more annotations, and began acquainting myself with the topography of the Land of Desolation.

It turned out that the guerrillas only wanted ten bucks. They also asked us to take a leaflet that promised "escalated actions" if the governor of Chiapas did not respond to what seemed like completely reasonable civic demands. All they wanted, apparently, was a meeting with the guy.

At approximately 2 p.m. we emerged from the mudslides and gloominess and roadblocks onto a ridge that was dry and spacious and positively blooming in sunlight. We'd crossed from the coastal side over to the valley side of the mountain range. Spread before us was the radiant Chiapas Valley, a softly sloping patchwork of fields that resembled a boundless bed covered by a quilt patched in every green shade of earth.

We'd all read in the Book of Mosiah of the "small number of men" who had been sent "to search for the land of Zarahemla; but they could not find it, and they were lost in the wilderness."

And it came to pass that we, who had waited our whole lives, yea, we who had been lost even that very day in a wilderness of murk and mire, we pilgrims were blessed at that moment to have lived and, with our mortal eyes, to behold the emerald land of Zarahemla in all its grace and splendor.

That evening all uncles and aunts, without exception, broke their diets and toasted Zarahemla with much chocolate cake. And I finally finished a coherent essay on ventriloquist dummies.

Having finished writing, I could finally try to relax and enjoy the charmed air of Zarahemla. Moments after sending my editor the long-overdue article, I drifted out of our hotel, onto a busy street full of shops and fumes and food carts emitting aromatic smoke. Tuxtla, Mexico, was sufficiently small that you'd occasionally be enveloped in a country breeze, clear and sweetened by grassy wildflowers.

Uncle Hugh was out there too, standing on the curb, eyes

closed, hands sunk into his pockets, taking in big, meaningfully deep breaths. As I approached, I said, "Well, here we are."

"Zarahemla," he replied.

We began to walk. As we passed a little barber shop, Uncle Hugh told me of his tradition of getting a haircut in every foreign country he visited. He'd made a habit of it during his many journeys. If I wanted an adventure, he said, I was free to join him tomorrow morning.

I asked him about his travel style, the sensual nature of it: the touching of ruins and artifacts, the haircuts, the tasting of new foods (unlike most of our fellow travelers, Uncle Hugh always gravitated toward the most exotic offerings). He made systematic use of the five senses. What was it Uncle Hugh was learning that we weren't?

He explained that he wanted to physically imprint these places and things onto his body, archive them in his nerves so that he might access them in the future—a kind of pilgrimage preserved as muscle memory.

"Everywhere I go," he said, "I'll have them with me. Even when I can't go anymore."

We continued walking and reached a giant crowd that had gathered on the town square to listen to a band. Uncle Hugh conceded that imprinting the world's enchantments on one's body is hard work. He wasn't sure his success rate was all that high. There were some frustrating moments along the way. He had, for example, gotten stalled on his journal project. His secret goal for this trip had been to write a little book, a pilgrimage narrative of *Book of Mormon* lands. He'd been flooded with so many sensory impressions the day before, when we were looking at the Tree of Life stone, that he hadn't written any of them down—and now he was already forgetting them. His book wasn't coming together, he said.

But I envied Uncle Hugh. To me, his writing troubles suggested that he was actually a happy, healthy person, that he didn't *need* to write. Happy people don't write books, just as happy people don't see angels. The kind of person who writes a book is the kind of person who feels that something really important is missing or lost or not right with the world, that some story needs to be told, to be preserved. For people who write bibles, the situation is even starker. The thing they are missing, the lost cause they hope to preserve with their book, is nothing less than the story of faith itself. It is one of the great ironies, one of the secrets of religion, that bibles are actually written by those who have lost faith.

In a way, the critics have always been right about Joseph Smith: there was something inherently heretical about his book project. Even his followers concede that he was stubborn in his refusal to join any existing sect. To them, his rejectionism is a mark of pride, a sign of his truer true faith. But a more worldly, plainer perspective is that Joseph, like all bible writers, simply lacked faith and, being a modern person, tried to replace it with a new version: faith in himself, which took the form of his book, a new bible that had him listed as "Author & Proprietor." Wanting his book to be a sequel to the Bible hinted at this larger loss of faith, because it suggested that the original was not sufficient—which is to say, not divine—and that past bible writers were all merely as authoritative as he, plain old Joe Smith. Maybe this faith in himself came, and could only come, with a loss of faith in something greater. Maybe that's the best any writer can hope for.

I noticed that Uncle Hugh and I had parted ways. He was now all the way up front, next to the police barricade that separated the band from the bulging audience of Zarahemlans. Uncle Hugh was clapping along with the accordion music, do-si-doing with strangers, and with his free hand, snacking on a cluster of piñuela, a fruit whose taste had been described to us as something between a banana and a pineapple. Meanwhile, I'd somehow retreated back toward the edge of the town square, to the gray and befouled pigeon-land behind the crowd, where I found myself sitting alone on a bench, scribbling and scribbling away.

Based on the evidence of a short drive through Tuxtla, it was reasonable to conclude that there were an abnormal number of kick-
boxing studios in town. Even our hotel housed a large dojo of some
sort. At all times of day the hotel elevators were full of young mas-
ters in training, clad in fight gear, nagging parents for ice cream.

It wasn't where we had planned to stay. Apparently there had
been some kind of mix-up with the hotels. Minutes before we
arrived in town the day before, a call informed us that in fact no
rooms were available because "the German embassy has taken over
the hotel." Everyone in our group had been duly alarmed.

That morning we were shocked to discover that our leopard-print
bus was gone, replaced by a much smaller and less illustrious zebra-
print bus. The zebra would frankly take some getting used to. For
one, its dashboard had the unfortunate habit of emitting a beep-
ing noise that exactly mimicked the movie sound effect for a time
bomb. Nevertheless, it was our bus now, and on this day we were
taking it to the zoo. Chiapas/Zarahemla, home to 30 percent of
Mexican wildlife, was, after all, also *The Book of Mormon*'s "land of
wild beasts," a hunting ground for the story's Jaredite people.

The zoo was inhabited almost exclusively by local animals that had been trapped in their natural habitats, a situation that seemed simultaneously less tragic and significantly more tragic than what I was used to seeing in zoos. We visited with the usual cast of nonplussed lizards, extroverted birds, and spiders prancing around like disembodied hairy man-hands. As usual, the zoo's *Homo sapiens* young were excited out of their minds to finally meet their primate cousins. In the nocturnal exhibit, a little Mexican girl sang a lullaby to a baby armadillo who was having a nightmare.

Meanwhile, a good-natured rodentlike creature about the size of a schnauzer was strolling around outside the cages on the pedestrian path, as though he too were enjoying a day at the zoo.

But we weren't in Zarahemla's only zoo to screw around. There was business to be done—to wit, exploring the world of jaguars, that ubiquitous symbol of Mesoamerican and therefore *Book of Mormon* royalty, and spending some time at the tapir cage. Lee explained that this animal, which looks like an oversized, nerdy pig, might have been the creature the book meant when it spoke of horses. (Historians believe that horses were a much later European import.)

Later, at Vips, the TGI Friday's of Mexico, we ate our dinner spaghetti Bologneses in a collective stupor as the trancelike video for "It's Raining Men" played overhead on a giant screen. I thought about Captain Moroni riding his gentle, chubby tapir into battle, and for some reason the image depressed me. When I was in a bad mood, all the wonders of our voyage, all the lovely correspondences between Mesoamerica and *The Book of Mormon*, felt diminished by these occasional glitches, by the details that didn't quite add up.

——

But I couldn't stay mad at *The Book of Mormon* for long. Every time things looked bleak, something came along to restore my faith. A day cruise on the Río Grijalva (which Lee identified as the Sidon, the major river that runs through *The Book of Mormon*) brought nothing but that crispy, quenchy, refreshing forgetfulness you feel when you descend into a water-chilled canyon on a blazing hot day.

We sightsaw a canyon side covered by a colony of gigantic elongated fungi that grew like fantastically long mouths drooping deeply in silent song. Every few minutes our guide, using his angel-like vision, would locate distant crocodiles sunning themselves with their mouths also frozen wide open, as though locked for eternity in an expression of jaw-dropping astonishment. We made frequent stops to observe spider monkeys sitting on tree branches, playing cat's cradle. Maggie, in better spirits today, brought hope to all by showing the group that her nasty knee bruise had scabbed over into the exact shape of her native land, Australia.

When our river guide cut the engine and gave us a few hushed moments to absorb the surroundings, Uncle Ian was heard to say wistfully, "And can you just imagine this whole river full of dead Lamanites?"

But nobody took him up on the offer. Instead we joyrode at full throttle and luxuriated in an even cooler and more life-affirming breeze. When we arrived back at the dock, each pilgrim in our group emerged in turn from the ship like Charlton Heston descending from the sacred mountain in Cecil B. DeMille's *The Ten Commandments*: with a shining face (in our case, from sunblock) and a large halo of fabulously blow-dried hair.

||||||||||||||||||||||||||||||||||||||||||||||||||||||||||||||||||||||||||||||||||||||||||||||||||||||

After two weeks in Mesoamerica, I happened to encounter my own face in a mirror and noticed that my eyebrows had grown noticeably bushy and profuse. I attributed this new bounty to the tropical climes of these fertile *Book of Mormon* lands and especially to the wisdom gained during my travels therein.

But on the bus later that morning, I picked up Uncle Hugh's Spanish grammar book only to discover that for a good part of this journey, at least since we'd departed from the Land of Nephi, I'd been brazenly referring to myself in the third person, as though I were a nobleman of high rank. I still had much to learn.

On this day my learning would happen in the great city of Palenque, one of the sites that inspired Joseph Smith to endorse Mesoamerican settings for his *Book of Mormon*. Because of its unusually well preserved art and architecture, Palenque is one of the Maya ruins that has most impressed foreign travelers and fired their imaginations.

Near the gate of Palenque, our group huddled for a talk from Lee. He pointed to one of the city's picture-perfect towers and told us that it absolutely was *not* the Tower of Alma. One of my fellow American travelers lowered his camera.

After we walked through the ruins, I approached a Lacandon

tribesman standing at the gate of the park. I was attracted by Lee's suggestion that this native tribe may be directly related to Lachoneus, the illustrious chief justice of the Nephites who took office in the year 1 CE. Today the Lacandon people are dwindling fast, down to just hundreds.

The Lacandon men at the gate of Palenque were dressed in simple white robes, unlike any others I'd seen in Mesoamerica. They looked like the wingless angels I'd encountered in *Book of Mormon* illustrations. There was a debate among my fellow pilgrims about whether these men actually dressed this way or were trying to boost sales of bow and arrow sets, handmade chocolates, and hand-rolled cigars.

The robed Lacandon and their dignified wares stood out in contrast to the unscrupulous guys who blindsided tourists with jaguar-shaped noisemakers that made a roaring sound when you manipulated their buttocks.

As I bought a pack of cigars from one of the men, I sensed that Uncle Ian had materialized on my left. I knew what this was about. He was demonstrating "ghost walking," a deer-hunting technique he'd introduced to me that morning (to my untrained eye, it had looked indistinguishable from Elmer Fuddesque skulking).

I slid the contraband cigars into my bag.

"Didn't see me, did ya?" said Uncle Ian.

"Nope—you got me."

"And I see you got yourself a little souvenir there."

"Oh, yeah," I said, awkwardly pulling out the cigars. "Couldn't resist."

He examined the cigars with disdain and yearning. Stately, plump Uncle Ian would surely have been a cigar man if his creed had not forbidden it. It was a shame we wouldn't be able to sit on the hotel veranda that night—overlooking the beach upon which the people of Jared, survivors of Babel, once landed their ship— smoke cigars made by the people named for King Lachoneus, and together ponder the mysteries of *The Book of Mormon* and Palenque into the wee hours. But rules were rules.

In the Palenque site museum, Uncle Ian and I stopped at a life-sized diorama of a Maya home. We were joined by Ian's younger sister, Pam, mother of Maggie and Tara. The three of us quietly read the panel by the diorama. Before someone built a home, we read, he would first bury his ancestors on the site as a way to effect ownership of the plot of land and also to create a bond between the dead and the living, which served as protection from evil.

Pam turned to her brother. "Do you remember when Dad was at the end? Do you remember what happened?" she asked.

Uncle Ian looked away and nodded vaguely.

She explained to me that they'd been sitting with their dying father and a presence had entered the room. Everyone had felt it. The next day, when their father was more with it, they'd told him about the visitation. He replied, "I know." This happened for six days, Pam said, and each day she urged her father to speak to the ghostly visitor. But he was too scared.

Uncle Ian wanted to change the subject. He jumped in and added that when he, Ian, was six years old, he too had died and had an out-of-body experience during which he floated into another room at the hospital and witnessed a nurse changing into her uniform.

"That's what a little boy remembers," he said.

But Pam was still in her own reverie. I could see that her eyes had welled up. She was still gazing at the life-sized diorama of the little home, at the beds of the living family members placed almost directly on top of the graves of their ancestors. At night they would be only feet apart, dreaming together in a kind of cosmic bunk bed.

Though we knew it was coming, the grand finale of the tour, indeed of the entire Nephite saga, arrived unexpectedly and without much fanfare. After more than two weeks and almost a thousand miles, we pulled into the parking lot of a small, canary-yellow conference center and made our way to the backyard, which overlooked a dazzlingly green valley and tree-dotted foothills. On the horizon, cast under a shadow that in the circumstances implied the sound of a really deep voice, sat an imposing mountain. Here was none other than Cumorah, the *real* Cumorah, the place where Mormon perished and Moroni emerged, alone, with the gold plates in hand. Not once during the tour had I observed Lee, a veteran of these sites, take a photo, but at Cumorah even he snapped away.

The grand scale of this land, Lee told us, accords better with the story than the modest topography of upstate New York. Despite the text's use of the word *hill*, Cumorah was more of a mountain. And the valley below it had once been the site of a big city. "The whole face of the land had become covered with buildings," reads the book, "and the people were as numerous, almost, as it were the sand of the sea." And during the apocalyptic battles described at the end of the book, the entire population was killed there.

"It's a beautiful day today," Lee said, "but let's not forget what happened here. This is a hill of great sadness."

The hill in New York, he said, was misnamed Cumorah later, in the nineteenth century. He seemed kind of defensive about it. But to me it seemed appropriate, more like a naming-after than a misnaming. *The Book of Mormon* is full of repurposed names, from

Nephi to Joseph. Geographically the twin Cumorahs are far apart, but in the saga they are connected, like a story and its sequel: one starring Moroni the man, and the other, Moroni the angel.

According to *The Book of Mormon*, the Cumorah where we now stood was the burial site of many other books. Mormon was given access to the entire library of the Nephite people, a millennium-old collection. He entered the cave archive where they were stored and pulled out the plates of Nephi and all the other Nephite writings—those by Jacob, Ether, Omni, Alma, Mosiah, and company—edited and abridged these works, added some comments of his own, and bound them into the gold plates. He then deposited all the original books in a secret cave in Hill Cumorah—the very Cumorah we were now photographing. Eventually he dispatched Moroni to bury the gold plates elsewhere, in an unnamed place. Lee wanted us to understand that the text pretty clearly says that everything *but* the gold plates was buried in a place called Hill Cumorah.

Some people believe that the other books buried here in Mexico might one day be revealed—maybe next week, maybe in a thousand years. And not only those. There could be other buried books.

"The records of the Nephite people were revealed to us in the 1820s," Lee was telling us. "But any and every nation can have buried plates. New plates can appear *anywhere*."

Seeing Cumorah in the distance, still pregnant with buried books, I, for the first time on the trip, sensed the presence of the gold plates, that physical link between this land and Joseph Smith's life and my own. Like everyone on the tour, I had built up this moment in my mind, and now that it had come, that I could see Cumorah on the horizon, I really did feel something, and it felt undeniably true. You can fly all the way down to Mesoamerica and follow the story told in the plates, from Nephi's landfall all along the thousand-year sojourn of his people through Central America; you can go into the land where the gold for the plates was originally mined. You can, in so many ways, get as physically close to the plates as possible, but you can never touch them.

And that's how it always goes: every book is really two books. There's the book that is published and then there's another, private edition—an original version engraved, so to speak, on gold plates—that is never seen by anyone but its author. Even its author gets only the slightest look at it. Joseph's gold plates had chapters that he described as "sealed" and that he didn't, or couldn't, translate. Every book we read is really a translation, an imperfect copy, of those unseen and ultimately untouchable gold plates. All stories are approximations of some lost story. I wasn't yet sure what this meant to me, but I knew it would somehow be important to me in the future. It took going all the way to Mesoamerica and physically seeing Hill Cumorah for me to understand that the gold plates were gone forever.

The sadness of that thought wouldn't register until later. At the moment I saw it simply as something that was true and that happened also to be beautiful because it came in the form of a dark and mysterious mountain.

Lee, now chatting about topography, was suddenly interrupted. Uncle Hugh had gone missing again. The usual search party was dispatched. Lee, accustomed by now to the disappearance of various uncles, went on with barely a pause. "And it came to pass," he read to us, "that there were sorceries and witchcrafts, and magics . . ."

This is still true in this region today, Lee told us, looking up from his book. "This is a witchcraft capital here. In October, witches come from all over the world for conventions here." Some of the women exchanged creeped-out looks.

As Lee resumed his reading and continued to draw Mesoamerican parallels, we heard Maggie shout, "*There* he is!" A few of us jogged over to the edge of the yard just in time to see Uncle Hugh in the near distance, scaling a short fence in a field down the hill. It wasn't clear how or when he'd gotten down the slope. His family shouted to him. We all shouted to him. But he either didn't hear the calls or didn't care to reply. He just kept trekking. It was suggested that Uncle Hugh may have been seeking a different vantage point from which to take a photograph.

"No," his wife said, with deep resignation, "I think I know where he's headed."

We all did. Uncle Hugh wanted to reach the mountain. And when he reached the mountain, he wanted to climb the mountain. This, as we all well knew, was in the nature, in the very essence, of what it meant to be Uncle Hugh. His pilgrim soul left him no choice in the matter. He would lay hands on Cumorah.

"It'll take him a day at least, maybe more," said Lee, with an uncharacteristic edge of irritation. It had been a long trip.

For weeks now—and in fact since he had been a child—this landscape had been presented to Uncle Hugh as an allegory. Now that he was here, what choice did he have but to see himself inside the allegory too? How could he just stand by and take a picture?

I wasn't surprised, but I still felt a bit jealous that it was Uncle Hugh who had the honor of being the trip's one Cumorah syndrome sufferer. Some part of me wanted to join him. Perhaps the time had finally come to put aside the trappings of tourism, to remove my shoes like a proper pilgrim, and approach the distant, sacred mountain.

In Werner Herzog's documentary *Encounters at the Edge of the World*, a herd of penguins move from their colony toward the ocean to hunt and then return home with food. All but one. In a wide-angle shot we see a single little black dot standing still, barely visible in the diabolic expanse of white. "He would neither go toward the feeding grounds at the edge of the ice nor return to the colony," Herzog tells us. "Shortly afterward we saw him heading straight toward the mountains." Nothing could stop the pious little penguin's will to walk toward the sublime. The last shot we see is this solitary soul waddling into the interior of the vast frozen continent, five thousand kilometers with no prospects for shelter, food, or water.

The Book of Hebrews describes it too. The people who kept faith all their lives but died "having not received the things promised" and, even more poignantly, "having seen them from afar"— these people embraced their fate as "strangers and pilgrims on the earth . . . looking for a better country." For some pilgrims, arrival is everything—getting the picture, sharing the picture, leaving a votive offering. Being present in the sacred space and marking that presence. And then there are pilgrims for whom the holy is always on the horizon, and their votive offering is their life.

Jesus was one such pilgrim. In the gospels he walks circuits along the paths of Judea; according to *The Book of Mormon*, he was also a sojourner in the New World. They all wandered: Adam after leaving Eden, Abraham venturing westward with no destination, Joseph into Egypt, Moses leaving Egypt. But *The Book of Mormon*, more than any Bible story, was fundamentally a story of "strangers and pilgrims on the earth . . . looking for a better country." Nephi and his descendants in the New World were farther from home than anyone in the Bible. Moroni was a pilgrim, carrying the plates thousands of miles, with no family or friends. And so was Joseph, who, from the moment the gold plates came into his life, never stopped roaming.

It's possible, even likely, that I saw Uncle Hugh sometime later. But I honestly have no memory of seeing him again. Nor does he appear in my notes. The last I remember of Uncle Hugh is his back and his little hat moving toward distant Hill Cumorah. As far as I'm concerned, he's still on his way there.

HILL CUMORAH

ONE

According to Google Maps, it would take well over a month to walk the roughly 2,500 miles from Hill Cumorah in Mexico to Hill Cumorah in upstate New York. That was the trek Moroni made at the start of the fifth century, gold plates in hand. And yet, according to most counts, thirty-five years or so elapsed between the "great and tremendous battle" at Cumorah and Moroni's burial of the plates in New York. What took him so long? He doesn't tell us.

We do know he took some time to put a few last touches on the gold plates by editing a short account of the people of Jared and doing some writing of his own. But I can't help wondering if he was just too depressed to do much of anything. In a brief account, Moroni describes his dire situation: "I even remain alone to write the sad tale of the destruction of my people. But behold, they are gone . . . Therefore I will write and hide up the records in the earth; and whither I go it mattereth not."

The only thing worse than writing his sad tale, it seems, would be finishing it. Maybe all those decades passed because Moroni just couldn't bring himself to complete the project. With his people gone, his sole purpose in life became finishing the book. But doing so would also mean acknowledging that the Nephites' story—his story—was truly over. In burying the plates, he was burying more than just the plates.

Even his last gasp of creative resolve, his own writing, was doomed by circumstances: "I would write it also if I had room upon the plates, but I have not; and ore I have none, for I am alone. My father hath been slain in battle, and all my kinsfolk, and I have not friends nor whither to go."

It seems Moroni, the last of the ancient American writers, ran out of writing supplies. (Maybe that's how all literary traditions end: for lack of basic resources.) We are left to imagine Moroni, having finally buried the plates in New York, disappearing into an immense continent, a lonely and broken man. *The Book of Mormon* ends on a dark, aimless, almost nihilistic note. If, as tradition has it, ghosts are the spirits of people who died unhappy, whose lives lacked satisfactory endings, it isn't surprising that Moroni's specter continued to wander years after he died.

Readers have long felt unsettled by the mysterious fate of *The Book of Mormon*'s last hero. In Spanish Fork, Utah, over fifty years after Joseph died, a man named Higginson recalled that a man named Marsh, one of Joseph's deputies, had once become "very anxious to know something of the fate of Moroni." In response, a vision had come to Joseph:

A wild country and on the scene was Moroni after whom were six Indians in pursuit; he stopped and one of the Indians stepped forward and measured swords with him. Moroni smote him and he fell dead; another Indian advanced and contended with him; this Indian also fell by his sword; a third Indian then stepped forth and met the same fate; a fourth afterwards contended with him, but in the struggle with the fourth, Moroni, being exhausted, was killed.

In archives you can find two rough, hand-drawn maps—both made by contemporaries of Joseph—that trace Moroni's journey through the American continent. As it turns out, he didn't walk directly from Mount Cumorah in Mexico to the hill in upstate New York. According to these quirky maps, he lugged the gold plates from "Sentral America to the Sand hills Arizona then to Salt Lake U[tah], T[erritory], then to Adam on Diammon, Mo, then to Nauvoo, Ill, then to Independence Mo [which Joseph had identified as the Garden of Eden] then to Kirtland Ohio then to Cumoro NY"—all the places to which Joseph and his followers would eventually bring *The Book of Mormon*. Joseph's whole life, in other words, was a sequel to Moroni's travels, a reverse journey along his trail.

According to this lore, Moroni charted out almost the entire length of the future territory of the United States; his quest to bury the gold plates was a kind of mythic founding of the country. Brigham Young reported seeing this ghostly native founder of America walking around the Utah wilderness. Physical traces supposedly remain: Native American inscriptions in Fillmore and Cedar City, Utah, have been attributed to him. But Hill Cumorah, New York, is the last place we know for certain that Moroni visited during his life.

My drive to the hill, on Interstate 90 west from New England— roughly the same route the Smith family originally took from Vermont—was a tour through the haunted lands of the American imagination. That stretch, which cuts from Massachusetts to Ohio, is a fertile region full of glacial lakes, long favored by human settlers. Until Europeans moved in, it was populated by the five nations of Iroquois, and when the tribes had been mostly pushed out, their artifacts and long-standing burial sites remained scattered over the frontier.

Finding themselves suddenly removed geographically from the constraints of Puritan New England, the settlers experimented with new forms of spirituality, new social structures, and new narratives. The region became synonymous with fiery religious revivals. As we were all taught in school, this area, thick in woods and hellfire cults, was known as the Burned-Over District. Occasionally these upheavals resulted in entirely new sects, most of which have since moved on or died out.

The Puritans weren't completely wrong about what went on in the forests on the outskirts of their settlements. People practiced witchcraft well into the nineteenth century and enthusiastically assimilated local Indian conjuring, or what they imagined was Indian conjuring. Most fused these pagan magical practices with their old-time religion, which had long been preoccupied with ghosts and demons.

America's distinct storytelling tradition crept out of that wooded wilderness. The encounter with the New World's frontier lands—the domain of the Devil, as the Puritans called it—played no small part in creating American literature. Eager to cultivate an independent, homegrown literature distinct from European writing, nineteenth-century Americans wrote stories unique to the frontier. Often this meant tales about Indians, specifically about Indians who either were vanishing—like the best-selling *The Last of the Mohicans*—or had vanished, then returned, like *The Book of Mormon*, which was revealed by Moroni, the last of the Nephites.

During the Andrew Jackson years, Indian ghosts were on everyone's mind, probably as a kind of nationalist wish fulfillment and also as an expression of guilt and anxiety over national crimes, all mixed in with the old existential terror of and erotic fascination with Indians. Everyone was writing stories about Indians. Hawthorne said that he couldn't tolerate another Indian story—which he mentioned in a preface to an Indian story. In the mind of the American reader, the Indian—fearsome, noble, tragic, and, most important, departed—was the bestower of land but also a gothic curse on its inhabitants.

Critic Leslie Fiedler identified the gothic as the quintessential American mode of literature: "Until the gothic had been discovered, the serious American novel could not begin," he wrote, "and as long as that novel lasts, the gothic cannot die." It was not an accident that the rise of America as a political entity coincided with the rise of American gothic literature. A society that viewed itself, on the one hand, as a reason-based experiment in liberty—a break with the superstitions and bloody feudalisms of Europe—but whose deepening commitments to slavery and to the brutal dispossession of native peoples matched that most basic of gothic themes: the divided self, the outwardly upstanding citizen who harbors an unspeakable secret, the person with a deformed soul hidden from view yet still grotesquely present and constantly on the brink of being unmasked. Hawthorne's scarlet *A* may well have stood for *America*, after all.

At the heart of the gothic is a fear, bordering on a dread certainty, that the past hasn't passed but rather continues to metastasize into a terrible, inescapable fate, that the land is pregnant with ghosts, alive with death. European gothic plots often involved long-decaying ruins, haunted castles, and degenerate monasteries—the rotting corpses of the aristocracy and the Church—but in America, a land with no history and no ancient curses, free of Europe's millennia of ghosts, a country that indeed defined itself in opposition to Europe, anything was possible. That, at least, was the story. Except that frontier people like Joseph Smith, who lived among the mysterious, impressive Indian burial mounds, believed that America too sat on ruins as cursed as anything in England or Germany. Hill Cumorah was believed to be one such haunted site.

The gothic vision lurked even more sinisterly in America, in fact, precisely because the official national story of Jefferson's Enlightenment rationalism suppressed it and declared itself free of such medieval backwardness. Whereas Jefferson literally cut the ghosts from the Bible—he used a razor to remove any spooky, irrational elements from the text—Joseph and his fellow gothics made it their job to add phantom shadows to the nation's stories.

The Book of Mormon was sold as an epic history of the Indians who had very recently, and for ages, lived in the land; it told of the connection between those peoples and the American reader. The Indian angle was *The Book of Mormon*'s original and rather savvy marketing campaign. It was presented to the public as one of the more go-getting renditions of the popular Indian ghost story—a true account!—and, as it's turned out, one of the longest-lasting. It was published in March of 1830, less than two months before President Jackson signed the Indian Removal Act into law. Even as native peoples were being pushed away, their specters were emerging in the forests and in the visions of frontier seers like Joseph.

Although *The Book of Mormon* saga tells of native ghosts in the woods, starting with Moroni himself, and contains many typically gothic aspects—a buried ancient manuscript, an undeciphered language, occult objects, the hint of unspeakable secrets—it is rarely included in the conversation about gothic literature. In a recent academic study that focuses specifically on the theme of Indian ghosts in early nineteenth-century American literature, *The Book of Mormon* isn't even mentioned in a footnote.

On my way to Hill Cumorah, I drove through the green hills of western Massachusetts and passed by Nathaniel Hawthorne's old home. It wasn't an incidental crossing. Hawthorne and Joseph Smith were born a year apart; their families both came from around Salem, and both their paternal patriarchs participated in the town's notorious witch trials. In fact they collaborated with each other. A Smith boy who had accused his aunt of making a compact with the Devil gave his testimony directly to Hawthorne's ancestor John Hathorne, a respected magistrate and pillar of the Massachusetts Bay Colony. Blameless Mary Easty was eventually found guilty, and on September 22, 1692, she was hanged.

Nathaniel and Joseph were haunted by their Puritan ancestors, each in his own way, and spent their respective creative energies distancing themselves from the grim hypocrisies and subjugations of New England culture. Both undertook their projects by re-creating themselves in literature, revising the story of their people, searching for, as Hawthorne said of his own writing, "somewhere between the real world and fairy-land, where the Actual and the Imaginary may meet, and each imbue itself with the nature of the other." With every tale and novel, Hawthorne—who placed the *w* in his last name in order to distance himself from the notorious Judge Hathorne—plumbed deeper and deeper into the pit of the Puritan soul.

Joseph took the opposite approach. He decided to leave it all behind, to replace America's Puritan past with a bold new history. As far as he was concerned, the narrative he'd inherited could suffocate in the soil of New England; he would remake it in the West. Young Joseph Smith, like Hawthorne's Goodman Brown, that Puritan boy of Salem, brazenly entered the uncharted woods, the endless American wilderness where demonic forces had long reigned, and he never looked back.

On my way to Hill Cumorah, I passed the exit for Talcottville, New York, once a home to literary critic Edmund Wilson. As part of his research on the Dead Sea Scrolls, Wilson visited Hill Cumorah in the late 1960s, and in his resulting book he briefly described climbing to the top, taking in the view, and imagining how Joseph had imagined it.

Wilson's interest in the Dead Sea Scrolls—the fantastic library of first-century Hebrew books that were found in a desert cave and which, in some suggestive ways, echoed the lore of the gold plates—culminated in a series of *New Yorker* articles that were among the first and most serious popular accounts of the discovery. But even as Wilson traveled to the Middle East to investigate these ancient relics, he found Joseph's narrative, which had grown in his own Anglo-American backyard, to be of little merit, a mere con.

For a serious American reader, *The Book of Mormon* can be kind of embarrassing. In Wilson's case, it probably didn't help that a relative on his mother's side was one of Joseph Smith's closest confidants, a husband to no fewer than forty-five wives, father of sixty-four children. Perhaps the proximity of his home to Hill Cumorah and his family ties to Joseph Smith were precisely the problem. It had always been Joseph's closest neighbors, after all, who most vehemently rejected him. The book was boycotted even before it was published. That was the major reason Joseph went west to begin with. Maybe Wilson too felt the need to distance himself from the book because it was too close for comfort, rooted in the same soil that had nurtured him.

Recounting his—and Joseph's—view from the peak of Hill Cumorah, Wilson, however, tried to be generous. "I could see how he might imagine himself a Moses," he wrote, but he stopped short of acknowledging that any of the writers who had composed the original biblical saga, the one about Moses, might be described in similar terms: as standing on a small hill on the edge of nowhere, imagining himself a Moses.

What, after all, makes the bizarre cult of obsessive-compulsives and alleged misogynists behind the Dead Sea Scrolls any more legitimate, any less problematic, than Joseph Smith's cohort? Wasn't that one of the lessons of the scrolls: that sometimes it's the sect of separatist weirdos, those who are unreasonably committed to scribing their odd books, who end up preserving something important from their time?

But Wilson's read is representative. My conversations with Americans about *The Book of Mormon* were often characterized by a casual condescension, a lack of curiosity, even among those who are usually curious and open-minded. But maybe this reflexive distancing betrayed the recognition, the anxiety, that the book came from us, that it could only have come from us, that it bears the telling family resemblances.

In its day, *The Book of Mormon* was dismissed as un-American, as a crypto-Islamic text. In an early case of Islamophobia, Joseph Smith was routinely defamed as a "Yankee mohamet." This charge, coded for polygamy, was a convenient way to incite mass panic and ultimately to justify violence against Joseph and his followers. But it was precisely that renegade status and its provenance in the exotic East that attracted the freewheeling Herman Melville to *The Book of Mormon*.

On my drive to Hill Cumorah, I stopped for lunch near the Massachusetts–New York border, close to Herman Melville's home, which he'd named Arrowhead after the Indian artifacts he'd unearthed in the yard. I pulled over at a spot overlooking Mount Greylock, the view Melville had from the window of his study. Hawthorne, his neighbor and friend, wrote that in the winter months Melville would look out the window at the white landscape, "shaping out the gigantic conception of his white whale" from the humped silhouette of Mount Greylock. In the story, Ishmael indeed describes Moby-Dick as resembling a "snow hill in the air." Like Joseph's Indian mounds, the shapes of the New York landscape suggested the story.

It was during this period, when Melville was working in his study at Arrowhead, that he became interested in *The Book of Mormon*. It's rarely cited—not even by many biographers or scholars— but Melville was a fan. Starting with his incredibly weird novel *Mardi*, which features a prophet named Alma, one of *The Book of Mormon*'s great heroes, Melville had Joseph's narrative on his mind. In an 1850 letter to one Evert Duyckinck, he spelled out his personal connection to *The Book of Mormon* narrative. This was around the time that *Mardi* was failing in the market and irritating critics, and when he was at work on *Moby-Dick*. Melville had mailed Mr. Duyckinck a copy of *Mardi* and kindly requested that he give refuge to the unsuccessful book, "which almost everywhere else has been driven forth like a wild, mystic Mormon into shelterless exile."

That formulation—"wild, mystic"—also appears at a critical moment in *Moby-Dick*, when Ishmael grapples with his guilt for having been swept away, along with the pagan harpooners, by Captain Ahab's rousing, bloodthirsty pep talk. "I, Ishmael," he recalls, "was one of that crew . . . a wild, mystical, sympathetical feeling was in me; Ahab's quenchless feud seemed mine." A wild mysticism is how Ishmael identified himself with the mad Ahab roaming the seas, and also how Melville identified himself with the Mormon storyteller who was wandering the American deserts. In his letter, Melville makes the meaning of these sympathies plain and personal: they are the distressed feelings of a writer who has created an unappreciated book.

It makes sense that Melville related to *The Book of Mormon* at the same moment that he was transitioning into the underground, mystic strain of American storytelling, fully and fatefully slipping into commercial failure. Nor was it any accident that wild, mystic Melville identified with *The Book of Mormon* while Mark Twain, literary realist and rationalist, and a successful author, famously had no patience for it.

Melville had prefaced *Mardi* with a little joke: since many readers had regarded his first two books as fiction, even though they had been sold as nonfiction, he wondered if perhaps *Mardi*, his first official novel, or "romance," would be received as factual. He was testing to "see whether the fiction might not, possibly, be received for a verity." This question was central to the story, as he wrote in the preface. Maybe part of what he saw in *The Book of Mormon* was the way it had created an American story that confidently did exactly that: cultivate a fiction that was received as a verity.

And not just any kind of verity. As Melville wrote in a letter to Hawthorne during this period, "Though I wrote the Gospels in this century, I should die in the gutter." It was the conviction that he himself was writing nothing less than a new scripture that made his failure so bitter and disillusioning. Perhaps in *The Book of Mormon* Melville found a kindred literary soul, a uniquely ambitious American book, a new gospel that was likewise unappreciated, assaulted, and chased into exile.

A year later Melville gave *The Book of Mormon*—the book itself—a cameo in the novel *Pierre: or, The Ambiguities*. Melville was working on *Pierre* during the painful period when *Moby-Dick* was being roundly ignored or worse. *Pierre*, one of his most experimental and, in places, angry books, was a kind of defiant reply to the treatment he had received for *Moby-Dick*. But the oddness of *Pierre*, of course, only sealed his fate. (One review headline read simply: "Melville Crazy.")

In the story, Pierre proudly places a copy of *The Book of Mor-*

mon on the shelf of great Eastern and eclectic masterpieces and offers it as a gift to the mysterious Plotinus Plinlimmon, a man described as a "hat-lifting, gracefully bowing, gently-smiling, and most miraculously self-possessed, non-benevolent man." A popular lecturer who repudiates books, Plinlimmon doesn't touch *The Book of Mormon*, much less read it. As Melville was watching his own work being pushed off the shelf, he seemed to recognize that *The Book of Mormon* was similarly situated.

Perhaps in Melville's turn into a wild, mystic Mormon, there's a hint to Joseph's gold plates. Ishmael tells us that he was much struck by a drawing "representing the old Indian characters chiselled on the famous hieroglyphic palisades on the banks of the Upper Mississippi. Like those mystic rocks, too, the mystic-marked whale remains undecipherable." Maybe the white whale was Ishmael's gold plates—and the gold plates, engraved in undeciphered hieroglyphs, were Joseph's Moby-Dick. And whether that would make Joseph like Ishmael or like Ahab is itself an undeciphered mystery. Just as Ishmael becomes seized by the terror that he is *becoming* the lunatic Ahab, Joseph, from the moment he climbed Cumorah and laid hands on the gold plates, struggled with his identity: was he the naive, adventurous youth or the charismatic cult leader? Like Ishmael, Joseph discovered the gothic secret that he could be both.

The Book of Mormon in fact contains a minor character named Ishmael, who dies just before boarding the ship that will sail across the world in search of the Great Idea. I like to think of Melville's Ishmael as a sequel to *The Book of Mormon*'s Ishmael. Maybe it's just my imagination. But when I picture Melville's Ishmael, when I see that unschooled boy enamored of the pagan prince Queequeg, when I see his identity merge with that of the monomaniacal Ahab and imagine him setting out on his giant, doomed quest to interpret the mystical hieroglyphs on his whale, I see the wide, dreaming eyes and the mischievous grin of Joseph. And it's not the craziest theory. Melville's Ishmael is after all a masked man, a persona: he asks us to call him Ishmael, but maybe his real name was Joe Smith.

Today the stretch of Interstate 90 that runs from New England to New York to Ohio—the literarily rich, fire-singed lands in which Joseph grew up and published his book—is home to our culture's sanctuaries. In geographic order, from east to west: the basketball, boxing, baseball, football, and rock 'n' roll halls of fame. Somewhere after the boxing and baseball but before the rock 'n' roll shrines, you'll see a sign for sacred Hill Cumorah.

The earliest images we have of the hill show a clean-shaven prairie land. In the old photos and etchings you can see the hill's distinctive form, which looks like a kindergarten line drawing of a hill, the naive shape of an overturned letter *V*, more like a pictograph that represents "hill" than the actual three-dimensional thing. It even has a whimsical-sounding classification: it is a drumlin, a word from the Gaelic, which sounds like some bald-headed, impish manchild from Middle Earth but which in fact denotes, in geology, a rounded hill formed by the movement of glacial ice sheets over rock. I can report that this particular drumlin is a satisfying form, a thing that looks exactly like what it is: a hill from Faërie.

Today Hill Cumorah looks a bit different than it did to Joseph. The west face—the view of the hill you see from the old road—is a swath of grassland, a sloping field framed by dense forest, which, depending on how you look at it, is either a really crappy ski trail or a really great sledding course.

When I arrived there, during midsummer humidity, the site was buzzing with activity. The large meadow next to the hill had been cordoned off into a giant parking lot. A cheerful little village of striped, multicolored carnival tents created a county fair environment. In the wooded areas closer to the hill, people had set up camp with stoves and generators and refrigerators. They were there for a long haul.

The picnickers had come from all over the country and the world to toil together as the cast and crew of the Hill Cumorah Pageant. Since 1937 devoted readers of *The Book of Mormon* have made an annual pilgrimage to the site. There, right on the hill where the gold plates were excavated, they stage a giant show, an elaborate dramatization of the book, with water cannons and shooting columns of fire and dancing girls. The opening scene of the pageant—or, as insiders call it, Pageant—features a processional of the show's seven hundred cast members, all dressed in elaborate, colorful *Book of Mormon* costumes, hybrids of biblical and Maya cloaks, headdresses, turbans, jewelry, beards, spears, swords, and sabers. Together they march onto a seven-story stage built as a scaffolding directly on the hill. Sitting in the grassy meadow below, the audience watches this spectacle at night, under stadium lights and giant penitentiary-style spotlights. The show runs for over a week. But as the cast and crew are repeatedly told, the experience will last for a lifetime and beyond.

A little over a week before opening night everyone was gathered in that meadow for a giant casting call. I learned of this at the show's office, where I registered. The office, like so many official spaces associated with today's Saints, had the satisfying smell of the recently renovated, the tangy aroma of wet paint and factory-fresh carpeting, that ever-hopeful new-religion smell. The smiling Swedish woman who worked the desk handed me my kit, complete with neon orange pageant T-shirt and cast handbook, and offered to sell me postcards from previous pageants. To the uninitiated, these past shows would resemble debauched disco-era beach parties, with bonfires and symmetrically built hunks in tribal garb with lewdly greased biceps. I bought three postcards.

"They're giving out parts now," the Swedish woman said. "Women go first. If you get there quickly, you can stand with the men and ogle the ladies."

She pronounced the word "oogle," which sounded a shade seedier than "ogle."

The casting call in the meadow was a scene from a benign but eventful nightmare. To my left, dozens of teenage girls were dropping to their knees, clutching their hearts, dying theatrically, their soft suburban faces twisted into masks of deep Oriental suffering, each trying to perish more slowly and more anciently than the next. Older women in mom jeans and sensible shoes begged for alms and wailed to the heavens like Sicilian mourners. A woman with frenzied eyes and hair inflated by humidity repeatedly thrust an accusing finger at a nearby shrub and bellowed, "He's crazy! A *madman!*"

Amid these scenes of woe, a group of tweens, the younger sisters and cousins of the dying teenagers, hopped about in a merry circle dance. Other children, whose supervision had been neglected by auditioning parents, could be seen cartwheeling madly and playing badminton in trees. A flamboyant casting director stood by and shouted, "I'm gonna say this one last time, ladies. If I told you that you were either a"—he paused to read from a clipboard—"a boat child or a spoils-of-war woman, then you are dis*missed*. That means get out."

On a golf cart, whizzing by at a reckless speed, three identical church ladies, firmly set hairdos unmoving in the wind, giggled with glee. Meanwhile, we men waited at the edge of the meadow, oogling the ladies.

Soon it was our turn. Standing in our preassigned casting groups, stratified by age, we were surveyed by Hanson, the show's director, a svelte, stylish man whose bouffant of thick and meringuelike white hair, deep tan, unshakeable calm, and fabulously oversized turquoise ring would have made him a fine archduke. Hanson and his entourage of anxious walkie-talkie-bearing stage managers scanned the hundreds of hopeful men and boys, singling out candidates. After the fifth six-foot-three, two-hundred-pound man had been separated from the pack, it became clear what kind of guy was going to get a speaking role in this play.

A short fellow standing to my left, whose moist, freshly shaven cheeks resembled turkey cold cuts, began grumbling:

"Are they putting together a cast or a football team?"

There is a tradition in *Book of Mormon* paintings, going back to the official commissions made by Arnold Friberg—best known for his design work on Cecil B. DeMille's film *The Ten Commandments*—of depicting the story's characters as men of vein-popping, mountainous musculature, guys who would be comfortable stepping into the ring at WrestleMania. Joseph may have started this tradition with his description of the angel Moroni as "above the common size of men." By all accounts, Joseph himself was a large and athletic boy.

In his essay "Joseph Smith's Athletic Nature," Alexander Baugh cites the argument that superstrong people make better prophets. Baugh's own, somewhat defensive position is that being strong doesn't *prevent* one from being a prophet. This jock-prophet thesis intrigued me, especially as it seemed to be the aesthetic principle behind the casting of the Hill Cumorah Pageant.

Joseph's preferred sport was freestyle wrestling, or "catch-as-catch-can," as it was known then, which permitted any hold short of strangling your opponent. When you read accounts of Joseph's contemporaries, it becomes clear that the prophet positively loved to throw down, and he did so at any opportunity, even when it wasn't appropriate. Later in his life, when he became a well-known figure in the West, the prophet would ambush visiting dignitaries. One man, a respected minister, shocked by the prophet's request to spar following their meeting, stood silently, unsure how to respond; Joseph took this silence as an invitation to grab the man, twirl him around, and slam him to the ground.

Joseph also pestered a guy named Wandle Mace, one of his followers, to mix it up. In his memoirs, Mace, who was physically large but a pacifist, reported that the prophet would consistently shake his hand and "pull me to him for a wrestle."

Joseph apparently told another guy, "I wish you were a little larger—I would like to have some fun with you." Flattered by Joseph's attention, the man insisted that he was in fact prepared to fight. As the man would later recall, the prophet "began to trip me, he took some kind of lock on my right leg, from which I was unable to extricate myself. And throwing me around, broke it some three inches above the ankle joint."

Joseph's reputation as a bone-crusher extended beyond his circle. During his final days, when he was languishing in a Missouri frontier prison, one of his jailers challenged him to a match. According to those present, Smith threw the guard onto his back into a pool of water.

The job description of the prophet has always entailed physically demanding actions. He must live like a fugitive, hiking through deserts, wrestling angels, smashing idols, climbing mountains, carrying crosses, creating eye-catching spectacles. He must appear to have the power of a god even when being beaten, which for a prophet is an occupational hazard. After chiseling away at rock for forty days, alone atop a mountain in the middle of the desert, was it any wonder that poor eighty-year-old Moses dropped the stone tablets? Maybe Director Hanson was right: prophets should be cast like a football team.

The muted exasperation of my average- and below-average-sized counterparts at the casting call only deepened with the second round of selections, which privileged not statuesque men but mere fat dudes.

"C'mon. You gotta be kidding me," said the malcontent to my left when a shorter, stockier guy made the cut. Wielding his finely formed, turquoise-studded hand like a scepter, Hanson calmly made and dashed fortunes.

The rest of us, the scrawny masses, were forced to watch the audition, which consisted of twenty-five hand-selected hulks who took turns stepping forward with one arm extended theatrically and declaiming, "Touch me *not!*"

Hanson was unmoved. Gravely he huddled with his assistants. The auditioners were instructed to do another round, but this time, instead of reciting a line, each man was called upon to step forward, shake both fists over his head, and simply roar as loudly as possible. As we watched this spectacle, an awed silence descended on us average-sized men, and on the women and children too. After the last alpha male growled, the entire tribe replied as one with a lusty and appreciative war cry.

Hanson, only slightly less unmoved than before, conferred with his deputies; selections were made. In under half an hour, each speaking role, from Nephi to Joseph, was filled with beefcake. The rest of us, who hadn't been granted the dignity of an audition, were assigned roles more or less at random.

Alas, the role I was assigned didn't feel random. In fact, it felt all too apt. When I'd first signed up for the Hill Cumorah Pageant,

I had made a seriously bad decision. For reasons that aren't entirely clear—even to me now, as I write this—I had told the organizers of the show that my name was Yosef Green. Strange as it seems, I don't recall choosing to do this, much less the reason why. It somehow just happened; at least, that's how it felt.

I suspect it had to do with my desire to enter completely into the world of *The Book of Mormon*. For much of my journey thus far I had bracketed my inner skepticism and opened myself up to all possibilities. This had served me well on my trip through the Mesoamerican lands of the book. But now, as I began to explore Hill Cumorah, New York, the land of Joseph, I wanted to dip a bit deeper into the waters of Jerusalem syndrome, to know, to really feel what it would be like to be ravished by this story. In trying to believe the story completely, I thought it might be useful to simply imagine what it would be like to be a person who really believed completely and simply, with no baggage.

Of course, imagining a self with no baggage is a sure sign of having major baggage. The anxiety that had come over me during my first night in Guatemala City lingered on. Some part of me still wondered whether I had embarked on this project as a way to run away from nagging troubles in my own life, and whether most quests were just escape fantasies, as may well have been the case for Joseph himself. Problems in my marriage had only deepened. In trying to create a practical future with my wife, I found that our love, which had always been so mutually sustaining and had come so naturally that it seemed to be of nature, was getting lost in translation. My way of dealing with this painful situation was to actively avoid it—to buy plane tickets and train tickets, to rent cars. I continued to fear that I wasn't being honest with myself or others, and that I was inching ever closer to a precipice.

Still, I'd concluded that the experiences of traveling through the Nephite lands of Mesoamerica, seeing the real Hill Cumorah, had not been merely escapist. There really was something there, something precious. And in fact I'd been able to recognize it partly because of my troubles. That trip had been a true pilgrimage precisely because it had helped open my eyes a tiny bit more. I hadn't forgotten the feeling I'd had at Hill Cumorah in Mexico, the tangible sense of loss, of realizing that *all* stories begin as gold plates and that all gold plates are lost forever, that the stories we tell about ourselves are always some kind of translation, a flawed rendering. I hadn't forgotten that acutely sad, helpless feeling that something can be really important and real and yet gone and unrecoverable. In the presence of the mountain where the Nephites perished, the birthplace of the lost gold plates, I had been, I later realized, preparing for a serious personal loss—a relationship, a home, a story that I was telling about who I was. Another Jerusalem lost. But knowing all that, or rather, having strongly sensed it since I'd returned from Mesoamerica, hadn't diminished my desperate desire for control, or, lacking that, escape. On the contrary.

I'd been taken by the idea that the Hill Cumorah Pageant was a theatrical performance and had, I suppose, decided to adopt a kind of method-acting approach. Or something. The truth was, I hadn't thought it through. Nor had I considered what it would entail in practice.

Only while packing my car and beginning my trip to upstate New York did it fully dawn on me that for the next two and a half weeks I would be going by a random name. And not a particularly interesting one. Instead of being a Jewish guy named Avi, I would be a Jewish guy named Yosef: what had I really gained? Surely what I'd lost—a sense of normality, of good faith with my kind hosts— was hardly worth the exchange. Anytime someone would say my supposed name, I would be reminded again of what a bad idea it was. It also posed a practical problem. I would have to habituate myself to answering to it. My heart was weighed down by sin and doom. I should have turned back. But Yosef Green isn't the kind of guy who turns back.

As I'd put the car key into the ignition, I'd cursed the day Yosef Green was born. But when I pulled up to a stop sign and caught a glimpse of him looking back at me in my rearview mirror, with his eyes of an indeterminate swampy greenish hue, I just felt bad for the guy. He looked sad.

Before I hit the highway, I stopped at a vegetarian sandwich shop—an attempt to be virtuous—only to find that it had been ransacked, laid waste. It had apparently gone out of business. All that remained was its sign, which I swear on my mother's eyes said, CLEAR CONSCIENCE CAFÉ. Could there have been a clearer warning?

When I arrived at Hill Cumorah and waited at the casting call, I knew for certain that my fate was sealed when the flamboyant stage manager tapped me on the shoulder, squinted at my nametag, and said, "Yosef Green? You, sir, are rotten to the core." I went into a cold sweat as he handed me a card that read "Wicked Priest." I was instructed to wear it at all times.

Standing nearby, a frowning man with alarmingly sunburned ears turned to me and, in a thick, lazy Russian monotone, said, "Vant to know vhy you are vicked priest?" I told him I did indeed, sort of, yes, but not really, want to know. "Because you have skinny head," he explained, with the help of hand gestures, "vith very tall facebone."

The casting call carried on in full force past sunset. Having been dismissed by the stage manager and left to my own devices, I wandered up the steep winding path toward the top of Hill Cumorah. All around the hill, people asked one another which roles they'd been given. This was how you made small talk at Pageant. In disappointed tones, people revealed that they'd been recruited to join this or that angry mob, this or that group of slaves. Near the top of the hill, I encountered a guy sitting lumpily on a bench, eating a chicken wing. He was an evil Lamanite, he told me.

Each casting decision offered a small commentary on the story. It was becoming clear that the rank-and-file Lamanites were interpreted as a tribe of mostly hooligans (that is, your leftover burly men and fatsos) but also, mixed in, you had your lethargic depressives, like the guy with the buffalo wing. I tried to commiserate by telling him that I'd just been cast as a wicked priest. Instead of troubling him with the emotional issues raised by my assigned role, I just shrugged and said, "Oh well, right?"

"Actually," he said, "I would have been really excited to be a wicked priest."

At the top of the hill, by the monument marking the (estimated) spot where the gold plates of Mormon had been buried, I saw a young man in cargo shorts and a polo shirt, kneeling in prayer. His BYU cap lay on the ground beside him. He knelt there on both knees, as perfectly still as the statue before him—head bowed, hands clasped together in front of his chest. He was whispering. In the background, the frenzied sounds of the audition, still raging at the foot of the hill, reached us. In casting a crew of battle men, a role with a great deal of fight-dancing, the show's choreographers had been blasting the disco song "Kung Fu Fighter" on a soul-crushing loop. But up here those sounds were thin and inconsequential. Even though this spot at the top of Hill Cumorah had become a tourist destination, it was still remote enough to maintain a sense of intimate seclusion, the kind implied in that old hymn:

"The golden plates lay hidden deep in the mountainside / until God found one faithful in whom he could confide."

At the spot where Moroni confided some secret to Joseph, where now a gilded Moroni statue floated motionlessly at the top of a giant obelisk, the boy continued whispering. Until, finally, he jumped up, fastened his cap to his head and adjusted it to the desired angle, then stretched. He was a tall, muscular guy. I recognized him from the audition. He had roared mightily, earnestly, with unruffled confidence, not dementedly like some of his colleague hunks. Yes, I recognized him now. Here was none other than young Nephi himself.

TWO

There's an old theory, almost as old as *The Book of Mormon* itself, that charges Joseph and his associates, most likely Sidney Rigdon, with stealing an unpublished novel and using it as the basis for *The Book of Mormon*. Rigdon, a highly regarded minister from Ohio, is typically cited as Joseph's first major convert, the first person of social standing and learning—that is, not one of Joseph's family or his rustic neighbors—to affirm Joseph's claim to prophethood. That's the official story.

A counterhistory holds that Rigdon was actually the mastermind behind *The Book of Mormon* and that his later conversion was a ruse. According to this theory, Rigdon, a highly literate man, was the primary editor/author of the text we have today. This is known as the Spalding theory, after Solomon Spalding, the author of the unpublished and allegedly stolen novel, whose working title was *Manuscript Found*. It's sometimes called the Spalding-Rigdon theory.

Rigdon once worked in a Pittsburgh print shop that the hapless Spalding had tried—and failed—to persuade to publish his novel. The Spalding-Rigdon theory maintains that Rigdon somehow got his hands on the Spalding manuscript, used material from the pilfered novel, edited it to his liking, and added a few layers of his own, mostly in the direction of making it more preachy. According to the theory, Rigdon and Joseph Smith must have been in cahoots in the 1820s, at some point before the publication of *The Book of Mormon*.

The official history—the version Rigdon swore was true, even years later, after he broke with Joseph—is that their first meeting happened a year *after* the book was published and that Rigdon had nothing at all to do with the creation of *The Book of Mormon*.

The forgery and plagiarism accusations were leveled in a newspaper in 1834 by a disgruntled Mormon named Philastus Hurlbut, who interviewed a bunch of villagers in Ohio, including members of the Spalding family, all of whom swore that as early as 1814 they'd heard Spalding read aloud from an unpublished novel that featured characters named Nephi, Alma, et al., and that had included place-names such as Zarahemla. They also recalled that Spalding's tale concerned the discovery of a manuscript containing an ancient saga of America unearthed in Indian burial mounds.

In a few testimonies, witnesses recalled Spalding's compulsive use of "and it came to pass," the phrase that appears with astonishing frequency in Joseph's *Book of Mormon*. They recalled this verbal pattern precisely because it had annoyed them so much. Behind Spalding's back, they called him "Old Come-to-Pass."

The Spalding theory has gone in and out of favor. Even though it's made a recent comeback, there's still no conclusive evidence, no smoking gun. The damning Spalding manuscript that predates the 1830 publication of *The Book of Mormon*, which contains irrefutable parallels to it, has never been found.

There was one lead though. In 1884 an alleged Spalding manuscript surfaced in Hawaii and eventually landed at Oberlin College in Ohio. Devout readers gleefully pointed out that this Spalding manuscript sounds nothing like *The Book of Mormon* and contains none of the character names and place-names. The skeptics countered that it was close enough, and in a thickening of the plot, they posited a *second* Spalding manuscript, the real *Manuscript Found*, which they said would be chock-full of *Book of Mormon* parallels and would make their case beyond any doubt. Unfortunately, the manuscript of *Manuscript Found* appears to be lost.

I was interested in how the Spalding-Rigdon theory, a skeptical interpretation, turned out to be a mirror image of the devout viewpoint. Both theories produced a group of witnesses and hinged completely on a lost document: the gold plates for the devout and for the skeptics Spalding's lost manuscript, which might as well have been made of gold. Both sides were absolutely certain that their lost document existed, but both were ultimately systems of faith.

At the Hill Cumorah Pageant, however, you can easily find yourself some gold plates in the Props Department. The props area was set up like a booth at a carnival, with a guy penned inside a square counter, surrounded by overflowing rows of trinkets. Half the area looked like a Roman armory, with hundreds of carefully organized spears, swords, and sabers. The props guy was a big walrusy fellow whose face was dominated by a droopy mustache of the kind still seen in the less populated regions of our western provinces. I asked him if I might pick up the gold plates.

He rummaged behind him and in one rapid gesture placed the metallic-looking plates firmly on the counter. "There ya are," he said. "One set of gen-u-wine gold plates." He watched me as I picked them up. "Not as heavy as you'd think, are they?" he said. "If it's up to me, I say, make 'em heavy. Like how they really were."

The question of how they really were, how much the gold plates weighed, is taken quite seriously by readers of *The Book of Mormon*. A 1984 study published by BYU's Maxwell Center notes that a "surprising amount of consistent information can be gleaned from eyewitnesses." Joseph claimed that the length, width, and thickness of the plates was 6 inches by 8 inches by 6 inches. After factoring in some adjustments based on the testimonies of other people, the article offers some preliminary measurements: the plates measured .1666 cubic feet. And if this book were indeed composed of solid, pure 24-karat gold (1204.7 pounds per cubic foot), the final weight would be 200.8 pounds. Which is too heavy.

If, however, you factored in the research of metallurgist Reed Putnam, who argued that hammering plates of pure 24-karat gold would cut the mass by about 50 percent, the weight of the gold plates would drop down to 100.4 pounds. Which still seems too heavy.

If, however, the plates truly were written in ancient Mesoamerica, in the cities of the Maya, we can sharpen the measurements further. If the plates were made of the Central American tumbaga alloy—8-karat gold with copper—the weight would come out to roughly 53.4 pounds, which squares nicely with many statements made by members of the prophet's inner circle, including his brother William Smith. Willy once hefted the plates in a pillowcase and estimated that they weighed about 60 pounds.

With the tumbaga alloy theory, writes the author of the article, "other details fit into place." For example, coloring. Treating the red-toned tumbaga with any simple acid, a procedure used by the Maya, would remove copper from the surface, leaving a brilliant .0006-inch, 23-karat gilt coating.

We can also deduce that each individual plate was probably about .15 to .02 inch thick, or, allowing for air space and irregularities, about .03 to .05 inch. A 6-inch-thick book would therefore have contained between 120 and 200 plates. If both sides of each plate, front and back, were engraved, as described, you'd end up with a nice 240- to 400-page book.

"Thus," concludes the BYU article, "reasonable sense can be made of the physical description of the plates and of their possible metallurgical composition."

What is truly astonishing is exactly that: how reasonable it all sounds. Were you to tell an outside person that Joseph Smith dug up a gold book that was written in a Semitic language and buried in upstate New York by an ancient Maya who then returned as an angel, your listener would probably laugh. But in an article that is presented dispassionately, and with the great authority bestowed by reams of dull data, making reasonable sense of one technical aspect of the story, the humor is swallowed up by the numbers. And while a detailed analysis of the dimensions of an imaginary object might seem like a deeper kind of joke, what it actually achieves is something more sincere: realism.

Nabokov was thinking along the same lines as *The Book of Mormon* metallurgists when, as an act of literary criticism, he sketched entomological diagrams to determine what kind of insect, taxonomically speaking, Kafka's Gregor Samsa had transformed into, ruling out a cockroach and concluding that it must be some kind of beetle.

But realism cannot be manufactured by mere measurements. The missing nose in Gogol's story "The Nose" is plausible not because the dimensions make any sense but because the rest of the man's ruddy face, his well-starched collar, his pathetic lie about being an army major, his distress at having lost his social standing because of his missing nose, are each described with the precision of the painfully familiar. With Kafka too, it's the realistic details of

Gregor's life—his bed, his dead-end job, the family dynamics—
that make his transformed body seem possible.

Like Gogol's nose or Kafka's beetle, the plausibility of the gold
plates is drawn from the realistic details that surround them, the
ways in which this fanciful-seeming object mingles so easily with
everyday life in, for example, all its hiding places on the Smith farm:
a pillowcase, Joseph's smock, a pile of flax in the cooper's shop, a
stone under the fireplace, a barrel of beans, a wooden chest—all the
details that Joseph and his family members mention in their oral
histories and letters. And, in one of the loveliest and most comic
gestures in the story, when Joseph's wife, Emma, doing her house-
cleaning, momentarily lifts the cloth-covered gold plates so that she
can dust under them. Like the sister in *The Metamorphosis*, entering
Samsa's room and sweeping around his fantastically transformed
body, the realism of the plates emerges organically from the comedy
of housekeeping. Isn't the act of sweeping around something proof
that the thing exists?

The work of digging up and sorting out details, of co-creating
the story, continues today by writers, scholars, toy manufacturers,
tour guides, prophets, and gossipers—and also by the cast and crew
of the Hill Cumorah Pageant. Just as *The Book of Mormon*'s metallurgists spin realism into the story through an alchemy of precise
measurements and geographers trace it out in the distance between
Guatemala City and Lake Atitlán, the stage production creates a
reality through drama, by inviting its readers to inhabit it, to go to
the place and live inside it together for a few weeks. Casting those
hulking guys, those young BYU jocks, as leads in the show was part
of this process. So was getting a chance to play with gold plates in
the Props Department.

Sensing that I wasn't going away anytime soon, the props guy took a break from organizing his doodads. As we drifted outside the booth and loitered there for a moment, he reached into his breast pocket and whipped out a cigarette—strictly forbidden to a Saint—which amazed me until I realized that it was in fact a goofy swirl-shaped lollipop, which in its way amazed me even more. He tossed the pop into his mouth. There was something in the deftness of the gesture that suggested to me that the props man perhaps hadn't always been a Saint.

"Want one?" he asked.

"Nah, I'm good," I replied.

He gave me a sidelong glance.

"Is that right?" he said, with what I took to be some kind of wry cowboy skepticism. He was from Wyoming, born and raised.

"Well." He smiled. "That's fine. Don't got another one anyways."

At that moment, I looked up toward the top of the hill and saw Nephi (the actor playing Nephi) and Joseph (the actor playing Joseph) exchanging an immense, leaping high five, followed by a resounding chest bump.

THREE

During my first night at the Hill Cumorah Pageant, I heard a strange sound. I was lying in my dormitory bed at Finger Lakes Community College, shifting uncomfortably on a mattress made of a heavy plastic which I associate with bed-wetting resistance. The show's cast members were being housed by the college, about twenty minutes down the old road from Hill Cumorah. I'd been placed in a suite with three other single men, in what was, it soon became clear, the show's haven for eccentrics.

When I heard the late-night commotion, I left my room to investigate. One of my suitemates was in the kitchen, opening and closing the cupboards haphazardly like a zombie looking for his morning cereal. I was somewhat surprised by this but, tellingly, not as surprised as I might usually be. When I'd met him earlier that night, he had also been haphazardly opening and closing these empty cupboards.

A few hours earlier I'd been sitting in the kitchen with another of my suitemates, Greg, a software programmer from Salt Lake City who was into comics, sci-fi, video games—anything that mingled calculated rational decision-making with fun characters and explosions. He was explaining to me why it mattered that George Lucas was a sellout. Goateed, sleepy-eyed, and balding, Greg wore a rigid, deadpan expression and didn't appear to move his lips when speaking. With his arms crossed and propped on his large belly, he would sit and deliver candid, affectless opinions. By stringing together a steady stream of short pronouncements, he somehow managed to be, oddly, both chatty and understated. Like the chicken-wing eater I'd met near the top of Hill Cumorah, Greg had immediately asked what role I'd been assigned in the show. And like the guy on the bench, Greg had sighed with resignation upon my disclosure of having landed the apparently coveted part of Wicked Priest #2.

Did I have any theater experience? Greg wanted to know. Not really, I confessed. He sighed again.

"Do you know how many wicked priests there are?"

"At least two, right?" I said. Greg didn't smile. I tried again. "I'm not sure, to be honest. Six, I think."

Now he laughed. Actually, he just said the word *ha*.

"*Three*," he continued, refolding his arms. "It's almost a talking role."

Being a wicked priest wasn't like being a destruction victim or a faceless member of one of the Jerusalem angry mobs, Greg explained. It wasn't even like having the pretty respectable role of a spoils-of-war woman. As a wicked priest, one wasn't part of a mass ensemble. A wicked priest was a nearly singular role, a character that a serious actor could really breathe dramatic life into.

Greg, however, had higher aspirations; it was his opinion that he ought to be King Noah. He spun his eyes in my direction to see how I reacted to this audacious claim. King Noah was more than a mere talking role; it was one of the leads. But now that he mentioned it, Greg was totally right: he could easily have played King Noah. Based on the iconography of the story's characters, as depicted in influential *Book of Mormon* paintings and illustrations from the twentieth century—the same images that continue to make their way into *Book of Mormon* merchandising, film adaptations, action figures, and video games—the guy was a dead ringer for the villainous, gluttonous, lascivious king, right down to the facial hair.

"Omigod, you *are* King Noah!" I said.

Greg humbly lowered his eyes.

"Thank you," he replied. "I'm glad somebody gets it."

Greg in fact had played King Noah in past Hill Cumorah shows. People had told him that he'd been the best King Noah they'd seen. And he agreed that he'd pretty much nailed the part. What's more, he added, the role is incredibly physically demanding. It's not for just anyone. King Noah has to wear an elaborate, outrageously heavy outfit. You sweat buckets out there, he said. You get home and sit around with ice on your back for the rest of the night—and for a week's worth of shows. Greg documented every stage of prep work required just to get the costume on: the makeup, the wig, the beard, the massive headdress. The level of detail, the litany of buttons and beads and straps and feathers and special shoes involved, described with torturously slow deliberation, left me experiencing the squishy black flashes I had once felt during the early stages of heatstroke.

Greg could do this to you. His conversational manner was what one might call "overinclusive." When he got going, it was impossible to prevent his search engine–like mind from steaming forward. Somehow the topic of ski resorts with proximity to the Salt Lake City Airport had come up. (Because he'd brought it up.) The question, he noted, depended on what you meant by *resort*—all-inclusive or just skiing?—and it depended on whether *proximity* meant half an hour or, say, an hour away. Greg processed all this information for me right there and began streaming the data in a matrix of proximity/type. Then he ventured to recall the names of these dozens of ski venues. All of them. Each one—and as slowly as they came to mind, which was so slow that enough time passed between names to give the impression that he had concluded his list, that he might in fact have stopped talking altogether, an impression that was dashed horribly each time he intoned yet another name.

It was during that moment—when the squishy-headed, early-stage-blackout feeling was descending on me—that our second suitemate entered the picture. Stormed into the picture, in fact. He seemed extraordinarily angry, possibly at us. But I didn't care. I was just thrilled for the change of subject.

"Hey!" I said, probably a bit maniacally. "*Great* to meet you."

Immediately this new roommate was deeply suspicious of me. It would not be an exaggeration to say that he hated my guts. He glowered at me, scanning me up and down and across—scrupulously ignoring my eyes—and taking a series of small measurements, each accompanied by a displeased pout, the way a tailor probes a new customer. He shook my hand with great reluctance, from as far away as our respective arm lengths would permit. He was a short, anxious, nerdy, neckless black guy who wore a complicated sequence of sweaters, and round glasses that were too big for his face. Like Greg, he was thinning on top, but somehow, perhaps owing to his boyish looks, his bald head was more poignant than Greg's. He insisted that he was from Manhattan, not New York. And, as it turned out, he was not a tailor but a United States Postal Service worker.

"Oh, that's cool," said Greg. "You deliver the mail. Do you get the uniform?"

The postman, whose name was Rob, now shot Greg a poisonous look. It was very likely that Rob, in addition to hating me, now also hated him. But Greg wouldn't have noticed in any case. Instead he politely reached out to Rob by telling him that he himself knew someone who lived in New York, a "really weird cousin" who moved there after high school to join what sounded to me like a radical leftist anarchist marching band. Oblivious of Rob's deepening disgust, Greg affably took up the subject of glue.

"You know?" he was saying. "To apply the costume beards? It's a special kind. I asked Ryan in costumes—or was it Stephanie—well, I asked one of them and they're actually using a new kind of glue this year, different than in past years . . ."

As Greg continued in this fashion, I noticed that Rob had stopped paying any attention, if he'd been paying attention in the first place. With Greg not paying attention to Rob's not paying attention, the men managed to have a perfectly cordial exchange wherein Greg spoke at length while Rob needlessly opened and closed the cupboards of the kitchen suite. All the cupboards were empty, a fact that Rob quickly ascertained but that nevertheless didn't deter him from pressing his investigation to its conclusion.

On my way to bed, I walked by another suitemate's room. I hadn't met him yet. The only evidence of his existence was the non-stop buzzing of an electric shaver behind his door. One could only surmise that our fourth roommate was a gentleman of uncommon hairiness.

Now it was about midnight. Down the hall, in his royal chamber, King Noah was snoring monstrously but contentedly; the hairy fourth roommate had silenced his electric shaver; and I'd drifted out of my room to check on the sound I'd heard. That was when I saw Rob. He was at it again, compulsively opening and closing the kitchen cupboards. He was apparently asleep. The kitchen was completely dark. But in the ghostly light emitted from the empty refrigerator—which he'd also opened—I could see the postman's face. He wore the exhausted, unnerving, smudgy expression of a man without his glasses, eyes like scars, features all jumbled, as though his own blindness prevented him not merely from seeing but also somehow from being seen.

For what seemed an eternity but was probably more like a few seconds, Rob continued opening and closing the cupboards. He was sweeping his hands along the shelves in a desperate, blind search for something. He needed this thing, whatever it was, and he needed it *now*, but he wasn't finding it. He moaned angrily, agonizingly. Until, finally, he quit.

Sliding along the wall in a full embrace, the postman dragged himself back to his room. I thought of Kafka's traveling salesman turned beetle, scuttling upon his bedroom wall. A life spent circulating about endlessly can do this to a man.

Down the hall, in his room, Rob collapsed, with a crunch, onto the piss-resistant rubber dorm mattress. I returned my gaze to the kitchen and almost gasped. In the creepy fridge-lit space, the empty kitchen, with every cupboard thrown wide open, looked truly haunted.

I tried to soothe myself to sleep by picturing Jesus—the actor playing Jesus—being lowered in a harness on a crane way above Hill Cumorah, the no-kidding-around deus ex machina scene that was the spectacular finale to our play. I imagined being him. The cozy harness, the breezy, warm-but-cooling summer air up there, the slight tingle of the messianic stage beard—the best money can buy—the reassuringly regular cranking sound of the crane (heard only by me), the vast enveloping silence that hovered over the entire countryside and softly blunted the din of the trumpet blasts rising from the stage below, the tiny car headlights streaming by on a distant road, the modest glow of Rochester on the horizon, the feeling of being all alone but deeply part of something, of being exactly where I was supposed to be, of the air streaming up the gown that, according to suitemate Greg, is made of some top-shelf, highly specialized fabric chosen specifically for the gloriously, blazingly white way in which it radiates in the spotlight.

What was that like? What went through the mind of the guy in that harness? He was full of the kinds of summer concerns that occupy any rising college sophomore. He had his whole life ahead of him—a thought that never came into his head, nor had to, because he knew it as a self-evident solidity of the bones. He was from a wealthy family, a star student-athlete, a sweet kid who spent his time helping less fortunate children, the pride of his tight-knit, prosperous community. He was their future and he was glowing brightly. He was their Son. He was Jesus. I imagined the cool air up there and tried to hypnotize myself to sleep with it. But it didn't work.

When the distracting busyness of the day was done and I was alone with my thoughts, all the anxiety that had taken on the name Yosef Green came creeping back. In the dark, I couldn't quite erase the specter of the mad postman's face from my mind. It wasn't helping me sleep, that image. Nor did it help that so many of the completely bat-shit, barkingly wild nocturnal events I'd read about in Joseph's life had happened right up the road, in the same creepy forests I could see looming from my dorm-room window.

According to some versions of the story, the spirit of Moroni insisted that Joseph bring another person with him during his annual September 22 pilgrimage up the hill. At first the spirit said that this person ought to be Alvin, Joseph's beloved older brother. But in a chilling twist, he continued to insist that Joseph bring Alvin even after Alvin had died. Did Joseph exhume his brother's body at the command of this spirit? Necromancy, the art of using dead bodies in the service of magical conjuring, was a known practice connected with treasure-seeking.

And what about the murder that opens *The Book of Mormon*,

when Nephi beheads Laban? It seemed as if everywhere I turned, I found the sword of Laban. Usually a murder weapon is something to be disposed of. The sword had been introduced into the story as an object of fascination: even as Nephi struggles over whether to commit the murder, he is drawn to the shapeliness of the weapon. The narrator—the killer himself, after all—subtly suggests that it was the beauty of the sword, its fine metalwork, that helped sway him to put it to use. There is something grotesquely sensual, almost taboo, in that moment of lingering over, of savoring, the pleasing form of the weapon before using it to savage his victim. A murderer motivated by aesthetics is the most sinister kind.

When Joseph first opened the box buried in Hill Cumorah, there it was again, the sword, the murder weapon. According to Brigham Young, when Joseph and Oliver Cowdery returned to the hill to deposit the gold plates back in their proper place and saw the hidden cave full of books, they also saw Laban's sword hanging on a wall. Throughout the story, the thing appears and reappears like an obsessive thought.

Watching rehearsals of the play under the stars, I'd seen the actors and the director, svelte Hanson, working on the scene in which Nephi returns triumphantly with the book he'd stolen from Laban, placing it in his father's hands. I'd asked one of the actors whether they'd be rehearsing the scene that preceded that one, the murder. That scene, I was told, was not in the play. The murder of Laban, the theft of the book, those critical pieces of the narrative, had been omitted; the action picked up with Nephi running in, stage left, with the book in hand. No explanation of how he'd come by it or why he was running in breathlessly.

The conspicuous presence of the sword throughout *The Book of Mormon* saga, from the beginning of the book and for thousands of years afterward, and finally in the life of Joseph, made its omission from the Hill Cumorah play all the more noticeable.

But what was the meaning of the sword in Joseph's life? It's tempting to take a psycho-biographical approach to the story. Maybe Joseph was excavating his own dark dreams on Hill Cumorah. Maybe he was enacting a very literal version of Freud's archaeology metaphor of digging out and recovering painful experiences buried deep in the unconscious. Late at night, Joseph, haunted, would pick up a shovel, go deep into the woods behind his home, and dig and dig. Wasn't that a description of a psychological process as well? The old human myth of the boy who finds hidden treasure almost always boils down to the discovery of a long-buried secret, a taboo. What was the dark secret? What was he digging for out there?

Maybe the discovery of the sword in the same box as the plates was just a matter of presenting evidence: the hieroglyphs on the plates proved that the book was ancient and the sword proved that its story was factual. But even so, why *that* object? Why the weapon of dismemberment? Why not Nephi's sandal or Mormon's pinkie ring?

Some have suggested a rigid Freudian reading. Joseph underwent a childhood trauma in which he suffered a prolonged illness that culminated in a series of excruciating surgeries on his leg, without anesthesia. Even though the operations were successful and he grew into a strong man, Joseph, according to some people, suffered a lifelong phobia of dismemberment at the hands of a man with a long amputation knife.

A psychiatrist named William Morain wrote a book in which he theorized that Joseph associated this particular trauma with his father because his father, not his mother, was in the room during the surgery and hadn't protected him from the knife. In other ways too, Joseph felt betrayed by Joseph Senior, a loving father whose drinking and treasure-hunting and failed business schemes nevertheless made life painfully insecure for the family. According to this reading, Joseph, conflicted, split his father in two: on the one hand the beloved Joe Senior—in the story, Nephi's father, Lehi—and on the other the evil Joe Senior, represented by the drunken Laban. In slaying Laban, Nephi castrates the bad father while saving and vindicating the good father.

The people around Joseph certainly seemed haunted by his story. Decades after Joseph was murdered, David Whitmer, a member of the original inner circle, told the *Chicago Times* that he'd been back to visit the hill three times over the years. The stone box that Joseph had unearthed all those years earlier, said Whitmer, was right where Joseph had left it. "Eventually the casket had been washed down to the foot of the hill," Whitmer was quoted as saying, but it was still there. Even after Whitmer had parted ways with the prophet, he couldn't stop visiting the hill, thinking about it, talking about it. The casket that Joseph had excavated on Hill Cumorah remained there for many years; its uncanny presence would not be denied.

It was this casket that came to mind during my first night in the dorm, as I lay awake in bed. The gold plates were unearthed in the dead of night; to find them, you had to seek them in the dark, as Joseph had. It was no wonder the sword of Laban didn't appear under the bright lights of the pageant. It had originated in a much earlier, more primal version of the story, the one that had emerged whole, like the living corpse of a buried trauma, late one night in the life and nearby woods of young Joseph.

Maybe Joseph was excavating his own dark dreams on Hill Cumorah.

FOUR

The time had come for me to take the stage—in rehearsal—to inhabit the role of Wicked Priest #2. Or, to be more precise, to inhabit the role of Yosef Green playing Wicked Priest #2. The scene seemed straightforward enough. The wicked priests would enter at one of the high stages, Stage 5, then march in a slow, eerie processional to the sounds of imperial trumpets, drum rolls, and other ominous royal flourishes. We were instructed to "act seriously arrogant." While walking single file, projecting a nauseating degree of confidence, we were to descend a tall flight of stairs, at the top of which was evil King Noah's giant gaudy throne tricked out with a massive jaguar head that looked like a college team mascot afflicted by rabies. Arrogantly, we wickeds were to take our positions at the foot of the stairs, where we were to chat with each other in an arrogant manner about matters that even an audience member sitting all the way down in the meadow, well over six stories and hundreds of feet away, could plainly see concerned the worst kind of arrogance. A big drum roll signaled us to halt abruptly, kneel, and thrust our arms skyward, toward the throne, in a double-barreled "Hail, Caesar" salute. This was evil King Noah's cue to enter stage left, next to the rabid mascot, and fly into his maniacal spiel. That was the opening.

The challenge of the grand entrance was twofold. It went without saying that you had to act really arrogant, but, more pressingly, you had to refrain from giggling. This latter effort was made nearly impossible by the sight that confronted us the moment we entered. On a stage below, a group of what appeared to be not quite ninth-grade girls hoisted gold bowls above their heads while doing a suggestive, stutter-step circle dance. These were the notorious court dancers, a much-sought-after role among the younger set of cast members. As we wicked priests entered, these nubile court dancers were cued to stop suddenly and salute us with their bowls, which was supposed to add a layer of sleazy innuendo to our arrogance. But the effect of suddenly seeing a group of gawky, brace-faced suburban schoolgirls dressed as courtesans made it nearly impossible to maintain our arrogance and not laugh.

The music stopped. From down below the director yelled, "Guys, seriously. Let's get through this."

We gave it another try. After retreating back up the stairs, we stood at our marks—behind the throne—ready to enter again, redoubled in our professional commitment to behave arrogantly or, failing that, to do our best to avoid making eye contact with the girls in braces.

"Hold it, hold it, hold it," the director shouted. "Spoils-of-war women! We need you to take a more craven, conquered attitude. Can we do that?"

Hanson had proved to be a fine director. Earlier I'd observed him wrangling a giant tween-aged angry mob. "Don't all shake your fists," he told them. "We don't want everyone's hands going up together in that *Chorus Line* effect. Everyone, choose an angry action, make it personal."

A few stages below us, the spoils-of-war women tried out some craven poses, as per their instructions. I peeked out further and saw

Hanson nodding. The dreadful music was cued again. We arranged our arrogant faces and prepared to enter stage left.

This time we made it as far as the entrance of King Noah. The moment he stepped onstage, it was entirely clear that this Noah was 100 percent schmuck. He gave off a strong Mussolini vibe, by way of the *Arabian Nights*. Like all villains in American epics, he spoke with a British accent. He marched and strutted and emoted recklessly, alternating between a greasy grin and a bulldog scowl. In accord with *The Book of Mormon*'s description of him as a "wine bibber," Noah slurred his proclamations in a deranged but formal manner, partly declaiming his lines and partly vomiting them out, the way John Belushi might have played Richard III. Though I remained loyal to my suitemate Greg, who'd been shafted at the King Noah auditions, I had to admit that this actor was absolutely killing.

As we stood at our marks, I looked around and appreciated some of the show's other fine casting decisions. I was struck with one man in particular, who stood apart from the sporty, back-slapping-American-guys' guys who dominated the field. He was a man of mystical aspect: tall, dark, and lamblike, hunched and sunken-shouldered, with a long bushy black beard, wire glasses, and eyes of deep sorrow. He lacked any Mormon crispness and seemed to be from another, significantly more melancholic tribe altogether, more like a young Armenian Orthodox monk. It turned out he was a marine recently returned from the front, where he'd done a few tours in both Iraq and Afghanistan.

In our present scene, the young veteran suffered a gruesome martyrdom. Amid the nonstop disco inferno that was Noah's palace, the king eventually stood up and, to amuse his hard-partying courtiers, jubilantly slashed the throat of a shackled war prisoner, played by our poor monklike marine. His lifeless body was then tossed off the side of the stage, which had a jarring realism for those of us standing on set who were able to see him free-fall a story or so offstage onto some kind of cushion—we hoped.

Killing for sport was par for the course in King Noah's world. The country was run by hypocritical plutocrat-mobsters, allied with a thoroughly corrupt priesthood (my cohort). The land was plagued by licentiousness, taxes, and liquor—standard den-of-sin stuff.

Then came a man who dared to stand up and question King Noah. His name was Abinadi (rhymes with *a big hog pie*).

Pro-Noah loyalists immediately stood up and angrily denounced Abinadi as a madman, a coward, a traitor. A woman—one of the show's few female speaking parts—stood up and delivered an annihilating indictment. Noah concluded the lynching with a spitting, rabble-rousing condemnation of Abinadi to death by fire ("Burrrrn him to death!").

Even Noah's subjects, accustomed to the king's excesses, were shocked by this turn of events. Sure, Abinadi had behaved brazenly, but still, he was just a pious beggar, a bit quirky perhaps, but not an enemy of the state. He was just one of the regular people. But Noah would not relent. Abinadi was bound and dragged violently down three staircased stories of our stage (from high up, you could hear the set clanging against the grass of Hill Cumorah) to Stage 1, where a stake was being hastily erected for his execution. That was the cue for the sound effects of a bonfire, loud crackling and gusting flames, a terrible thing to hear in this context. When a row of real flames shot up, the actors onstage didn't need the director to tell them to take a step back in fright.

This was where I and my fellow wicked priests came into the picture. King Noah, who supposedly ruled by law, was forced to consider an eleventh-hour legal appeal to his execution edict. He delegated this judicial review to that ever-objective and august body, the wicked priests. We were the brain trust, the gatekeepers of the divine mysteries. We, learned yes-men, drenched in gold rings, jade jewels, and jaguar prints, were asked to put our evil turbans together, to stroke our sleazy beards, to project an air of solemn contemplation for the crowd, and, within roughly five seconds, to render judgment. The verdict, of course, was clear: the boss wanted this loser dead; therefore, it was the right decision. King Noah winked and thanked us for our wise counsel.

That was Alma's cue. Without any warning, Alma, one of my fellow wicked priests, suddenly stood up and publicly accused the king of a litany of crimes. If this weren't shocking enough, this once most loyal of loyalists turned to his colleague priests and exposed our corrupt tricks before the crowd. (Hanson instructed us to look particularly flabbergasted at the unmasking of our whoredoms.)

Having momentarily halted Abinadi's execution, Alma concluded his speech by officially defecting to the condemned man's side. King Noah, shaken, and personally wounded by this treachery from within his own ranks, condemned him to death as well—but only halfheartedly. It would be politically unwise to kill Alma, a hero of the people. Instead Noah ordered his goons to chase him into exile.

The next section of the story had been a favorite of my trusty guide, Lee, back on our tour through Mesoamerica. Alma's wanderings in exile were full of juicy geographical details. His travels through the wilderness, from the City of Nephi—the seat of King Noah's court—to the Waters of Mormon to Zarahemla, had blazed the critical part of our trail from Guatemala City to Lake Atitlán to Chiapas. As I watched our Alma flee the set during my scene at the Hill Cumorah play, I imagined this young hunk traveling through the densely forested miles west of Guatemala City down to the majestic lake, a journey of eight days, as we had learned. Perhaps he would sustain himself on mangoes and the occasional tropical turkey, but in pious deference to the law of Moses, he would pass on wild boar. As it was nearly a thousand years before the Mel Gibson suite, with its abundance of pillows, Alma would have slept right on the banks of Lake Atitlán/Waters of Mormon, a giant moon rising over the volcanoes and reflecting on the crater waters.

The actor who played Alma spoke in the sleepy, weary manner common to the burly man, as if being a burly man were in itself a terribly exhausting thing to be. Or maybe he was just tired of answering the same questions about his football career. As we awaited further directions from Hanson, an older gentleman, one of King Noah's grubby commoners, started bothering Alma, a rising freshman at BYU recruited to play left tackle. The man asked the young tackler if he had plans to play in the NFL.

The boy shrugged. "If it happens, it happens," he said. Sensing that his elder wasn't satisfied with the answer, he added, "Even if I went pro, I'd only do it a few years and get out."

With Alma, who stood a few Greek statuary heads taller than the rest of us wicked priests, the play's casting of hunk-heroes had finally backfired. The which-one-is-not-like-the-other effect of our walking single file during the entrance created a wildly mismatched look, like a Humvee leading a line of geese down the street, which spoiled Alma's surprise defection and gave the scene an unexpected, but to my fellow castmates not unwelcome, moment of slapstick.

FIVE

As opening night approached we were asked to participate in a "spiritual rehearsal" in which cast groups gathered together by scene to discuss the moral implications of their particular parts in the performance. When I arrived, Director Hanson was already speaking. His plush hair was having a particularly plush day.

"You may not think that playing a bad guy is a great way to spend your time here," he said to an ensemble of wicked priests, court dancers, assorted lynch mobs, and execution victims. "But you'd be wrong. Don't take my word for it, folks. I present to you His Royal Highness, King Noah." With this, our director bowed elegantly.

I exchanged a look with Greg, my suitemate and King Noah doppelgänger, who rolled his eyes.

When our King Noah—who was actually a pretty calm, personable guy—was done speaking, the director patted him on the back and took the mic. "So our message to you here: be willing to be bad. Say it with me: *be bad*." Everyone repeated it. "That's right, people, be wicked. Have fun with it!" The assembled Saints seemed happy to accept this message. But I must confess, my heart sank under the continued burden of being Yosef Green.

I needed a break from the dramas of the show. I needed to feel grounded again. When the spiritual rehearsal concluded, I got in my car and made a trip to the Grandin Print Shop, the site where Joseph's completed translation of the gold plates was transformed from a manuscript handwritten on foolscap paper into the leather-bound first edition of *The Book of Mormon*. In the midst of the fake beards and stage personas, there was something satisfyingly tangible in that.

When I arrived at the shop, located on the main street of downtown Palmyra, I was met by a shaggy but distinguished mutt who bore a close resemblance to Oliver Cromwell and guarded the door with an unsmiling but consummate professionalism. A few cast members from the Hill Cumorah Pageant were hanging out nearby, eating ice cream and showing each other, and me, photos of themselves eating ice cream at other *Book of Mormon* pilgrimage sites. Most photos, it seemed, involved someone standing in front of a statue of Joseph or another character from the story and replicating its pose.

In Grandin's old print shop, now a fully restored museum, you can see how the type was set for *The Book of Mormon*, how each printing plate was laid out by hand, letter by letter, how the pages were printed into large sheets, folded into fourths, and bound by hand. A tour guide takes visitors through every step of the elaborate process of tanning leather, pounding and sculpting it into a book cover, branding it with the title, and finally painting gold flourishes on it. Each book was handcrafted; each cover had its own quirky shade of leather and grain texture. It was a long and exacting process to produce the first print run of five thousand copies. I could understand why Martin Harris had to mortgage his farm to finance it.

It's odd to see a sacred text, an actual divine oracle, undergoing such a worldly production process. Like so much else with

The Book of Mormon, the nitty-gritty real-world details, laid out so plainly and with such plausibility, were a large part of the appeal.

But the deeper you walked into the museum, the less you saw. In the exhibit on the second floor of Grandin's shop was a display, a life-sized diorama representing the family kitchen that belonged to Joseph and Emma Smith during the first years of their marriage. On the table sat a bulky square object, the gold plates, covered by a linen cloth—an image personally resonant to me, from my childhood, for its resemblance to the traditional covered loaf of Sabbath bread. The concealment of the gold plates is typical of many depictions in *Book of Mormon* paintings and postcards: we rarely see it in Joseph's house, because in his real life no one was permitted a view, not his friends or family—not even today's museum visitors. The veil is never lifted.

Is there any way to see the gold plates in Joseph's life? Is there any way to lift the veil? Where would you start? At the Hill Cumorah Pageant? In the Grandin Print Shop? Was the answer in the archives?

Before I made the trip to Hill Cumorah, I'd spent days at Harvard's Widener Library sifting through Pittsburgh-area newspapers from the 1810s. Some of Joseph Smith's early debunkers had claimed that Solomon Spalding's manuscript, the alleged source text for *The Book of Mormon*, had progressed far enough in the publishing process to be advertised in a Pittsburgh newspaper under the title *The Book of Mormon* more than a decade before Joseph published his book. This advertisement, if it existed, would be the slam-dunk document in the controversy over who wrote the book and how it came together. Nobody has been able to track it down (possibly because it doesn't exist). So I figured I'd give it the old college try.

I started out more than hopeful. I was cocky. What doesn't Widener have? That place is lousy with erudition. On my first day of searching for the ad, the back of my scrap paper, which had been repurposed from an academic article, yielded a snippet of a footnote that began "It is not my purpose to offer an origin for the Huns." This struck me as a wise philosophy of life, a kind of koan.

The old newspapers were full of catchy ads for corn and mules and also personal notices taken out by people who wanted to publicly disavow responsibility for certain wayward relatives. There was also no shortage of ads for books; I was certain I'd see *something* that hinted at Solomon Spalding. The entire city of Pittsburgh in those days was all of six thousand people or so. How many of them were aspiring novelists? Every day I sat with a big cup of coffee and examined page after page of old newspapers on microfilm.

My search brought mixed signals from the universe. I took it as a good sign that the friendly archivist happened to resemble a critic who'd given my first book a positive review. In contrast, I saw a Bulgarian woman who sported gigantic earmuffs, a scarf long enough to roll through the full length of the library's fifty-seven miles of stacks, and a long cloak that was highly suggestive of death. It is critical to note that she wore these heavy garments *indoors*, with no apparent discomfort—even though the microfilm room was grossly overheated—and that she paced back and forth endlessly, her hands knitted gothically behind her back, her death cloak sweeping horribly along the floor and concealing her feet, giving the impression that she was floating across the room. I seemed to be the only one who noticed her.

I wasn't having any luck with the microfilm. Two days in, just when I felt that I was close—even though there's no close in this kind of thing—a fire alarm sounded. When I stepped out into the cold, a grad student in the Department of Statistics, smoking anxiously, told me that the old building was afflicted by all kinds of mechanical problems. There had been many fire alarms of late. Pointing his cigarette at the colossal library, he said, "One day all of this is gonna go up in flames."

Things finally came to a head in the little cafeteria space on the library's first floor, near the vending machine that rationed out gloomy minicans of tuna and sandwiches identified by their NASCAR-print wrappers as "rib-shaped pork." All the tables were empty except for one where the Bulgarian death-incarnation lady with the earmuffs sat. She was using a fork and knife to work over a full head of cabbage, in what was clearly a symbolic stand-in for her own head, and/or my head, and/or all of our heads. When she paused for a moment to look at me with her dead eyes, I immediately left the library and vowed never to return to the microfiche room again.

I decided then that the best place to find solid hints of the gold plates was in the text itself. After all, the complicated nature of authorship, the story of how life becomes a text, is one of the book's major themes. If you read the story, you sense it—the book is positively obsessed with the question of how it came to be. It started with Laban's book, which Nephi stole and which each subsequent writer expanded upon. Without Laban's book, there would be no gold plates. The book in our hands today came about as the result of Nephi's theft, the same way that Joseph's book allegedly came to be.

This connection came to me a few months before I visited Hill Cumorah. I had been chatting with some missionaries about Nephi when it hit me. In my notebook I quickly scrawled this note: "If Nephi = Joseph, and Nephi murders Laban for a book, then . . . Joseph murdered someone for a book. *It's a confession.*"

It was so clear to me. I was certain of it. The story of Nephi killing Laban and stealing his brass plates was Joseph's, or Rigdon's, or
some author's, grim admission to and justification for the murder
of someone, possibly Spalding, and the theft of this person's book.
It was just too much of a coincidence. There was no question in my
mind: someone had written it into the story. If this were a Sherlock Holmes novel, Joseph would finally confess that his book had
indeed been a confession to murder but that he did it for love. This
wouldn't be too far from Arthur Conan Doyle's *A Study in Scarlet*,
the very first Sherlock Holmes book, which takes place mostly in
the Utah frontier and concerns a wild Mormon plot twist.

Is it possible that Joseph killed someone for a book? Spalding
died in 1816, at age fifty-five, supposedly of natural causes. There
was no report of foul play. There was also no report of no foul play;
my written requests regarding the exhumation of Spalding's bones
for lab testing have been routinely ignored (possibly as part of a
cover-up). Joseph Smith would have been eleven years old when
Spalding met his possibly untimely end, a bit young for the business of murder. However, Nephi is twice noted to be young but
of large physical build (similar to the way Joseph was described).
Indeed, the difficult decision to commit this heinous act is a kind
of coming of age for young Nephi. Maybe that's what it was for
Joseph as well.

This reading is supported by another important text. Consider
Mormon. When he was ten years old, Mormon was approached
by a man named Ammaron, who told him that when he turned
twenty-four or so, the plates would come into his hands. This is
similar to Joseph's story: when he was a kid, Joseph was visited by
a divine personage (two, in fact) who told him to be patient, as his
purpose would eventually be revealed. As with Mormon, this task

consisted of creating a book, and as with Mormon, this happened when he was twenty-four years old.

Perhaps Joseph received a visit not from a divine personage but from Sidney Rigdon. According to biographer Fawn Brodie, a proponent of the Spalding-Rigdon theory, Rigdon would have known Joseph by reputation as the child seer of Palmyra, New York, and may have decided that this strapping youth was exactly the prophet he needed for his book in progress. So Rigdon tracked the boy down, and the rest is history.

A weirder possibility is that Joseph wasn't informed of the scheme. Maybe Rigdon conned him too. In an official history dictated in 1839, Joseph described the events of his first vision, as a boy alone in the woods: "Immediately I was seized upon by some power which entirely overcame me and had such astonishing influence over me as to bind my tongue so that I could not speak. Thick darkness gathered around me and it seemed to me for a time as if I were doomed to sudden destruction."

This terrifying assault was followed by a beautiful light and encouraging words from a divine personage. But maybe the aggressive visitor who Joseph insisted was an "actual being" really was an actual being, and wasn't a demon but just Rigdon ambushing him in the woods. Maybe Rigdon drugged Joseph, created a sound-and-light show for him, and told him he was God. Maybe Rigdon was also Moroni. Maybe *all* the strings were being pulled by the nefarious Sidney Rigdon. *Something* bizarre happened there in the 1820s—maybe that's how it went down.

If the text is your only guide, nearly any theory can be supported. It is certainly possible that the sensational Laban beheading was included just to excite readers; perhaps it was nothing more than that. But whether the murder of Laban and other such stories were thinly veiled confessions or just the twisted imaginings of fiction, or were indeed a true prophetic history, the stories take us into a dark place with them. And once we are there, what isn't possible?

The Spalding-Rigdon theory doesn't seem to want to die. It got a high-tech revival recently. Three Stanford scholars published an article in a journal called *Literary and Linguistic Computing* in which they applied a statistical technique called nearest shrunken centroids (NSC), a method originally used in cancer research. "The problem of authorship attribution," they wrote, "is surprisingly similar to that of a cancer diagnosis. Rather than classifying tumors by cancer subtype, we classify texts by author, and instead of using gene expression measurements to perform the classification, we use word frequencies."

Computing chapter by chapter, these literary techies analyzed the text of *The Book of Mormon* in comparison with the literary styles of possible authors. They quantified each potential author's literary style by reference to certain patterns of speech and grammar—for example, the frequent use of an unusual word or quirky punctuation patterns. They compared likely suspects, including Sidney Rigdon and other possible Joseph Smith associates, and used controls such as Henry Wadsworth Longfellow, who wrote a contemporary American Indian epic, and the Book of Isaiah, which *The Book of Mormon* quotes extensively. They computed the probability that any particular author wrote any given chapter. So, for instance, the study determined that whereas there is a ~0 percent chance that Longfellow wrote Chapter 9 of the Book of Moroni, in which Mormon laments the "depravity of my people," the odds that Rigdon wrote that section are roughly 90 percent.

Overall, chapter by chapter, Sidney Rigdon is the best bet in

Vegas, the odds-on favorite. His textual DNA was found all over the scene. It should be noted that Solomon Spalding's prints also appear with significant frequency, particularly in the Book of Alma's adventure sections.

I urge the patient and inquisitive reader to sit down one afternoon with a strong cocktail and sift through the details of "Reassessing Authorship of *The Book of Mormon* Using Delta and Nearest Shrunken Centroid Classification" (and its rebuttal). But I'll skip the details and jump ahead to my dramatic emotional conclusion.

The Stanford study suggested an answer to an old question of mine: is writing a disappearance act? Translating yourself into scribbles on a page seems like a good way not to be seen, to put something of yourself—sometimes a lot of yourself—into the world without actually being in the world. The cliché of the writer as recluse holds some truth. For some writers, maybe most, burrowing seems to be not an occupational hazard but actually the allure of the job, or at least one of its perks.

For some reason, film directors aren't asked to put their faces directly on their art (possibly because their art offers audiences many other faces to feast upon), but a book without an author photo is unsatisfying, unsettling even, to readers today. In fact, most readers don't want to see the faces of a book's characters; the only face they desire to see is that of the book's author. But it's possible that the author photo doesn't really satisfy that need so much as suggest how needy we are as readers.

It's an old problem. Consider God, the author of the Hebrew Bible: he declared it a mortal sin to reproduce his image. The lesson there was that the author was in the word itself, was seen in the word, *was* the word. But there's something unsatisfying about not seeing God the author, something tricky and discomfiting. Is it any wonder that the author of the Hebrew Bible spends much of that bible complaining that his readers are betraying his wishes by carving little figurines of his likeness? People can't help it: we need to see the author. Is it possible? Where would we even look?

There in the bar graphs of the Stanford study was an actual image, not of a person smiling in a portrait but of the *author*, the thing itself, his ghost, his literary soul distilled from the text by the magic of shrunken centroids.

In the language of the study, the bars of the graph represented an author's "signal" in the text. That made a lot of sense to me. An author doesn't put himself into a story exactly, but sends signals of

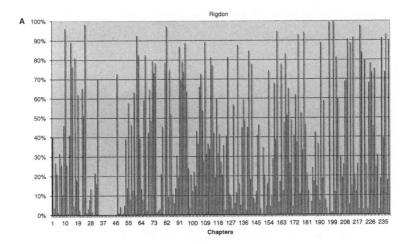

himself, from some distant place, into the text. Even many years later, even after the mortal author has departed, there they are, the signals, as strong as ever, like light from a star as distant as death.

Joseph's traditional credit as "translator," which appears on all editions of *The Book of Mormon*, does seem to capture something of his role in the book's creation: deeply involved and yet somehow peripheral. Almost nobody would dispute that his life in some way peeks out from behind the story.

Like a character from a gothic novel of his time, Joseph is an entombed figure, unseen and not quite named throughout the story. He is like Mr. Rochester's mad wife locked in the attic, whose dark presence is sensed as anxious rumblings, late-night footsteps, anonymous ambushes in dark corners, and sudden unexplained conflagrations. *The Book of Mormon* wasn't just buried in Joseph's life; his life was buried in it.

This absence lurks behind the Stanford study too, in a small but significant detail: the researchers didn't include a writing sample from Joseph Smith in their analysis. They argued that no verifiable writing samples of Joseph's exist. Or, rather, that none have been verified yet. Most of his "writings" were in fact dictated to a scribe, including his letters and speeches. Since he always worked with a scribe, we can't be certain that the words, grammar, syntax, and punctuation in a given sample are truly his, and thus we don't have any way to establish his literary DNA, said the researchers. They had no choice, therefore, but to leave him out of the study.

This was, to say the least, a major omission. It is amazing to consider the possibility that Joseph was technically unknowable. Everything we know of him is secondhand, at best. Everything he said is actually something attributed to him.

Shortly before he was murdered, Joseph delivered a famous talk in which he radically revised his own and much of Western theology, erasing the distinction between men and gods. All gods, including the Most High, Yahweh, were once regular men, he said. During this period of his life, when he'd become the mayor of a big city in Illinois, Joseph had come under siege from all sides. He was running into more and more political opposition from outside his community, ostensibly because of polygamy but mostly because he'd begun wielding a lot of electoral clout. Often these battles turned violent. Joseph became authoritarian and did things like order the destruction of an opposition newspaper's printing press. He also alienated his trusted inner circle. Even his closest friends, people who continued to believe in his earlier prophecies, began abandoning him, calling him a "fallen prophet." In that speech, which he delivered at a funeral, before a crowd of ten thousand people, he struck a defensive and boldly defiant note.

"You don't know me," he told his followers. "You never knew my heart. No man knows my history."

Thus saith the prophet Joseph. Unless he didn't say it at all.

SIX

After another long day of rehearsals, we made our way to the Costumes Department, where we were to be outfitted in our robes, beards, turbans, and assorted bling. The small costume shack located halfway up Hill Cumorah was identifiable by a clothesline strung between two trees, from which wigs hung savagely like the scalps of vanquished enemies. Inside, the shack was bursting with racks upon racks of fabulously ancient attire. Cloaks, tunics, mantles, sashes, shawls, wide belts, headbands, all in muted tones and fabrics, some with stripes that somehow suggested the Old Testament. Wigs and fake beards and headdresses, all handmade, were a major operation in their own right and got a separate department with its own staff.

It was of course the accessories that made the outfits: the feathers, the inlaid plastic stage jewels of sapphire and ruby and Central American jade, the patches of jaguar print and baubles made of shell and bone. The hybrid design—half Hebrew, half Maya—gave the outfits a daring, couture feel. We wicked priests were encouraged to go nuts with the costume jewelry, to trick out with gold rings on every finger and pile on the bracelets, earrings, and arm cuffs.

As I sat on a bench in Costumes, waiting for my fitting, I chatted with the young marine who played a martyr in our scene. His spectacles were riding down his nose. I was still having a difficult time imagining him in boot camp at Parris Island, much less in full battle gear. He was as warlike as a warm and thoughtful muffin. I complimented his whiskers. It was a beauty, this black beard, strong and Slavic. It resembled the winter pelt of a Siberian marten, wide and bushy in a way that conveyed the bursting, generative energy, the hearty and gallant and deep-feeling soul of its wearer. He was quick to tell me that he hadn't grown it for the Hill Cumorah show.

"Between the shaving cream, the shaver, and all those extra razors," he explained, "it's just too expensive. It really adds up."

Overhearing us, one of my fellow wicked priests cut in. "So, wait," he said, "you're just gonna wear that thing . . . *forever?*"

A good-humored little smile peeked out from deep within the whiskers. The marine gave his Siberian marten an affectionate caress. "I dunno," he said. "Maybe."

The time for fitting had arrived. We repaired to the changing area with our priestly vestments. As we stripped down, things got a bit elephant-in-the-roomy. Under their clothes the men were piously clad in their two-piece white temple garments, the much-ballyhooed, much-speculated-about Mormon "magic underwear." Whereas there was nothing magical, much less pious, about my frog-print boxers. I detected, or thought I detected, the men making a slight mental adjustment with regard to me. Since commenting on a guy's underthings is generally considered bad form, I observed the silence. I had to restrain myself from revealing that I too had grown up wearing magic underwear—the four-cornered, tasseled undersmock that Orthodox Jewish men wear at all times, pursuant to the Book of Deuteronomy—and that I was well aware of and completely on board with the idea of drawing inspiration from your undies. As a kid, I felt that my *tzitzits* bestowed a powerful secret identity, like the Superman outfit Clark Kent wore under his newsman's suit. (No coincidence that Superman was created by two Jewish kids who'd grown up in Orthodox homes.) For members of small tribes, there's a certain pride at passing for regular old American on the surface, but underneath, closer to your body, you wear a truer skin.

After the fitting I wandered to the meadow in front of the set, where people were practicing their parts or else playing the parts they inhabited in real life. I saw a girl of about seventeen sitting on a bench, reading. She was dressed exactly like Lenore Stonecipher Beadsman from *The Broom of the System*, David Foster Wallace's first novel: white dress, black Converse Chucks on her feet, two long wisps of hair framing her face. Sitting on the next bench, with a far-off look on his face, the gentle warrior-monk dipped a flaccid scrap of bread into some kind of white potage, like a guy in a Gogol story. At the top of the hill, the young man playing Jesus was being lowered by a crane from at least ten stories up, in preparation for his grand deus ex machina entrance. The walruslike Wyoming cowboy guy who ran Props strutted around like a character from *Shane*. When I looked around, I saw characters from other stories too. That's the difference between books and life. In Gogol stories the characters are Gogol characters, and in the Bible they're biblical, but in life it's always an odd mix of characters from many stories.

Later, as the sun set into a mellow tangerine glow, I wandered to the top of the hill, to the garden with the statue of the angel Moroni, a spot I'd been returning to often during downtimes. When I arrived there, I discovered my marine friend sitting on a bench, his long arms spanning the back of it, his head thrown back so that he was face-to-face with the heavens. We chatted some more. This time he brought up the beard.

"Everyone is interested in it," he said, still gazing deep into the cosmos.

"It's a great beard, man," I replied. "Pretty hard to miss."

"It makes you more visible," he said, stroking the subject of our discourse as though extracting data directly from it. "But it also makes you less visible."

Later, in my notebook, I would discover that I'd written this gloss while I sat there on the bench: "the beard as universe." What that means, I'm not entirely certain. But that was the mood up there atop old Hill Cumorah that evening.

We sat there for a while silently contemplating the mystical puzzle that is the beardness of beards. There would be many stage versions in this show: the artlessly bushy whiskers of sages and the sleazy, overgroomed, almost pubic hair-masks of the villains.

"I started growing it when I got out," the marine said. "When I got back home."

With that, he stood up and wandered over to the edge of the hill and looked down over the massive seven-story set and into the valley below. Then he turned and, without another word, continued on into the dark woods.

The next day I wandered into a missionary training session. The cast was being trained, or retrained, in the art of casual schmoozing so that they'd be ready to approach audience members, while in full costume, and chat them up before going onstage. When I arrived, two college-aged missionary sisters had already begun running the session, which was, as it turned out, made up mostly of children.

One missionary was very tall and had really long blow-dried hair, and the other was tiny and also had really long blow-dried hair. The tiny one also had an exceptionally high-pitched, Muppety voice. As I took a seat, I learned that we were engaged in an "icebreaker" in which you were supposed to say your name and something that you loved. The Muppet girl beamed out a smile wide enough to be seen from outer space. "Hi!" she said. "I'm Sister Stephens and looove the smell of . . . *bug spray!*"

Just as I was about to leave, my turn came. I announced my fake name and then blanked completely on everything that I love. Or maybe I couldn't think of something that Yosef Green loved. Whatever it was, I couldn't name a single thing on God's green earth that might be deemed lovable. I felt hundreds of young eyes pointed in my direction and the shining faces of the missionaries, whose patient smiles, it seemed, were beginning to go slack waiting for me to declare my love for something, anything, just so we could all get on with our lives. Growing increasingly hopeless, I finally blurted out, ". . . and I *also* love the smell of bug spray."

My rendition of the bug spray line, however, seemed only to depress people.

For appearances, I stayed on for an extra few minutes, during which I learned an excellent lesson in how to overcome the fear of talking to new people ("Use love!") and was treated to a little boy's answer to the question, What is charity? "Charity basically means nicenessness," he explained. As I walked out, I heard the children shouting in unison, "*Always. Be. Nice.*"

Sitting in my car, with the AC blowing on me, I wasn't feeling too nice. I had found myself needing longer and longer breaks from being Yosef Green. If the idea of being this Green character was to somehow get out of myself, to inhabit another self, it was having the opposite effect: it was forcing me to dwell on my identity way more than any healthy person should. I decided to take the afternoon off and make a visit to the Smith family farm.

As I shifted the car into reverse, an ad came on the radio with the same snarky, soulless know-it-all who seems to narrate every ad on earth.

"Heyyyy," he said. "Bet when you decided to be a *rock* star, you didn't plan on being a *loser* living in your parents' basement . . ."

It was an ad for a local night school. I turned the radio off. Then I pulled the key out of the ignition. I decided to walk to the farm.

I'd been meaning to do this hike for a while. Next to the pleasures of trekking the green Central American landscapes of Zarahemla, there was something satisfying about the particular three miles of far northern New York between Hill Cumorah and the Smith farm. With so much of the book's geography still a matter of conjecture, this particular parcel of earth offered something substantial, something calmingly quantifiable. We know exactly the hill Joseph identified as the source of the plates, and we know exactly where the farm was. The forest between these spots is roughly the same forest that Joseph recalled running through once he got his hands on the gold plates, the same woods where he said he'd hidden them.

The region is still dotted with deep ditches burrowed out by treasure-seekers; some of these mine shafts surely are the very same ones Joseph worked on. The country highway that snakes through these forests, today's Route 21, is the same road Joseph traversed countless times, north to Palmyra's center, south to the big town of Canandaigua. The book itself entered the world along this path: it was the road that Joseph rode with manuscript in hand, on his way to the Grandin Print Shop, the road on which the book emerged as a bound edition. This stretch of *Book of Mormon* land was as geographically solid as it got.

I'd driven on this road many times already, but it wasn't until I walked it, at an easygoing nineteenth-century pace, that I could appreciate how suggestive this landscape might have been to Joseph. The hills in this area were sufficiently curious-looking, few enough in number, and significant enough in size to suggest that they weren't natural but rather placed there by human hands. But in the end they were just little hills, in the same way that Don Quixote's windmills were just windmills. It took an act of imagination, of desire, to spin them into something more.

In paintings we see Joseph walking between tall trees, kneeling in a pile of leaves, sitting in a cabin in the woods. *The Book of Mormon* was born in the forest. It was a woodland tale, haunted by an ecosystem of supernatural beings. Joseph's recollections of his encounters with spirits near his home and on the hill are full of the sounds of feet running through the forest. Behind all the cosmic speculations, epic grandiosity, and marvelous tales of antiquity was probably something more basic: just a boy alone in a dark wood until, like Dante, he arrived at the foot of a hill . . .

I reached a mark by the side of the road. I took a scrap of paper with scribbled directions on it. A guy in a pizza shop in downtown Palmyra had drawn a little map for me. After I'd ordered my slice, I'd asked the pizza man if he knew of any old-time treasure ditches in the area. I felt somewhat awkward asking the question. But the pizza guy didn't blink. He knew of what I spoke. Unfortunately, he didn't know any exact locations. He did, however, have a buddy who could help me. As he reached into his apron to retrieve his phone, another customer, who'd overheard my question, appeared next to me at the counter.

"I can tell you," he said, still chewing. "Sure. Real easy."

He gulped and wiped his hands on his Levi's and made me a little map, prefacing every direction with the phrase "You're gonna wanna . . ." This created some confusion on my part. In one instance, "You're gonna wanna take a left" meant simply "Take a left." But another time, "You're gonna wanna take a left" seemed to mean "Take a left" until he added, "But *don't*. Go right."

Even as he was giving me his directions, it became evident that there was no way I was going to be able to find a spot in the woods with pointers like "You're gonna see a stump . . ."

Still, I gave it a shot. I'd kept the directions for just this hike. As I was standing by the side of the road, trying to determine whether a certain stump was *the* stump, the spot at which I was gonna wanna enter the forest, a car rocketed past me. A boy who'd stuck his head out the window shouted at me in that distinctive way in which a guy yelling at you from a fast-moving car can be at once a clamor of blurry, whizzing nonsense yet eloquent in his ability to convey a clear message of youthful hostility.

This seemed to happen a lot up here. Since I'd been in the area, either on this road or near my lodgings at the college, I'd been shouted at by passing cars at least once a day. These were the rural boys targeted by that taunting radio ad I'd heard earlier.

"Bet when you decided to be a *rock* star, you didn't plan on being a *loser* living in your parents' basement . . ."

This species of guy was also part of *The Book of Mormon*'s nature setting. It was a story not just of being lost in the forest but of that typically male reaction to feeling lost: rage, resentment. It was the story of a frustrated, impoverished young man from the provinces with a lot of energy and nowhere to direct it. Maybe, like those boys yelling out of cars, Joseph Smith was a rural kid who dreamed of being a rock star, with the fame and the girls and everything, and he wasn't going to let anyone get in his way, even if it meant coming off like a loser living at home with the folks.

I hadn't quite appreciated how rebellious Joseph was in quitting his farm labors in order to focus completely on his manuscript. Even in our decadent times, this kind of behavior is regarded with suspicion. But in those days, and particularly for a boy of his class on the rural western frontier, forgoing labor to do creative work was not done. In 1823, Joseph hadn't founded a religion or presented himself as a leader—he was just some migrant worker, deeply in debt, talking up the amazing book that he was supposedly going to publish. This went on for seven years until the book finally did emerge.

Instead of doing farm gigs to support himself and his parents—as his brothers and he had done since they were children—Joseph cut out for months to scribble his stories on foolscap. In the eyes of his farming neighbors, Joseph's days spent indoors, working with his pals on his book, were only another version of digging for treasure. One of the early libels spread around by his hostile neighbors was that Joseph was a lazy good-for-nothing. Joseph was many things, but lazy surely wasn't one of them.

In turning these remote surroundings into the site of an epic saga, he was doing what many writers have done: imagining his humble upbringing as important enough to matter. And like many writers, maybe he secretly hoped that his stories would be the thing that would carry him away from this place forever. That's certainly what ended up happening.

He never shook that rebel attitude, that need to make it big, American style—to be famous, and in his own way. So many stories contain little hints of his rowdiness, his restlessness. And then there's the big untold story, about his rock-star inclination for collecting groupies, including, allegedly, a fifteen-year-old girl. Many

Mormons today still aren't taught about this. But in his day polygamy caused division among his deputies and closest friends, almost all of whom eventually broke with him (partly out of fears for their own wives and daughters). As *The Book of Mormon* got into more hands, as his renown grew, Joseph became more audacious, more self-destructive, more flamboyant.

When I finally arrived at the Smith farm, two companion missionary sisters were seated in front of the visitor center. One was reading aloud to the other from *The Book of Mormon*; the latter seemed to listen only vaguely and mostly basked in the sun. The sight of two young women in long dresses, reposing on a bench in a garden, reading in this way, struck me as an image from an old painting. Deciding not to disturb the picture, I turned around and headed back to Hill Cumorah.

SEVEN

It was well known at this point that I was the acting talent behind Wicked Priest #2. What wasn't known, not even by me, was that I'd also been cast in another role. I learned of the new role when my suitemate, good old reliable Greg, asked me about it. I told him I didn't have a second role. He grumbled a bit and rolled his eyes.

"You gotta look *behind* your casting card," he said. "There's another one there."

Sure enough, on my lanyard, attached by a rubber band to my wicked priest card, was another card. As I pried open the unreasonably tight rubber band, I saw Greg cross his arms over his chest.

"So what'd they give you?" he asked.

"Destruction Victim," I read.

He smiled faintly and let his arms drop.

"Pretty minor role there," he said. "But it's a fun one. They give it a lot to children."

The destruction victim scene portrayed the tumultuous moment in *The Book of Mormon* after the great, dark prophecy has finally come to pass. The sign had arrived in the Central American jungle cities of the Nephite people: *It is finished.* The much-discussed savior had just been killed on a hill overseas, back in Jerusalem. Darkness and chaos descended on the earth.

This is the central moment in *The Book of Mormon*, when its ancient, eyewitness account matches that of the Bible. It happens at the center of the book, almost exactly halfway into the story. Like a rare alignment of earth, moon, and sun, this moment of literal darkness marks the point at which the narratives of the Old Testament, the New Testament, and *The Book of Mormon* are perfectly synced. The same global blackness that is foretold in the Old Testament and that comes to pass in the New—as Jesus dies on the cross—is experienced by the Nephites living in Mesoamerica.

The three-day period of total darkness described in the New Testament is corroborated by the Nephite writers all the way in the Western Hemisphere. According to *The Book of Mormon*'s account, this darkness brought with it catastrophic natural disasters (possibly including volcanic upheaval, as Lee had explained during our trek around the volcanoes lining the Waters of Mormon/Lake Atitlán). The survivors of this devastation were rewarded with the arrival of the savior—for a short visit—in the Land of Bountiful, which we'd passed in southern Mexico. In the Hill Cumorah show, however, I would not be among those lucky enough to witness this spectacular event, for I was one of many victims of the Great Destruction.

As Greg had predicted, the destruction scene in our play involved mostly children. (Concerning any detail of this production, large or small, Greg was never wrong.) As a member of a large crowd, I now had a firsthand look at our director's talent for handling big ensemble scenes. His directions for us were similar to those I'd overheard at the angry mob rehearsal.

"Each one of you, look at your neighbor," he told us, "and see how they're dying—okay? Now die a different way. *Die your own way.*"

This talk of bringing about my own death ratcheted up my Yosef Green–themed anxiety. In trying to talk myself down, I made the decision to keep my demise simple and generic: the old-fashioned clutch of the chest, the drop-to-one-knee thing, the theatrically vain attempts to stand, and finally the potato-sack fall. A textbook epic fatality, Cecil B. DeMille–style. Nothing fancy or personal.

As I practiced, I came to understand why they drafted children as destruction victims. You needed to be nimble and energetic— you needed good knees—to perish efficiently and then immediately jump up to exit the stage when the lights went to black. Dying isn't for the weak.

As I rehearsed my death, I heard someone yell my name. Or rather, I heard someone yell the name of my tormented soul.

"Yosef!"

After days of hearing the name and cringing, I found that my horror had diminished somewhat—which was far more horrifying.

The man waving at me from offstage at my destruction victim rehearsal was an older, smiling gent. He was wearing a missionary's dark slacks with a button-down white dress shirt and dark tie— very much like the captains at the prison where I once worked— and a baseball cap with a preposterously long, floppy brim that gave him the affable look of Goofy from the old Disney cartoons. He was the chief of the Hill Cumorah production.

"Hey, there," he said. "Can we talk? Just been trying to find you."

"Oh, yeah," I replied. "How about in forty-five minutes or so? I've got this rehearsal."

"That's okay," he said to me. And then he shouted to the director, "I need to speak with him."

That's when I knew something was wrong. Besides God, rehearsal was the god we all worshipped in this show. Nothing trumped rehearsal. If he was pulling me out of rehearsal, someone had died.

But of course I was overreacting. Nobody had died. He patted me on the back. We did a walk and talk. Suddenly from the show's giant speakers we heard an ocean-liner horn of a deep voice intone *"I AM JESUS CHRIST."* It was unnerving and thrilling to hear the name said the way it was meant to be said.

We walked down to the hut where I'd registered, to an improvised office that had the feel of a command center. The sounds of people working phones, simultaneously trying to defuse crises and manage egos—that, along with more men wearing captain's whites—again took me back to my time working in prison.

We were seated for not more than three seconds when the chief tapped the mouse on his desktop, refreshing the image on his darkened monitor. To my horror, the image was of me. He took a deep breath. I stopped breathing altogether.

"Do you know that person?" he said.

"Yes," I replied.

"What is your relationship to this person?"

To such an unexpected and pointedly phrased question, I had no obvious answer. I stared at the image of "this person." The picture had been taken in Jerusalem by an old family friend, a professional photographer who'd also taken many of the nicest photos of me and my sister as children. For sentimental reasons, I'd enlisted her to take this shot of me and had used it as the author photo for my first book. I remembered that time in Jerusalem, finishing and also trying not to finish that first book, wandering around the Old City, looking for *The Book of Mormon*, beginning to reread the story of Nephi. My relationship with my girlfriend-then-wife had been happier then. Though it hadn't been that long ago, I honestly wasn't sure what my relationship to that person was. So much had happened since then.

Maybe I was staring too hard at the screen, but as I regarded the image, something in it started to move. I witnessed a kind of mortification pass over the face, then shadow into it, through the eyes. It was horrible to behold. But I saw it. At first the face appeared wooden, then waxen, then the flesh melted away. I distinctly remember saying to myself, *You* are *seeing this, you're really fucking seeing this!* The flesh slithered away, as though sucked into itself through an invisible straw behind the eyes. What remained was a grinning ghoul, unrecognizable to me.

"I am that person," I said.

I'm pretty sure I didn't black out, because I have some memories, albeit sketchy, of what came next. For days I'd taken copious notes. But that night, or any after it, I wasn't able to bring myself to write anything but a few quotes and jots. I never fully recorded that moment, or what happened next. I couldn't bring myself to commit the squalid details to paper. I especially didn't want to remember that hallucination, or whatever it was, with my photo.

Here's what I do remember: I apologized for making up an identity and said, truthfully, if not coherently, that I wasn't sure why I'd done that. The head of the show said that he forgave me and he'd pray for me—which alarmed me, since where I grew up, you mostly pray for people only when they are gravely ill. Then he said it was time for me to pack up my things and move on.

Like many a sinner, I felt somewhat relieved to be caught. There was nothing I wanted more than to put Yosef Green behind me. I thanked him. And apologized again, this time more abjectly.

"We forgive you," he said. "But pray over it, okay?"

I told him that his kindness was overwhelming.

"That's kind of the point," he said.

———

On my way back to the dorm, I would be accompanied in my car by the show's head of housing, who I suspected was the one who sniffed out Yosef Green. He was a former FBI man.

This ex-cop was waiting for me when I came out of the office. He patted me on the back and said, "Love you, man." Before my disgrace, we'd gotten along well. As I drove south toward the college dorm, on Route 21, the old Joseph Smith road, I could see the usually gregarious FBI man staring out the passenger window at the passing countryside, silent and preoccupied. Finally he began to speak, midthought.

"I mean, yeah, it's true," he said. "There were a lot of crazy things—and some weird things—going on around here back then. Joseph Smith was a *man*, you know?"

He paused. I could sense him looking at me. Then he continued.

"Those were some strange and difficult times back then. Hard for us sometimes to understand."

"That's very true," I said.

"But all of us here have faith. And we know what faith brings because we see it in our lives, every day. That's real. You gotta understand that."

I told him that I was also in search of faith.

"Good" was all he said.

After throwing all my clothes into my bag and gathering up my belongings, I saluted my suitemates' thin, bedraggled man-towels, which hung in the bathroom like the flags of small but proud republics. I tossed my bag into the car and left the show, two days before I was to take the stage.

For the next half hour I found myself driving aimlessly on the old carriage road. Because the FBI guy was truly a saint, he had already texted me, inviting me back as his guest for the opening night of the show. But I was feeling sick and horribly embarrassed and didn't quite know what to say. Without noticing, I'd driven back into Palmyra and parked in front of the Grandin Print Shop, the place where Joseph's manuscript had been painstakingly transformed from a giant pile of handwritten sheets into a bound book. Until I arrived at the Grandin shop that last time, I hadn't been conscious of my fixation on the life-sized diorama of Joseph and Emma Smith's kitchen on the second floor of the museum. But as soon as I entered the building, I found myself walking directly to it.

There was something dreamlike about encountering this everyday domestic scene abstracted in the embalmed darkness of a museum. The spareness of it, the uncanny stillness, presented itself with all the burnished salience of a memory.

In a lecture to his colleagues, Freud once said that his patients "suffer from reminiscences." As an illustration, he drew a comparison to a person lingering in front of a public monument. Imagine a man who is so taken by the pathos of the devastating London fire of 1666 that he stands before the city's monument to that long-ago event, compulsively gazing at it, incapacitated, unable to partake of life happening all around him in modern London. His patients, said Freud, are like this "impractical Londoner" who "cannot escape from the past and neglects present reality in its favor."

I stood at the Smith family kitchen, suffering from reminiscences. The gold plates resting on the table, veiled in linen, held my attention like a monument. At that moment the covered book filled me with sorrow, an odd and confusing reaction. I remembered a dream from a few nights earlier, the night I'd seen my suitemate, the postman, sleepwalking. I'd dreamed of this kitchen diorama. But instead of the gold plates lying on the table, I saw a dead infant, blanketed, an image that wasn't just devastating and grotesque but, set within this clean, cozy, brightly lit, perfectly tranquil family kitchen, simply impossible to grasp.

Nothing was as central to Joseph's life and yet as poorly integrated as his great book. When the plates entered Joseph's home, an impenetrable barrier appeared. We can still see it; it's as clear as a bandaged wound. Something important in Joseph went into hiding when he brought this book into his kitchen and immersed himself in its translation. In order for his story to emerge into the world, he or some part of him disappeared forever—yet remained shrouded in plain sight.

This was one of my big fears about writing. When you tell stories for a living, stories become a way of life. Those stories threaten to become the place where your real life occurs. But what happens to the self who isn't translated into words and put on the page?

At Hill Cumorah in Mexico, I'd felt the absence, the unrecoverability, of the gold plates—of all gold plates—which I later understood was a way of sensing the impending loss of a marriage, of a beloved, of a story we told, a true story. Here, in Hill Cumorah, New York, I encountered the plates more directly, more painfully, as a dead presence. It was something I would need to learn how to live with.

Skeptics like to portray the disparities in Joseph's story as proof that he was a charlatan. But maybe his retrospective revisions were really a way to venture further and further into uncharted terrain as a self-made person, becoming more and more embodied as this character, and in need of thicker and more secure masks in his daily life. Maybe he just wanted a less troubled story. Or maybe he just went too far and got lost. I'd nearly gone out of my mind in four days as Yosef; what would it be like to live an entire life as Joseph?

Maybe in his evolving stories he was looking for a way to balance the destabilizing effects of his imagination, or whatever it was he saw up there on Hill Cumorah.

What happens to a person who climbs the mountain? One ancient interpretation of the near sacrifice of Isaac atop Mount Moriah claims that the boy in fact *was* killed there that day, offered as a burnt sacrifice, and that his ashes were scattered on the altar. Needless to say, this is a drastic departure from the official biblical account, in which Isaac is spared in dramatic fashion, then descends from the mountain and goes on to live a long life. Isaac's survival is indeed crucial to the plot of the story; it's narratively impossible that he died on that mountain. The point of this radical revision of the story is that somehow both versions are true: after Isaac ascended that mountain, he both returned and never returned.

When Joseph climbed Hill Cumorah and dug for the gold plates, the angel struck him down; he died on the spot and was buried in the very casket in which he'd found the book. And then he descended the hill with the book in hand.

EDEN: AN EPILOGUE

At the end of that summer, as I was on my way to the Garden of Eden, I stopped at a bookstore in Kansas City to do a reading from my first book. The audience, five kindly older women, were being so nice to me that I felt compelled to spontaneously edit out the curse words from the piece I was reading, which happened to have a surprising number of curse words. A few minutes into the reading I noticed a sunburned guy leaning on a bookshelf. Offset by the redness of his face, two huge, hungry blue eyes came into focus. They were peering at me. The owner of these eyes, a nineteen-or-so-year-old, was smiling crookedly. For his benefit, I reinstated one of the curse words.

I'd been driving around in a giant rented black SUV, reminiscent of the kind used by the Secret Service, investigating sites in Missouri and Illinois. This land had been the end of the line for Joseph. He'd had high hopes for Missouri in particular, and when Joseph had high hopes, it meant they were out of this world. A Mormon primer for children from that period spells this out:

Q: Who made this world?
A: The Gods.

Q: Where was the Garden of Eden?
A: In Jackson County, Missouri.

In an 1831 revelation, Joseph had discovered that this region, the center of the American continent, was also the very centerpiece of the creation of the heavens and the earth. Greater Kansas City, Missouri, had provided the clay into which God breathed life; Jackson County had known the bare feet of Adam and Eve; the Tree of Knowledge once bloomed by the banks of the Missouri; the town of Far West was the site where jealous Cain killed Abel. Joseph praised this land at great length and in the most lyrical language he could muster. He wasted no time naming one area Adam-ondi-ahman, which meant, he said, "the place where Adam came to rest." That is, the place where Adam and Eve ended up after they were expelled from Eden. A few years after settling there, Joseph was also violently expelled from this Eden, by order of the Missouri governor.

After my reading, the sunburned kid approached me, handed me a sheaf of papers, and told me that he was also "kind of a writer." I agreed to read his stories, though in a somewhat vague way, as I was distracted by the effect of the sunburn, the white-blond hair, and the eyes: red, white, and blue, an all-American boy. Kyle was his name. He was touchingly skinny, with long bangs that he adjusted reflexively every few seconds with a quick shake of his head, giving the impression that he was extending a surreptitious invitation to step into the next room with him. Almost immediately it became clear to me that Kyle and I were going to have dinner together.

"Can I invite my girlfriend?" he asked. "She won't believe this. I was just reading your book last week and here you are."

I watched Kyle retreat into a corner, adjust his hair with two big swoops of the head, and begin to speak fervently into his phone in a way that suggested a dog gnawing on a juicy bone.

I liked Kyle, and suddenly became interested in reading his stories. I skimmed the first one. It seemed to be about Kurt Cobain. I skimmed the second one. Kurt Cobain figured prominently in that one as well. In the third, Kurt Cobain's name definitely came up. Before I could flip to the fourth, Kyle was standing in front of me, flicking his head toward the door.

Even after *The Book of Mormon* was published, Joseph continued writing himself into the story. As he moved west—usually under duress—he continued digging into the ground, unearthing artifacts and telling their stories. With each new move, from Ohio to Missouri to Illinois, he continued his work as a chronicler of the American continent. The landscape served as the hieroglyphs of his ongoing epic. As he pushed farther into the territories, he continued to find lands wide open enough for his expansive interpretations. The relics he continued to discover were the beginnings of the sequel to *The Book of Mormon,* which was already beginning to take shape during his lifetime. He continued writing and translating; a few of those texts were officially canonized.

In 1834, four years after the book was published, Joseph, then of Kirtland, Ohio, embarked on an expedition to explore sites for future settlement in Missouri. He and his men, an assortment of religious seekers, loners, and freelance body snatchers, trekked through western lands few of them had ever seen but all had read about in *The Book of Mormon.* As they made their way through Ohio and Illinois—Nephite lands, according to Joseph—*The Book of Mormon* was their travel guide. Never was the story more vivid to Joseph than when he was on horseback.

In a letter to his number-one wife, Emma, he wrote:

"Wandering over the plains of the Nephites, recounting occasionally the history of *The Book of Mormon,* roving over the mounds of that once beloved people of the Lord, picking up their skulls &

their bones, as a proof of its divine authenticity, and gazing upon a country the fertility, the splendour and the goodness so indescribable."

In Pike County, Illinois, they went treasure-hunting and unearthed a human skeleton with a broken femur and a rib cage punctured by an arrowhead. Joseph explained that these remains belonged to none other than the great Zelph. Not being prophets themselves, none of his men knew who this Zelph was. If they had lived in the days of old, however, they would have known all about him. Once upon a time, Zelph was a household name in America, Joseph said. Although his story was not told in *The Book of Mormon*, Zelph belonged to the story's Lamanite people and was a mighty prophet, or possibly a mighty knight, in the employ of one king, or possibly prophet, Omandagus or possibly Onandagus—the correct spelling is unknown. What is known, without question, is that Zelph's fame reached from "hill Cumorah to the Rocky Mountains." He was an American celebrity. The discovery of Zelph buoyed Joseph's weary men as they pushed farther west.

When I myself came across Zelph's bones—in a book—I felt a pleasure similar, I imagine, to what Joseph's men experienced during their excavation. For *Book of Mormon* readers, finding Zelph—who knew there even was a guy named Zelph?—suggests just how rich American soil is with sequels, how much yet unknown, still to be discovered.

Days earlier I'd driven my Secret Service SUV by the spot in Illinois where Joseph had received the revelation about Zelph. Now, at dinner, as I updated Kyle on the details concerning Zelph, it became clear to me that he'd be joining me on my long drive the next morning to Carthage prison, where Joseph Smith and his brother Hyrum met their sad end.

The prison proved to be one of the most pleasant, least bitter, and generally lowest-key martyrdom sites I've ever seen. After our prison tour, Kyle and I walked by the adjoining garden. As we sat on a bench, he asked me about the writing life. I told him about publishers and agents and book proposals and MFA programs. He asked me if I ever get recognized on the street.

I laughed.

We sat in silence for a while, soaking in the sun.

I asked him how he would describe his stories.

"They're kind of sci-fi," he explained, "but not. They're more like historical fiction? You know? But like with sci-fi plot twists at the end, sorta."

I wanted to tell Kyle that his writing historical fiction about Kurt Cobain made me feel old but realized that saying that would *really* make me feel old, so I just said, "Cool, can't wait to read them."

We sat in silence once more, watching a large family of foreigners sharing ChapStick.

I observed a local douchebag pacing through the garden, lightly but quite intentionally kicking his toe into defenseless tulips as he walked by. He was shouting into his phone, "'kay, not gonna say it again—just get it done." As I turned to Kyle to say, "God, what a *douche*bag," the douchebag threw on a pair of the very same red plastic sunglasses I was wearing, and so instead I just said, "Hmm."

"Wanna go to a rave tonight?" Kyle asked me.

"A *rave*?"

"I mean, I'm sure you've been to better ones."

"That's very unlikely," I said. "I'd be honored to go to your rave."

Before the raving began we stopped at Kyle's place for dinner. He lived with his mom, his older sister, and her five-year-old son. As we sat in his kitchen, Kyle told me more about himself. He'd graduated from high school the year before and was working as a security guard and in construction and other odd jobs. (He'd changed his shifts around so that he could attend my reading.) He was thinking of going to college but wasn't sure. High school had been torture for him. Just then, a little boy in full Superman outfit, including cape, materialized in the doorway. When he saw me, he stopped short and shrank back toward the door. Gingerly he walked over to Kyle and handed him a note.

"Thanks, bud," said Kyle. The boy smiled proudly and ran off as fast as he could. Kyle read the note and said, "Gotta do laundry and shit before we go out."

As he loaded the washing machine, Kyle elaborated on how horrible his high school experience had been. As he spoke, he stripped off his clothes and threw them into the wash.

"Senior year"—off came his shirt—"I started hanging out with my girlfriend." Off came his pants, belt tossed to the side.

"She's awesome." Right sock. "You'll probably meet her tonight." Left sock.

Kyle was now standing there in just his boxers.

"Honestly?" he continued. "I probably have two friends total from school."

He looped a thumb under the waistband of his underwear and began to remove it. Then he stopped and looked at me.

"But they're *definitely* friends for life, know what I mean?"

He peeled off his boxers, tossing them into the washing machine, and stood before me in the heroic nude, this heedless youth of Missouri.

"Let's make the nachos," he said.

We had dinner around a card table in the kitchen. (Kyle was attired in an oversized bathrobe.) The little boy joined us. It was touching to watch Kyle fuss over the child. He propped the boy on his lap with a practiced gesture.

The little boy opened up a bit to me. He had large, attentive eyes that inhaled his surroundings. You could almost hear his little brain buzzing with high-powered activity. He showed me a favorite truck and brought it over for my inspection. When the boy announced that he was done with peas for the night, Kyle, in one deft motion, picked up the plastic plate and flipped its tiny contents into the trash, then Frisbeed it into the sink. The little boy watched with wonder these feats of strength and agility in his young uncle, the man of the house.

"I'll wash that later," Kyle announced. Then he turned to me and said, "Can I ask you something?"

"Sure."

"Mind if I join you again tomorrow? It's really cool for me to see a real writer at work. I wouldn't get in your way at all. And I can totally help out. You said that you could have used someone back when you were looking for Zelph. I can make us sandwiches and carry stuff. I didn't know the Garden of Eden was right here, but I know the area pretty well. Been here my whole life."

I told him it would be a great pleasure to have him as a partner in my search for Eden. After a brief negotiation we agreed to the following terms: I would match the fee he got for a day of security guarding at the mall and he would make us sandwiches. He would guide me through the terrain and I would guide him through the research and writing steps I was taking. If we found any treasure, we'd split fifty-fifty.

Having settled business matters, we prepared for the rave. In seconds Kyle reappeared in a loose mesh tank top, thick sneakers, Kansas City Royals cap tilted backward, and camo shorts that hung low on his hips, with the strong suggestion of ripe fruit. As we approached the site of this party, my strong natural disinclination to attend the rave began to harden into outright refusal. By the time

I pulled up my Secret Service SUV to our destination, I was committed to doing pretty much anything else. But I figured I'd give it a few minutes.

It was a good deal smaller an affair than I'd imagined. I'd pictured a converted skating rink or barn. It was held in the garage of some guy's uncle's auto repair shop. The uncle was planning to redo the space and had lent it to the kids for the party. He was going to gut it anyway and didn't mind if they trashed it. So we were told. When we arrived it was already packed with flesh and wafting billows of booze, perfume, summer lust, and smoke. Kyle pulled out a joint and offered me the honorary first hit. As Kyle texted something, he whispered in my ear, "If you don't toke a lot, go small."

But it was too late. I was already completely ragtime. Small but powerful strobes were making my mind race like a colorful deck of tarot cards rapidly shuffling, cartwheeling at a pace that was becoming magnificent and terrifying and articulate of many meanings. Then it slowed. I was able to observe solitary flecks of dust journeying through the lights, casting gorgeously thin shafts of shadow. *We are all pilgrims floating through the lights, seeking a better country*, I thought. Then I laughed at how stupid that sounded. Then I considered the phrase "negative space" and wondered at length about what made this a "rave" instead of just a "party." But what I was actually doing, I finally realized, was just staring at the ceiling, at the light swirling around it like a sea anemone. I became powerfully thirsty—thirsty the way they get in the Bible before something really bad happens.

In Kyle's ear, I shouted, or tried to shout, "Think I'm gonna jet." He objected at first but then became distracted by a girl who'd grabbed two big fistfuls of his loose belt and was pulling him torso-first into the melee. Kyle turned to me and shouted, "Tomorrow, dude. Garden of Eden!" and was seen no more.

A desperate and fascinated search for the door reminded me that I was substantially stoned, which I'd forgotten because I was substantially stoned. I would put off driving for a bit and take a walk.

The garage where the rave was raging was located at the foot of a small hillock. I climbed it, then sat on a rock and looked down. To get here, we'd driven east for a while on the same road we'd be taking tomorrow. By my calculations, I was sitting near the edge of the Garden of Eden.

After digging up gold plates and translating *The Book of Mormon*, after all the traveling, all the sneaking around with his forty-eight or so wives, after building a large temple in Ohio and seeing the ranks of his followers begin to grow, Joseph moved into Missouri. He must have known the end was near. It had been only a few years, but so much had happened. He would go no farther. The demons he'd encountered as a child around Hill Cumorah, that pursued him to Ohio, all of that would catch up to him here. He knew that. But it was okay: he had dug as far as he could, as far as it was possible to dig, farther than anyone else had dared to try. He'd tunneled all the way to the Beginning, before all the trauma and hurt and betrayal, before the lies. He'd found his way back to the life that existed before all that, to the person he'd been when all was happy and safe.

"Can't repeat the past?" said Jay Gatsby. "Why of course you can."

To Joseph that past was a *place*. Of course it was. Like Jerusalem or Zarahemla, the past was a land you could find on a map and return to, live in. This was the land he'd come from—we'd all come from—and where, in a short time, he would die. Here was the Beginning and the End. When he first saw this good land, after fighting his way through the wilderness, Joseph was immediately relieved of all his troubles. He leaned back on his horse and shouted for joy. His dog too became excited. And both prophet and dog howled together toward the big prairie sky.

I grew suddenly tired. I pulled Kyle's stories out of my back pocket, leaned against the rock, and began to read. The first one was about two guys, one who was superangry and one who "was seriously zen." Soon there was a love triangle with an incredible girl, unappreciated, beautiful, and cool in every way ("she could list the starting lineup of the 2004 Kansas City Royals like it was.her street address"). She taught the angry guy how to love and shook up the Zen guy so much that he had major epiphanies about life. The angry guy got the girl because he knew "how to drive her wild," while the Zen guy embarked on a major solo road trip which, as the story's end implied, would be an ethereal, life-changing journey. "Treat her well," the seriously Zen guy said to the superangry guy. "I don't think I'm coming home." After so much fighting and unpleasantness, these old friends, brothers really, embraced and said goodbye. The angry guy was Kurt Cobain, before he became famous, and the Zen guy would be his anonymous lifelong muse. There were definitely some hints of historical fiction in the story, but I didn't detect any sci-fi. This was pure cowboy lit.

I gazed through my sleepy eyes toward the land Joseph had named Adam-ondi-Ahman. We were east of Eden: the spot where Adam and Eve were deposited after their expulsion from the Garden, the first stop in their new fallen world, in our fallen world. The entire surrounding area was mostly black and silent, except for the rave, which was anything but. Paradise sat shrouded somewhere on the horizon in a pervasive expanse of primeval darkness, and set against this, the sounds and colors and sweet-smelling smoke of the rave rose up to the heavens like a fire dance on the Neanderthal plain.

The offspring of Adam and Eve, having themselves never known

Eden, still too young to inherit their dire inheritance—the melancholy of eternal exile—these first-generation humans, immigrants to earth, wanderers though not yet pilgrims, surely raved all night, as abandoned and locked-up Eden lay so close behind them and as the waters of the Great Flood loomed before them. They must have known it was coming, or at least had some hint of it. Even at that moment I could smell the approach of one of those big crazy midwestern summer storms. Tomorrow Kyle and I would get into my Secret Service SUV and drive to Eden, that dark horizon.

In the Garden of Eden itself, nobody told stories. There was nothing to tell. There's no narrative where there's no feeling of loss, and there's no loss without a choice between good and evil. There were no stories, just trees. What you saw was what you got. Except for the Tree of Knowledge: that was forbidden. But that wasn't exactly a story either; the "do not" of that tree had in it the suggestion of story, an invitation to spin a tale, which was taken advantage of by the snake, Adam's jealous brother. But there were no human stories, not until Adam and Eve were exiled. That story, of what was lost, of how it happened, of what was to come, that was the first human story.

Once Joseph passed back into that original place, into the darkling valley I was looking into, he reentered the garden land where there were no stories to tell. That's how he knew he was home. That had been his destination all along. That's what all of his stories were for: to take him to the place where there would be no more need of stories.

I picked up my pen to scribble something. But I was too tired to write, so I just made indecipherable glyphs on the page that I would have to use the gift and power of the Lord to translate later.

I had a few more thoughts about Eden that needed to be recorded before I forgot them forever. I needed to jot down some thoughts about the rave. And to make a note to look into the possibility that Mount Greylock, Melville's mountain, was the true Cumorah. Or at least to rule it out. Oh, and I needed to consider a trip down to Louisiana, where people were excavating the remains of a settlement much bigger and more technologically sophisticated than had been previously known in that area. This Mississippian civilization had apparently included large cities made of wood, which is why there aren't many traces left. One theory is that these city-builders may have come from the south, maybe Mesoamerica. This development might put North America back on the Nephite map, just as Joseph had said it was. Even a late date could have *Book of Mormon* resonances. Who knows, maybe the last Nephite, Moroni himself, having trekked far north to bury the gold plates and keep his promise to Mormon, then traveled back south—he was Maya, after all—and spent the remainder of his years as king of the Lamanite-Mississippians. Or as their scribe. Maybe there were plates of Moroni somewhere in Louisiana that told this whole sequel. It might be worth a trip. I made a note to take more notes, and reminded myself to remember to read it.

As weird slumberland images began to press heavily against my eyes from inside my head, I tried to remind myself to write Kyle a note. My pen hand was useless now, so I composed in my head.

I'd start by giving him my take on his stories, then give him a pep talk about writing while also giving it to him straight. I would end the note by answering a question.

You asked me if I believe. I think everyone has to believe in something. Here's what I believe: I believe that Hill Cumorah is a real place. Maybe this belief is not exactly what the devout believe, but it's really not that different either. Nobody knows where the real Cumorah is. Some say it's in southern Mexico.

(Remember how I told you I saw it?) Some say it's Joseph Smith's hill in New York. Some say it's in Chile or Brazil. Or even the Rockies. The point is that it's all of them. It's right down the road from you. And it's also across the world. And it's the path between them. The world is full of buried books. They're there. That's no bullshit. Other people don't need to believe in that, but if you want to be a writer, you do. You must have faith. The gold plates are real: every book is a translation of them. The book that you find at Hill Cumorah could be the thing that saves you. More likely, though, you'll just break even. It might also break your heart, ruin you. I'm serious. You should know that. But you might as well be brave and keep your energy high. Just the way you are right now. You can go and find one of those books. Go there and dig for it. Start with the hill down the road. That's how it starts, Kyle. Confess that you are a pilgrim on this earth, in search of a better country—then go find it. See you tomorrow in the Garden of Eden! Don't forget the sandwiches.

ACKNOWLEDGMENTS

My deepest gratitude goes to my editor, Ronit Feldman, for her patience and foresight; to Nan Talese and the dedicated staff at Doubleday; to Jennifer Lyons, for all that she does. And to Emily Wong.

To my first responders, for their invaluable critiques: Kayla Rosen, Alex Chu, Ezra Feldman, Beverly Schneider, Sasha Weiss, Elif Batuman, Lamar Denton, Bernie Steinberg, and Alexis Coe.

To Adena Steinberg.

To the members of various LDS communities who opened their hearts and minds to me. To Blake Allen; and to Dwight Schwendiman and Bill Matthews for their Christlike forbearance.

To the biographers of Joseph Smith, especially Fawn Brodie and Richard Bushman.

A NOTE ABOUT THE AUTHOR

Avi Steinberg is the author of *Running the Books: The Adventures of an Accidental Prison Librarian*, which was a *San Francisco Chronicle* Best Book of the Year. He is a regular contributor to *The New Yorker*'s Culture Desk blog. His essays have appeared in the *New York Times Magazine*, *Salon*, *Paris Review Daily*, and *n+1*.

A NOTE ABOUT THE TYPE

This book was set in Adobe Garamond. Designed for the
Adobe Corporation by Robert Slimbach, the fonts are
based on types first cut by Claude Garamond (ca. 1480–
1561). Garamond was a pupil of Geoffroy Tory and is
believed to have followed the Venetian models, although
he introduced a number of important differences, and it is
to him that we owe the letters we now know as "old style."
He gave to his letters a certain elegance and feeling of
movement that won their creator an immediate reputation
and the patronage of Francis I of France.